823   Alden, Patricia, 1945-
Ald   **Nuruddin Farah /**

GAYLORD

PRINTED IN U.S.A

Nuruddin Farah

Twayne's World Authors Series

African Literature

Bernth Lindfors, Editor
University of Texas

TWAS 876

NURUDDIN FARAH
Louis Tremaine

Nuruddin Farah

Patricia Alden

St. Lawrence University

Louis Tremaine

University of Richmond

Twayne Publishers
New York

Twayne's World Authors Series No. 876

Nuruddin Farah
Patricia Alden and Louis Tremaine

Copyright © 1999 by Twayne Publishers

Twayne Publishers
1633 Broadway
New York, NY 10019

Library of Congress Cataloging-in-Publication Data

Alden, Patricia, 1945 –
    Nuruddin Farah / Patricia Alden, Louis Tremaine.
        p.   cm. — (Twayne's world authors series ; TWAS 876. African
    literature)
    Includes bibliographical references and index.
    ISBN 0-8057-1667-X (alk. paper)
    1. Farah, Nuruddin, 1945 –   —Criticism and interpretation.
    2. Postmodernism (Literature)—Somalia. 3. Politics and literature—
Somalia. 4. Somalia—In literature.   I. Tremaine, Louis.
II. Title.   III. Series: Twayne's world authors series ; TWAS 876.
IV. Series: Twayne's world authors series. African literature.
PR9396.9.F3Z54   1999
823—dc21   98-33279
                                                                    CIP

This paper meets the requirements of ANSI/NISO Z3948-1992 (Permanence of Paper).

10 9 8 7 6 5 4 3 2 1

Printed in the United States of America

Contents

Preface

We came by two separate but similar paths to the work of the Somali novelist and playwright Nuruddin Farah. In both cases, it was a political scientist and specialist on the Horn of Africa—not a fellow literary scholar—who first put one of Farah's books in our hands, recommending to us the insights of his political analysis. Since then we have discussed Farah's work with many other readers and been struck by how easily he becomes many different kinds of writer, depending on the reader and the context in which he is read. There is Farah the feminist, for example, whose first novel convinced some of his editors and reviewers that he was a woman writing under a pen name. There is Farah the innovative prose-poet and stylist, Farah the social scientist, Farah the committed activist, Farah the paradoxical postmodernist, and so forth. The originality and the intensity of Farah's work in each of these dimensions make him one of contemporary Africa's most important and challenging writers and have brought him several literary awards including the 1998 Neustadt International Prize for Literature. A natural consequence of this multidimensionality, however, has been a scholarly response that generally fixes attention on only one aspect of Farah's work at a time. The only book-length study to date, Derek Wright's *The Novels of Nuruddin Farah,* provides valuable interpretations of the fictional work, though he considers each novel in isolation from the others.

The problem facing a reader of Farah is evident to any teacher who has tried to include his work in a course on, say, African literature: Which book does one select? This problem arises with Farah more than it does with most writers because, far more in his case than in most, the meaning of each text is knitted into the larger body of work as a whole.[1] Our purpose, accordingly, is to provide an introduction to and interpretation of the novels and plays of Nuruddin Farah that articulates between each work and the whole work. Our thesis is that the various strands in Farah's writing are elements of a single pattern consistently developed from his first novel to his most recent: an ever deepening meditation on the complex relationship between individual autonomy and social responsibility. In Farah's artistic vision no value is more precious or essential than the individual's freedom to define and shape the life of the self. To claim this principle requires, however, that such freedom be extended to all, actively promoted within every relationship at every level of human affairs, and defended through collective action when necessary. This vision generates and incorporates Farah's political philosophy, his treatment of gender, and his use of language.

Our book is an introduction to Farah's work as a whole in another sense as well, treating not only his eight published novels but also his work as a dramatist. Of his four plays, the first was never publicly produced (falling victim to Somali censorship) and the text has been lost. The other three have all been staged and are as implicated in the pattern of his oeuvre as any of his novels, though only one, *The Offering,* has been published (in a literary magazine in 1976) and only one, *Yussuf and His Brothers,* has been the subject of critical study (an article by Jacqueline Bardolph). These three plays form part of the body of work we examine in the present study in an effort to provide as comprehensive a view as possible of Farah's art. We omit from consideration only his short fiction; the reason is that, by his own account, he produced these pieces primarily out of economic necessity and regards them as peripheral to his serious work.

We have described that work as centrally concerned with the freedom of the individual. Farah's source of material in developing this theme, in every text, is Somali society, and he draws on this source directly and in detail. The theme itself, in fact, has specific roots deep in the culture and history of Somalia, so we open our study of Farah's work with a consideration of the social history of that country. An equally important perspective on the work is to be found in Farah's personal history, to which we devote chapter 2. The dominant fact in that history is his long exile from Somalia. While others have followed his life up to the point of exile, we have felt it important to carry the story forward, examining in some detail Farah's experience since leaving Somalia and his developing understanding of the meaning of his exile, details and developments that have a direct bearing on the pattern of his work. Chapter 3 is a chronological survey of Farah's novels and plays, tracing basic stages of development in his work and summarizing the content and construction of each of the texts. For the reader who is familiar with only one or a few of Farah's books, this chapter is crucial to an understanding of chapters 4 through 6. For those more familiar with Farah's writing, chapter 3 raises new interpretive issues about each text that relate to our larger argument.

That argument is the matter of the remaining chapters, in which we analyze Farah's treatment of politics, gender, and language in his work as a whole. In chapter 4 we show that the primacy that Farah attaches to individual autonomy makes his vision more political, not less so, because it renders every act involving two or more human beings a political act. Negotiation of autonomy, for Farah, is at the heart of every relationship and every social formation, from the family to the nation. Attention by other scholars to Farah as a "political writer" generally focuses on the politics of resistance to dictatorship in the first trilogy; we argue instead that every one of his novels and plays is equally and essentially political in nature.

To locate politics, conceived in this way, at the center of Farah's work leads us to a reconsideration of his writing about women, which we develop in chapter 5. Here we discuss, first, the ways in which men in the patriarchal world of Farah's novels and plays imagine women and how these imaginings are rationalizations for male control of women. We then turn to the variety of women's responses to male domination in these works, focusing on women's opportunities for resistance, especially by cultivating their own imaginations and developing their own narratives. Farah also depicts men resisting patriarchal power by imagining different relationships with women, sometimes taking on unconventional gender roles themselves. Some characters, both male and female, imagine themselves as differently gendered, and we examine the extent to which their gender crossings are liberatory or oppressive. We conclude this part of the study by considering how Farah as a male writer extends his own imagination into women's experiences.

The construction of human possibilities, for Farah, is the work of the imagination and the instrument of the imagination is language. These are the subjects of our final chapter, in which we draw attention to the activity of self-narration by which Farah's characters express their own autonomy. This self-narrating of Farah's protagonists relates their imaginative work to that of the writer, for self-narration entails a concomitant invention of those who share one's social world. This activity is therefore, in Farah's terms, necessarily a political act. As a result, the imagination must be an ethical faculty, and it is this ethical dimension that both anchors and explains some of the most characteristic features of his voice as a writer: his indeterminacy, his extended metaphors, and his incorporation of other voices and texts into his own. It explains too a recurrent dilemma for Farah, the fact that the politician and the dictator, as well as the writer and his characters, use the same power of language to conceive themselves and others in their world. This insistence on the ethical role of the imagination defines Farah, cosmopolitan experimentalist though he is, as a politically engaged writer working in the tradition of the Somali verbal artist.

While we accept the entire responsibility for this reading, we feel greatly indebted for help in the work that led us to it. Our most important debt of gratitude is to Nuruddin Farah himself, who entrusted us with the manuscript of his most recent novel, *Secrets*, which had not yet been published at the time we began work on this book, provided us a current version of *Yussuf and His Brothers*, responded generously to our correspondence and telephone calls, and accorded us a long interview. Several portions of that interview (which has not been published elsewhere) appear in this book. We are especially grateful to Charles Sugnet for his encouragement, personal assistance, and insightful conversations with us about Farah and his work. We would also like to thank, among many others, James Currey, Pat Howard, Margaret Busby, and Sallie Hirsch for beneficial discussions. Eckhard Breitinger and Bernth Lindfors have both been helpful to us in identifying and locating materials, and a National Endowment for the Humanities seminar directed by Professor Lindfors provided the rich environment in which Patricia Alden first wrote on the work of Farah. Like all Farah scholars, we are indebted to the prolific and insightful work of Derek Wright and Jacqueline Bardolph, even though our approach will sometimes suggest different paths of entry than theirs into Farah's writing. Portions of the research leading to this book were carried out with support from our respective institutions, St. Lawrence University and the University of Richmond, and Louis Tremaine enjoyed significant assistance from St. Lawrence in the form of an appointment as visiting scholar-in-residence.

Finally, a word on the transcriptions and spellings of Somali words and names may be of help to the reader. Where common alternatives exist, we have retained the spellings of names as they appear in the texts of Farah: for example, *Mogadiscio* rather than *Mogadishu* as the capital of Somalia. Many of the words and names that appear in this book conform to official Somali orthography—again, because they appear that way in Farah or in other sources we cite. Two letters in particular in that orthography may give the non-Somali reader difficulty: *c* and *x*. In Somali, *c* represents the sound of the Arabic consonant ʿ*ayn* and never the sound of *k* or *s*. Thus the Arabic name that English readers know as *Ali* is written in Somali—and in the works of Farah—as *Cali*. *X* represents the heavily aspirated Arabic *h* and never the sound *eks*. Thus the Arabic name that English readers know as *Muhammad* is written in Somali as *Muxammad*.

Chronology

1945   Nuruddin Farah born in Baidoa, Somalia.

1947   Family moves to Kallafo in the British-occupied Ogaden (soon thereafter handed over to Ethiopian control). Farah attends Qur'anic, primary, and secondary school.

1960   The Republic of Somalia gains independence from Britain and Italy.

1963   Family moves to Mogadiscio, Somalia, to escape war in the Ogaden.

1964   Completes secondary school.

1965   Publication of first short story.

1966   Enrolls at Punjab University, Chandigarh, India.

1969   Receives bachelor's degree.

Marries Chitra Muliyil, an Indian student in Delhi.

Somali Revolution brings Siyad Barre to power.

1970   *From a Crooked Rib.*

Birth of son, Koschin.

First marriage ends.

1973   Somali-language novel serialized in government newspaper; publication cut short by government censors.

1974   Departure for England; beginning of 22-year absence from Somalia.

Enrolls in one year of postgraduate study in theater at University of London, attached to Royal Court Theatre.

1975   Continues postgraduate study for one year at University of Essex.

The Offering produced at Essex.

1976   *A Naked Needle.*

Decision to remain in exile from Somalia; beginning of three-year stay in Italy.

1978   *A Spread of Butter* broadcast by BBC African Service.

1979   *Sweet and Sour Milk.*

        Moves to Los Angeles.

1980   Awarded English-Speaking Union Literary Award for *Sweet and Sour Milk.*

1981   *Sardines.*

        Teaches at University of Bayreuth, Germany.

        Moves to Jos, Nigeria.

1982   *Yussuf and His Brothers* produced at Jos.

1983   *Close Sesame.*

1984   Moves to the Gambia.

1986   *Maps.*

        Moves to Khartoum, Sudan.

1989   Moves to Kampala, Uganda.

1990   First publication of *Gifts,* in Finnish translation.

        Mother dies in Mogadiscio.

1991   Marries Amina Mama, a Nigerian sociologist.

        Moves to Ethiopia.

        Father dies in refugee camp in Kenya.

        Awarded Tucholsky Literary Award in Stockholm for work as literary exile.

        Siyad Barre driven from power.

1992   *Gifts* published in English.

        Moves to present home in Kaduna, Nigeria.

1993   Birth of daughter, Abyan.

1995   Birth of son, Kaahiye.

1996   First visit to Somalia since beginning of exile.

1998   *Secrets.*

        Awarded Neustadt International Prize for Literature.

Chapter One
Farah's Somalia:
A Legacy of Contradictions

During this period, whenever anyone asked me why I wrote the kind of books I did, I answered that I wrote to put down on paper, for posterity's sake, the true history of the nation. . . . So why do I write nowadays? I write because a theme has chosen me: the theme of Africa's upheaval and societal disorganisation. And I write in order to recover my missing half.

—Nuruddin Farah, "Why I Write"

When Nuruddin Farah wrote these words in 1988 he had not seen his "missing half"—Somalia, the land of his birth—in well over a decade. In that time he had developed into one of Africa's most inventive, cosmopolitan, and independent-minded writers and one of its most outspoken critics of tradition; and yet, as his statement suggests, his art had become—and remains today—inseparable from the history of his nation. To read Farah without some working familiarity with that history would indeed be to miss half of the resonance of his writing. There are three reasons why this is so and why we therefore open our study of Farah's art with a review of Somali history.

One reason is that Farah writes in a language rich in references to a highly particular world of cultural and historical experience, a world strongly marked, for example, by certain forms of Islamic thought and practice, by a political and ethical temper with roots in nomadic pastoralist culture, by the role of clan relations in social institutions, by particular forms of social control experienced by women, and by other historical and cultural forces that we examine in this chapter. These references in Farah's work serve the purposes neither of local color nor of ethnography but are an essential part of the vocabulary of his ideas. Second, despite his formal and stylistic inventiveness and his choice of English as a medium of composition, Farah's practice as a writer places him directly within a Somali tradition of verbal art that insists upon critical attention to immediate and specific real-world problems. Third, the social history of Somalia is a story whose larger themes echo throughout Farah's novels and plays. To be a historically aware Somali writer is to inherit a legacy of contradictions, a story of tensions between a closely woven unity of cultural experience, on the one hand, and social forms and structures that are ever splitting, shifting, and recombining, on the other. These themes in Somali history are an important source of insight into related tensions that inform Farah's writing at several levels and that are, in turn, central to the argument of this book.

Among the forces that historically have unified the cultural experience of the Somali people are their language, their religion, and their nomadic-pastoralist tradition. These factors in the Somali cultural legacy bear some consideration because they play a complex role in the work of Farah. Traditionally their homogenizing influence has favored social balance, but as we show in subsequent chapters, that very influence becomes a problematic and destabilizing force amid the conditions of "upheaval and societal disorganisation" that Farah depicts in his novels and plays. Moreover, the specific ways in which these cultural factors operate in the Somali context have much to do with the potential that Farah finds in them as resources for political resistance.

With regard to language, Uncle Hilaal in *Maps* expresses a widely held view when he says to Askar that "a Somali . . . is a man, woman or child whose mother tongue is Somali. . . . The Somali are a homogeneous people . . . and speak the same language wherever they may be found."[1] Hilaal overstates the case slightly, for there are numerous dialect differences among Somali speakers, differences wide enough in some cases to interfere with mutual intelligibility. It is true, nonetheless, that Somalia is a land united by language to a degree unmatched by any other sub-Saharan African country of its size. One or another dialect of Somali is the first language of virtually all people born in Greater Somalia (comprising the Somali Democratic Republic, Djibouti, the Ogaden region under the control of Ethiopia, and the Somali-speaking region of northern Kenya), a population exceeding seven million. The Eastern Cushitic roots of this language in the Somali territories reach back two thousand years, and its major dialects have been relatively stable since at least the sixteenth century. In that time the Somali language has developed into a medium that supports a culture of open and vigorous public debate, detailed oral history, and poetry of exceeding complexity and refinement. Because Somali society has historically been primarily dependent on nomadic pastoralism and trade, that oral culture has evolved through continual contact and exchange throughout the Somali-speaking regions. Despite many attempts to devise a writing system for Somali, an official, standard orthography was not established until 1972, making Somali one of the last African national languages to acquire an official written form. The impact of the new orthography on linguistic homogeneity in Somalia, however, was far less significant than in most other African nations, because of the unifying social dynamics of language already long at work throughout Somali-speaking culture.

Most Somalis also have some familiarity with a common second language, Arabic, both as a language in its own right and through Arabic loanwords in Somali, and this familiarity is the result of a second fundamental source of cultural commonality in Somalia: religion. Unlike the populations of most nations in Africa south of the Sahara (including the bordering states of Ethiopia and Kenya), where one typically finds a mix of Islam, Christianity, and one or more indigenous African religions, over 99 percent of Somalis are at least nominally Muslim. Furthermore, to be Muslim is to incorporate into one's thinking a set of concepts and beliefs that stress unity far more than does any other world religion. The central tenet of faith in Islam is the oneness of God, a oneness that both precludes any other source or site of divinity and includes all of existence within the unified being of God. This tenet bears not only on spiritual life but on social life as well, and indeed makes little distinction between the two. Adherents practice their faith, and at the same time signal their faith publicly, by performing the acts known as the "five pillars of Islam": daily recitation of the profession of faith ("There is no god but God, and Mohammed is the prophet of God"), prayer five times each day, the giving of alms, fasting during the month of Ramadan, and pilgrimage to Mecca. The source of religious understanding is, likewise, a unified source: the Qur'an, believed to be God's own words delivered by the angel Gabriel (*Jibriil* in Somali) to a single recipient on behalf of humanity, the prophet Mohammed. The Qur'an, along with the *hadith,* or sayings of the Prophet, guides nearly every aspect of daily life, from the allocation of inheritance to the enjoyment of sex. There is no Qur'anic provision for priestly authority standing between the believer and God, but only for teachers to aid in understanding the word of God. All of these elements make of Islam a religion that notably encourages homogeneity in the community of the faithful.

Whether such encouragement is successful depends, of course, less on the abstract system of Islam than on its social practice. In this regard, Lee Cassanelli writes that "Islam's universalism has certainly contributed to the Somalis' consciousness of their common identity as a people, but Somali society has in turn given Islam as practiced in the Horn a distinctly Somali character."[2] Somali Islam is an ancient and relatively orthodox practice, probably dating from the eighth or ninth century. Popular religious belief in Somalia, however, incorporates unorthodox articles of faith as well. Notable among these for their appearance in the work of Farah are special spiritual powers to bless, curse, or divine, which are attributed to religious leaders and sometimes to uncanny others; the existence of jinns (mortal but supernatural spirits); the intercessionary power of saints; and spirit possession. These elements notwithstanding, Somali Islam is distinct from Muslim practice in many other countries in resisting the elevation of individuals into positions of political power through spiritual authority. Such authority is mainly limited to traveling Qur'anic teachers and to local *wadaaddo,* or religious men, who interpret religious law and celebrate rites such as marriage but who are typically excluded by these roles from political governance. As in other African Muslim countries, Sufi orders or brotherhoods gained influence in the nineteenth century and have remained important in religious and social life. Such orders emphasize particular interpretations of one's personal relationship to God and correct spiritual discipline, but they do not, at least in the case of the Somali brotherhoods, seriously challenge Islamic orthodoxy. The leaders of local congregations of these orders are known in Somalia by the Arabic word *sheikh,* which is sometimes used as a synonym for *wadaad.* Both usages of *sheikh* occur in Farah. The geographical mobility that is traditional in Somali society has worked to prevent the isolation of these brotherhoods and congregations and to favor, despite areas of regional consolidation, the circulation of popular religious ideas, legends, and practices throughout Somali culture.

If this traditional mobility is partially responsible for unifying Somali culture linguistically and religiously, it is in turn the consequence of a third basic element of the country's cultural commonality: nomadic pastoralism. Somalia's hot, dry climate and flat, sparse terrain leave almost no other choice for subsistence than herding, outside of the few areas that support agriculture along the coast and between the only two rivers in the country, in the south. As a result, about 65 percent of Somalia's population is pastoralist, the third largest population of pastoralists in the world. Where water and vegetation are adequate, Somali herders tend cattle, sheep, and goats, but in much of the interior for most of the time they are not adequate to support life by means of these animals alone. There human survival depends on the extraordinary survivability of the camel. For the Somali pastoralist in these circumstances, the camel can provide nearly an entire diet, material for clothing, shelter, and implements, a means of transport, a medium of exchange, and a rich source of metaphor. The management of this remarkable resource is a demanding task, requiring an ability to move great distances with the herd in search of water and pasturage. That ability in turn results in an existence that defines home as wherever one is able to find water and grazing and limits significant wealth to what moves or can easily be moved, that is, to the herds and to people themselves.

Animal wealth is easily calculated by the number of beasts under one's control, but the maintenance and extension of human wealth depends on a far more complex mechanism, one that grows directly out of the ecology and economy of nomadic pastoralism and that deeply affects the lives of almost all Somalis. That mechanism is the Somali kinship system. Ninety percent of ethnic Somalis are members of one of six major clan families, all of which acknowledge a common founding ancestor named Samaal. Of these six clan families, four are primarily pastoralist, accounting for 70 percent of the Somali population and living mainly in central and northern Somalia, while the other two are more settled and dependent on agriculture, living mainly in the south. Even in the towns, a majority of Somalis retain a strong sense of kinship and, very often, a direct involvement in the social, economic, and political affairs of their rural kin. Claims of responsibility to distant clan members are often asserted—and often resisted—in Farah's books. The pastoralist clan families are not only predominant in Somali culture by their numbers but preeminent by their prestige *as* pastoralists. These four groups, collectively called Samaal, project a system of values that has great currency in Somali culture. These values—physical toughness, adaptability, courage, fierce independence—take on imaginative life in the figure of the nomad who, unless he is a *wadaad,* traditionally proclaims himself to be both herder and warrior. The other two clan families are collectively called Sab, a pejorative coinage of the Samaal, who consider the settled Sab cultivators inferior. Of far lower prestige, though, are the riverine people inhabiting the valleys of the Jubba and Shabeelle. These are mainly descendants of pre-Somali peoples or escaped slaves and have historically occupied the role of serfs in Somali society. Other Somalis identify them as culturally and physically different from themselves. Their current place in society is reflected in the marginal service roles that unnamed "River People" occasionally play in Farah's novels. By contrast to these and to outsiders, both Samaal and Sab share a common consciousness of membership in a system of related clan families.

Each of these clan families comprises clans, and each of these clans consists of lineage groups, in a system of increasing segmentation whose base is the nuclear family. Near the top of these pyramids the force of identity is largely imaginative, but at the lower levels identity as a member of a lineage group becomes active and functional through participation in councils, open to all adult males, where decisions are reached democratically regarding matters that affect the survival and prosperity of the group and its members. Survival and prosperity can be fragile affairs for the Somali pastoralist and so these decisions are often of great consequence. Furthermore, the conditions of pastoral life do not support the maintenance of fixed centers and lines of authority but rather impose on the group as a whole the burden of agency and authority in matters affecting its interests. It is this consciousness of collective action and responsibility, not merely mutual affection or shared history and experience, that gives such life and meaning to an individual's sense of identity as a member of a lineage group.

The force of this attachment to the lineage group is graphically apparent in the manner by which names are constructed in Somali. There is no family surname that passes from one generation to the next. Rather, a child receives a single name of his or her own, which is then followed by the father's name and then the grandfather's. Nuruddin Farah's name, for example, is Nuruddin Farah Xasan, or Nuruddin the son of Farah and grandson of Xasan. (He uses Farah professionally as a surname, a practice we follow in this book, but in personal life he is Nuruddin. This explains why most of his characters seem, to the Western reader, to have only a "first name," except at moments of great seriousness or formality, when they may have two or three.) Thus, to mention one's grandfather by his full name is to refer at the same time to *his* father and grandfather; in other words, to bear a name is to bear an entire genealogy. Most Somalis, especially rural people, can recite their own genealogies as far back as the clan founder, usually a chain of 20 generations or more.

A still greater force of identity attaches to membership in a *diya* group. In an environment that has no centers of authority to turn to for the administration of justice, the *diya* group is a collection of families that bears communal responsibility for the rights and obligations of its members in disputes with people outside the group. If a member of the *diya* group is harmed or killed, the group exacts compensation (the meaning of the word *diya*), often in the form of animals, which it pays to the victim, his or her family, and members of the group as a whole;

and it provides compensation on behalf of any member who harms or kills someone outside the group. In this way the system avoids a good deal of violent conflict and retribution. In effect, the legal or ethical self in such a system is not the individual but the group to which one belongs. Some observers, in fact, mention this elimination of individual responsibility for one's actions through the *diya* group as one of the characteristic ways in which Islamic orthodoxy bends to accommodate pastoralist social practice in Somali culture.[3] Historically, then, this system of kinship-based communalism, arising out of the rigors and constraints of nomadic pastoralism, has been a major factor, along with language and religion, in the cultural homogeneity that characterizes Somali life.

A dimension of this way of life that requires particular comment is the tradition of patriarchy, a topic that is of enormous concern to Farah, for reasons we explain in chapters 4 and 5. Lidwien Kapteijns captures this aspect of Somali experience succinctly: "Precolonial Somali society was an unambiguously patriarchal society in which women were barred from autonomy in production and reproduction, were excluded from formal political or religious leadership, and were not acknowledged as autonomous legal persons."[4] More recently there have been changes in the status of Somali women (not entirely for the better according to Kapteijns's analysis), but in the traditional frame of reference against which Farah's female characters are explicitly sketched, women owe whatever legal status they possess to the men under whose protection they are held. Thus, decisions affecting the life of a girl or unmarried woman are made by her father and those affecting a married woman by her husband, with male kin of these men stepping into the role should the father or husband die. Conforming to Islamic tenets, men may (and in the rural areas usually do) practice polygamy; departing from those tenets, men generally exclude women from all inheritance. Marriage is strictly exogamous, so women leave their families and communities when they marry to live in communities where they have no kin other than their husbands'. It is common for men to divorce wives past childbearing age, who must then seek other male protection, which often comes from grown sons with whom, Kapteijns suggests, they intentionally maintain close ties against such a day.[5] They do not participate in group councils but are represented, when they figure at all, by the men responsible for them. Their value is openly reckoned at half that of men—in cases of homicide, the traditional *diya* paid for a man is 100 camels while that paid for a woman is 50.

Farah often represents the condition of women in Somali society by what is, for him, one of its most disturbingly emblematic elements: female circumcision. This is a procedure that takes various forms in the different societies, mainly in Africa, in which it is practiced. In Somalia it appears in its most extreme form, in which a great deal of flesh is removed from the external genitalia and the opening is then stitched together, a procedure called infibulation, which is typically performed on girls between the ages of five and eight and often repeated after a woman gives birth. Many infibulated girls and women experience, besides the trauma and frequently the infection attending the operation itself, other complications relating to urination, menstruation, sexual intercourse, and childbirth. A 1981 study indicates that over 99 percent of Somali women were circumcised and that a majority of them favored the practice and expected it to continue.[6] Another study shows that although some form of female circumcision is practiced by varying percentages of the population in many African countries, only in the Somali-speaking countries of Somalia and Djibouti is it practiced so nearly universally.[7] Here, then, is yet another dimension of the cultural homogeneity that marks Somali society.

That homogeneity indeed has been so marked as to prompt Cassanelli to claim that "unlike any other African territory, Somalia in 1900 was already an embryonic nation" (Cassanelli, 5). If that embryo has since come to birth (a question on which there is room for debate), it was not through the internal dynamics of the nomadic pastoralist system. Although we have been using the word *system* to describe the workings of this society, the social units that are its basic elements are in constant motion, forming, dissolving, and re-forming in response to circumstances that arise in the natural and social environment and in defiance of stable structure. While nomadic pastoralism is an important basis of cultural unity in Somalia, therefore, it is also historically the primary source of political disunity and of the tension between unity and disunity in Somali social relations.

How can this be, one might ask, if kinship is so much the principle of political group formation? One is born, after all, into a family and a lineage and, except through marriage, this location in social space does not change. The answer is that kinship only seems to structure group adherence in Somali pastoralist society. What it does in fact is to delimit the possibilities of political alignment. Within those possibilities, actual functional relations are spelled out explicitly in treaties and contracts to which people become party at their own discretion, treaties that are almost entirely contingent on context and that are highly sensitive and responsive to changes in context. For example, drought, a common occurrence in Somalia, may require cooperative efforts to dig wells or share pasturage; camel raiding may motivate those threatened or victimized to band together to protect the herds and conduct reprisals; or renewed rainfall or the departure of the raiding group may permit greater dispersal and remove the need to remain in contractual relations that now seem cumbersome to maintain over long distances. In a land of such scarcity that starvation is often a quite real and present threat, particular clan loyalties cannot withstand the force of circumstances like those on which survival may depend. Clans and clan families are relatively vast and there is considerable latitude for selecting *which* clansmen one chooses to align one's household with and therefore on which council one will sit and deliberate group decisions. This is especially true of the *diya* groups, through which it is not unusual for clansmen to be pitted against one another regarding the claims and compensations to which they are contractually joined. Thus, membership in functional political units is crucial but discontinuous as groups grow and shrink, dissolve and reconfigure with the ever shifting circumstances of nomadic existence.

In such a process constituted authority can have little relevance. The Somali clan does traditionally recognize a sultan (*soldaan*)—Deeriye in *Close Sesame* is such a figure—and smaller groups may have headmen of sorts, but they mainly serve ceremonial functions, and should they acquire power beyond such roles, it is not constituted power but is accrued through personal prestige. Actual power to make and execute decisions belongs to the council as a whole, and if it lies in anyone's personal hands, it is in those of whoever argues most convincingly. This resistance to hierarchy among individuals applies to political segments as well, and for the same reasons. Decisions made at a "higher" level of clan segmentation do not necessarily override those made at a "lower" level (the quotation marks are necessary here because there are no corresponding terms in the Somali language for these hierarchical distinctions). Ultimately, the only stable functional structure in traditional Somali society is the household, which can and does enter and leave political alliances at will. It is with some reason therefore that I. M. Lewis has characterized political relations in this society as "democratic to the point of anarchy."[8] The parallels are unmistakable between these ways of conceiving political relations and the radically nonhierarchical and pragmatic vision of democracy at the heart of Farah's own political thought.

Somali nomadic pastoralists, then, are bound neither by stable group
membership nor by stable lines of authority, and the primary reason this
is so is that they *are* nomadic. John Markakis comments that "pastoralist
movement generates conflict without end."[9] *Diya* groups and other
mechanisms operate both to diminish and to accommodate conflict, but
not to eliminate it, for conflict is endemic to a way of life that requires
the continual, unregulated, and far-ranging movement of large numbers
of people and animals in search of the resources needed to sustain them,
resources whose location is also in movement. Although particular clans
tend to be associated with particular regions, they do not claim ownership of territory or recognize the territorial ownership of others. Individuals and groups, rather, hold property—both livestock and territory—
by force, that is, hold it as a practical matter, not as a matter of
principle. Borders and deeds of title are not practical in such circumstances, any more than are titles of office or legal citizenship. "Pastoralist
production," Markakis observes, "neither needs nor can afford state
institutions" (Markakis 1987, 17). It is the very logic of nomadic pastoralism therefore that accounts for this anomaly at the center of the
Somali social legacy: a society that is culturally unified to a degree
unparalleled in the region but politically disunified in the extreme.

In such conditions oratory emerges naturally as an essential and powerful medium of political life. Where there are no established lines of
authority or policies grounded in fixed political entities, collective
actions and policies must be worked out anew and in public as each new
occasion arises. Where political relations are explicitly matters of treaty
and contract, the instrumental importance of words is especially apparent. Each pastoralist head of household has the right to participate in
the councils of the groups with which he is aligned, and the manner of
his participation is oral: the practice of formal public argumentation.
The degree to which an individual's arguments on a given occasion are
successful is partly influenced by the respect in which the community
holds him, respect resulting from age, wealth, reputation for wisdom or
courage, and so on, and the order in which individuals speak may
depend on such matters. The overriding factor, however, is his rhetorical
skill, his ability to use effectively the considerable resources of the
Somali language in arguing his position.

The greatest control over these resources, and therefore the greatest
potential for power within this rhetorical arena, belongs to the poet.
Said Samatar makes the relationship between oratory and poetry in
Somali pastoralist society especially clear: "Not all words are equally

effective in influencing public decisions and . . . rhetorical discourse gains in power in proportion to its formalization. Against this background, the hold of the poetic craft on the Somalis becomes obvious when it is understood that poetry represents for them the ultimate formalization. Somewhere in the interplay of lyrical beauty and fusion of thought with expression, poetic oration turns into a force of the most potent sort which as one Somali put it, 'strikes with irresistible force.' "[10] This "ultimate formalization" is complex indeed and is as structure-bound as the political culture in which it operates is structure-free. Somali poets have traditionally composed in several different genres, each with its own rules of prosody and characteristic uses to which it is put. The *gabay*, for example, requires a pattern by which every hemistich of every line in the poem must contain at least one word that alliterates in the same initial sound. Moreover, the most skilled poets command— and employ—rich and extensive vocabularies, including words that would be unknown or considered archaic in less formal settings. Such a vocabulary not only embellishes and lends nuance to the poet's meaning but also provides needed repertoire to a poet composing a *gabay* of 100 lines who must come up with at least 200 words that alliterate in the same sound and still suit his theme semantically.

Somali poets have traditionally dealt with as broad a range of topics as have poets in most other cultures, but the special rhetorical climate of Somali culture has made poetry a central feature of political life. Pastoral*ist* poetry in this context should not be confused with pastoral poetry as that term is understood in the European tradition, that is, with lyrical evocations of an idyllic existence far removed from the cares of the real world. The Somali poet in the pastoralist tradition, on the contrary, typically deals directly with the most local and immediate of public concerns: a feud between clans, the behavior of community members, ways of dealing with the growing pressures of a drought, and so on. What is more, poetry of this sort is not simply detached commentary delivered from the sidelines, as topical poetry often is in other cultures. Its explicit intent is to shape the course of events, and when the poet is skilled it often does just that. The poet may rise in the midst of debate in council and counter the opinion of another in the "ultimately formalized" speech of a *gabay* composed for the occasion, and in this way exert significant political power. It is common, in fact, for poets representing different communities to engage in continuing debates in verse form, one answering the other (or sometimes several others) in chains that may grow to several—or in some cases over a hundred—poems long.

Indeed, poetry not only influences political events but also may initiate them. This is the case with poetry, and with oratory in general, for example, that deliberately insults another group in order to declare enmity, assert priority, or avenge insults suffered. Such cases may give rise to an ongoing feud of words, which may in turn develop into physical violence. In these ways the poet, precisely because he *is* a poet, often exerts overt and recognized political leadership.

The reason we have been using the masculine pronoun in referring to the orator and the poet in the political arena is that women, as we have indicated, are largely excluded from that arena in Somali pastoralist society. It is therefore extremely rare (though not unheard of) for poetry created by women in the classical tradition of the *gabay* and similar genres to be heard. This does not mean that women do not compose or recite poetry in Somali society—Farah's own mother was a noted oral poet—but only that they do so in genres considered "lighter" and far removed from public debate, such as lullabies, work songs, and songs of entertainment. Amina Adan, however, suggests that verse of this sort may not always be as light as one might think, that Somali women have long used these forms for multiple purposes, singing a child to sleep, for example, and at the same time protesting their treatment at the hands of men and expressing solidarity with one another as women. In such material she finds evidence that "the woman's movement has deep roots in Somali history."[11]

It is likely that relatively private and intimate oral expression of this sort is put to comparable purposes in many cultural traditions. The more formalized poetry of the public sphere in Somalia, however, stands in marked contrast to other oral traditions in Africa. While there is enormous variety in the products and practices of oral societies across the continent, research in this field has uncovered certain basic patterns that have wide general validity. According to these patterns, in comparably respected forms of orature in the public sphere (the oral epic among the Mandinka of West Africa, for example), the text has no known author or origin. A griot, or bard (who in some cultures is always a man and in others may be a woman), learns the text from an older griot and recites it at appropriate occasions. The griot does not memorize the text verbatim but learns instead a detailed repertoire of textual components and formulae for deploying them in performance. A number of elements may enter into this performance, including gesture, musical accompaniment, audience interaction, and the incorporation of new or modified components relating to the particular occasion and the local situation of the audience. One cannot say in these circumstances that the griot is the original author of the text, which may have come into being many generations before the performance and which may be significantly reworked (and passed on to another griot in this revised form) in a frame of reference supplied by its current audience. To this extent the text may be said to be the product of the collective authorship of the culture and the community. The griot, however, is far from being a neutral vehicle of transmission but exercises originality and creativity in the necessary act of improvisation by which all these elements (as well as the griot's own personal touches) enter into a given performance. Though greatly simplified, this account corresponds to the most basic current understanding of "high" verbal art as it is practiced in the majority of African oral cultures. We describe this pattern in some detail here because most of the published commentary by non-Somalis on Farah's relationship to Somali orature assumes that the Somali tradition and the more widespread griotic traditions in Africa are of a piece.

The fact is that nowhere in Africa do we find a more complete contrast to this pattern than in Somali oral poetry. A Somali poem in one of the classical genres is held to be the work of a single identified poet to an even greater extent than is the case in the European written tradition—to a greater extent in that an "anonymous" poem may be published and read in the European context, but a Somali poem may be recited only after the poet is first named and the circumstances in which it was composed explained, if they are unfamiliar to the audience. As in other cultures, the poem may be passed along and recited by others and long after the poet's death, but the reciter must memorize and repeat it word for word, with no distorting improvisation or distracting elements of performance added to the words as the poet composed them. These rules are so strict and so widely recognized that B. W. Andrzejewski calls them an "unwritten copyright law," and strict sanctions apply to violations of this law.[12]

What these practices mean is that oral texts are not held to be communal property and are not freely available for reshaping to the changing needs of communal life, as they are in most other African oral societies. So long as they survive in memory and in circulation, they remain the sole property and responsibility of the individuals who compose them and must be passed along utterly intact, syllable for syllable. The importance of this insistence on individual authorship is clear if one recalls the political function that many poets and poems serve in Somali society. Because poetry, as the highest form of oratory, has a direct impact on affairs within and between communities, it is crucial that the positions and the arguments expressed in it be transmitted, heard, and distinguished from one another accurately. Because the poet, as the most accomplished of orators, may wield great personal power—power, it is believed, that can work to the benefit of the community but that can also deceive and destroy—it is vital that his audience perceive accurately from whom the power of the poet's words emanates and to what ends it is directed. Some of the functions of the complicated and rigid rules of poetic composition now become apparent as well. The degree of success with which they are manipulated helps to establish and maintain not only artistic reputation but also leadership credentials, and the complexity of the poem itself helps guard against distortion, interpretation, or falsification in transmission. The result is a tradition of poetry that is highly conservative in some of its formal aspects but that, because it is so fiercely individualistic, breeds innovation in thought and style. It is these features that lead Samatar to speak of "the dynamic, wildly experimental and ever-evolving nature of Somali poetry," which nonetheless "remains fixed in a stable traditional frame-work."[13]

Nuruddin Farah is neither a pastoralist nor an oral poet, and he disavows any direct connection to the work of such poets, cautioning "let us not be romantic about the oral tradition," which he calls "defective" for the purposes of a contemporary writer.[14] Our contention nonetheless is that the cultural legacy of this pastoralist and poetic tradition bears constantly on Farah's own work. The reasons for this are developed in later chapters; what is important at this point is to identify the features of that legacy that are of particular relevance. Some of these we have emphasized already: the highly integrated vocabulary of ideas, values, and experiences that binds together traditional Somali culture, the resistance to political unity and stability driven by forces in the natural and social environment, and the tension between these in Somali cultural self-understanding. These features explicitly shape the thinking and behavior, whether by sympathy or by antipathy, of virtually all of Farah's fictional characters; and the problems they produce for identity formation and political action are among the problems with which Farah's art is most centrally concerned.

Another relevant feature is the patriarchal nature of Somali society and its consequences for the physical, social, and intellectual condition of women. Perhaps no other dimension of his work so distinguishes Farah as an African novelist as his attention to these issues, not only in his social critique of patriarchy itself but also in his use of patriarchy as a

figure for other forms of domination and in his exploration of the conflicted nature of human consciousness as it develops in the context of
these gender relations. Yet another feature is the traditional role of
poetry and the poet in traditional Somali society. Farah, as we have said,
is at pains to maintain a distance between his ways of working, as a
writer, and those of the oral poet—and this too distinguishes him from
other major African writers such as Ngugi wa Thiong'o of Kenya and
Chinua Achebe and Wole Soyinka of Nigeria. The conception of the verbal artist that informs his work nonetheless is in many ways strikingly
identical to the one we have seen at work in Somali oral culture: self-
conscious exercise of powerful language; an understanding of language
as powerful; attention to the dangerous as well as the beneficial possibilities of such power; an assumption that verbal art should be a discourse
of ideas, treat political topics, and serve political ends; and an insistence
on the individuality, originality, and independence of the verbal artist
both as creator and as political player.

  This complex idea of Somali culture, then, is a vital dimension of the
artistic mind of Nuruddin Farah and of the Somali society that he writes
to and about. It is, however, as we have presented it thus far, *only* an
idea, a static representation of a people that is no more a stranger to historical change than any other. In turning to the process of change over
time in Somalia we move closer still to the subject of Farah's art. As he
says in the epigraph to the present chapter, in fact, he believes that one
of his central purposes is to write "the true history of the nation." He is
not, however, a historical novelist in the usual sense of the term; his
books are set almost exclusively in the time of writing (parts of *Maps*, in
fact, are projected a few years into the future relative to the time in
which Farah wrote them). What is "historical" about these works, then,
is their analysis of a contemporary state of affairs understood in part as
the culmination of patterns of change long in the making, patterns that
must therefore figure importantly in the working vocabulary of a reader
of Farah.

  While some of that change has arisen internally, from the natural
dynamics of a living society, much of the historical change that concerns
our reading of Farah has, prior to independence, been generated or initially provoked by interaction between Somali-speaking communities
and forces outside Somalia. What exactly constitutes "inside" or "outside" Somalia, in fact, is less than clear, for historians, as well as for
Farah's characters. The earliest Somali-speaking populations occupied
the northern area of the present-day state and began to expand south-

ward and westward in the tenth century, encountering and overcoming
Bantu- and Oromo-speaking peoples in a process that did not culminate
in the present pattern of Somali occupation until early in the twentieth
century. For most of that period of expansion, Somalis found themselves
encroached upon as well by various outsiders. Among these were Arabs,
a powerful fixture for many centuries, beginning before the advent of
Islam, in much of the north and in coastal areas further south. Arab
sheikhs were, according to legend, the founders and namesakes of the
major Somali clan families, and Arab traders were the most likely
founders of the longest-established coastal towns, including the present-
day capital of Mogadiscio, which dates from the ninth century or earlier.
Another significant force was the Christian kingdom of Ethiopia,
located to the west and northwest. Beginning in the fourteenth century,
Ethiopians and Muslim Arabs in the region fought a series of religious
wars in which the Ethiopians for a time prevailed. Then, in the sixteenth
century, the Arab state of Adal launched a new and successful effort to
drive the Ethiopians back onto their own highlands, and several Somali
lineage groups joined in this campaign.

These facts complicate the historical picture of Somali culture and
politics in several ways. One is that, although Somali society itself
appears indeed to have displayed the cultural commonalities we have
described, it was by no means culturally isolated in the territory it occupied. On the contrary, it was aware of and in contact with two powerful
groups (Ethiopians and Muslim Arabs) organized around ideas and
social practices very different from its own. One of the most significant
differences is that both groups, unlike the Somalis, were highly centralized. This means, in the case of Adal and the other Arab states in the
area, that Somalis had exchange with Muslims practicing an Islam
designed to accommodate the needs of fixed settlement and a high
degree of institutionalization, in contrast to their own religious life as
pastoral nomads. In the case of these states and of Ethiopia, they were
dealing with polities that not only claimed territory the Somalis thought
of as their own but that made very different kinds of territorial claims,
ones expressed in terms of specific borders and sovereignty within those
borders. To the nomadic pastoralist such boundaries serve no useful purpose and obstruct a freedom of movement crucial to survival. To cross
such a boundary, for the nomad, is at the same time to cross a line
between ways of thinking about social existence. Finally, to have joined
with Adal in the war against the Ethiopians was to introduce, however
fleetingly, a new mode of political organization, for it required that the

several, widely separated Somali groups that participated make common cause with one another against an outsider and that they accept, for the length of the campaign, a hierarchical structure of authority. What stand out as important elements in this precolonial history for our reading of Farah, then, are the experience of highly varied possibilities for social organization laid over a deeply nomadic consciousness; the sense of common identity as a relationship that is both fluid and pragmatic; the long-standing threat felt by Somalis from neighbors who, unlike themselves, are states; the willingness of Somalis to band together to oppose that threat; and the initiation of a history of conflict with Ethiopia.

From the eighteenth through the mid-nineteenth centuries, other small states or statelike presences established themselves in the region, including outposts controlled by Omanis to the south in Zanzibar and by Ottoman Turks to the north in Egypt, as well as small Somali sultanates. Their presence was felt almost exclusively along the coast, however, and had little impact in the interior apart from the opportunities they provided for commerce. This relative freedom enjoyed by most of Somali society in ordering its own political affairs came to an end, however, with the Berlin Conference of 1884–1885, an event that altered the historical destiny not only of Somalia but of the continent as a whole. At this conference the major European powers signed a treaty that legitimized (according to their own thinking) their geopolitical ambitions and established procedures for asserting territorial claims and exerting administrative authority in Africa. In Somalia the effect was to accelerate a process whereby the British, French, and Italians, all of whom had recently initiated small footholds along the coast for various commercial and strategic reasons, expanded their spheres of influence in the region. Ethiopia, faced with this rapid growth of European hegemony, strongly reasserted its own claims to Somali-occupied territories. As a result, by the end of the century, borders had been carved across the Somali lands that closely resemble today's political map of the region, with every inch of these lands falling under the claim of one or another of these four imperial powers. The far-northwest corner of the Somali-speaking territories became French Somaliland, located in present-day Djibouti. To the east of this and covering most of the northern coast on the Gulf of Aden was British Somaliland. The coastal areas extending south along the Indian Ocean were consolidated as Italian Somaliland. The most southwesterly of these areas were incorporated into the British colony of Kenya as the Northern Frontier District. The

central inland area known as the Ogaden (after the name of the Somali
clan to which most of its occupants belonged) fell under the control of
Ethiopia. These five areas today are spoken of as Greater Somalia and
symbolically represented by the five points of the star in the Somali
national flag.

All of this was accomplished by treaty, and Somali groups themselves
were parties to some, though by no means all, of these agreements.
Lewis quotes the terms of one such treaty that followed the final Egyptian departure and comments on the limits supposedly contained in it:

> "Whereas the garrisons of His Highness the Khedive are about to be
> withdrawn from Berbera and Bulhar, and the Somali coast generally, we,
> the undersigned Elders of the . . . tribe, are desirous of entering into an
> Agreement with the British Government for the maintenance of our inde-
> pendence, the preservation of order, and other good and sufficient rea-
> sons." Nor did the clans concerned expressly cede their land to Britain;
> they merely pledged themselves "never to cede, sell, mortgage, or other-
> wise give for occupation, save to the British Government, any portion of
> the territory presently inhabited by them or being under their control."[15]

As members of an oral society, the Somalis who entered into these agreements had little experience with written documents, but they did, as we
have seen, know a great deal about negotiated treaties. In the Somali
way of understanding the occupation and control of land, however, such
treaties addressed only matters of present usage and movement. The
European and Ethiopian signatories, on the other hand, used these documents to justify lasting claims of ownership and sovereign authority,
the boundaries to which were negotiated among the competing imperial
powers quite without the consent of the Somalis who lived there. These
claims, in and of themselves, were irrelevant to the nomadic Somalis.
Slowly but increasingly, however, such claims began to function as
legally reinforced imperatives, and nomadic Somalis found themselves
treated for the first time as subjects of states, expected to observe borders, pay taxes, and bend to centralized authority.

These unaccustomed circumstances elicited uncharacteristic responses:
political rhetoric cast in nationalist rather than clan terms and political
leadership by men of religion rather than warrior herdsmen. Sufi sheikhs
were naturally better positioned for nationalist leadership than were
clan sultans or pastoralist elders because the brotherhoods appealed to
constituencies that crossed clan lines and because, in their teaching and
organizing roles, the sheikhs often traveled even more territory and in

more different directions seeking the faithful, than the pastoralists did seeking water for their herds. The most influential of these sheikhs was Sayyid Maxamad Cabdille Xasan. Often referred to simply as the Sayyid (an honorific title), this now legendary figure, invoked in many ways in the work of Farah, was the spiritual leader of the Saalihiya order, which many Somalis in the Ogaden joined in the late 1890s in response to the pressures of the Ethiopian occupation. Caught up at first in pressing the complaints of his followers against the Ethiopians, he soon found himself under suspicion by the British, who saw him as a potential source of rebellion, assisted the Ethiopians with information about his plans, and dubbed him the "Mad Mullah" after an epithet first used against him by Somali rivals in a theological disagreement.

Sayyid Maxamad's political career from that point on was a complicated one whose elements—and whose complications—have significance for a reading both of later Somali political history and of the political fiction and drama of Nuruddin Farah. As the leader of a Muslim community growing increasingly restive under the intrusions of allied Christian powers, the Sayyid began an armed rebellion with his followers against both the British and the Ethiopians, experiencing in various battles spectacular successes as well as crushing defeats. In the midst of these campaigns he began, apparently for the first time in his life, to compose poetry, dismissing and taking over the functions of poets in his entourage whose efforts he judged inadequate to the needs of his movement. The poems he produced were among the most powerful weapons in his arsenal and to this day have a widespread reputation as some of the finest ever composed in the Somali language. The political and military machine he built to prosecute the war was highly structured and centralized and was sometimes turned against clans that opposed him or were thought to support the British. He faced a revolt among his followers in 1909 and executed many of those suspected of leading it. After this reversal his power and success spread for the next several years. During this time a new and more anti-British ruler came to the Ethiopian throne, and Sayyid Maxamad entered into a brief alliance with him. The Sayyid's own style of rule became increasingly distant and dictatorial and he developed a taste for the luxuries that his power made available to him. His end and the end of his movement came in 1920, when the British attacked his forces with airplanes and then organized an assault by allied Somali groups, and when a devastating smallpox epidemic swept through his army. Sayyid Maxamad himself died of influenza at the end of that year.

There are many references to the Sayyid in Farah's fiction (as there are in Somali political discourse in general), and one of Farah's most strongly drawn characters, Deeriye in *Close Sesame,* takes the Sayyid's career as a frame of reference for his own political options and dilemmas. Out of that career, in fact, arise themes that inform Farah's work far beyond any single character or text. It is, once again, a legacy filled with contradictions. Sayyid Maxamad virtually invented Somali nationalism by the terms of his appeal, the compass of his recruitment, and the target of his campaign, which was not just a single enemy but the combined threat of imperialism—and yet the coalition he forged was still far from Somali-wide, and he manipulated clan loyalties and entered alliances with sworn enemies when his purposes required it, much in the nomadic and not the nationalist political model. He courageously asserted the rights and interests of Somalis against the oppressive policies and practices of the occupying forces—and yet he used his position to increase his own personal power, even at the cost of political executions, and to enjoy luxuries and pleasures denied his followers. His virtuosity as a poet was inspirational and is still—and yet the degree to which he monopolized the public rhetoric of his movement made poetry's potential for abuse emerge as clearly as its power to inspire, especially given the disparity that sometimes existed between his words and his personal actions. In an examination of these contradictions it becomes inescapable that the dictator figures in Farah's writing are degraded versions of a model whose original may be found in the much revered figure of the Sayyid, and that in this model are to be found some of the most provocative problems that drive Farah's political fiction.

Despite the lengths to which they went to put down the Somali rebellion, the British expended relatively little attention and few resources on the colony they had successfully defended. The Italians, on the other hand, were a far more aggressive presence in the Horn, developing an extensive infrastructure in the Somali territory they controlled and in 1935 invading and conquering Ethiopia. A few years later they brought World War II to the Horn as well, attacking and occupying British Somaliland. The British then recaptured this territory and ejected the Italians from Ethiopia, in the process retaining control of the Ogaden. This meant that all the Somali-speaking lands apart from Djibouti were reunified and they remained so through the end of the war. Indeed, it might be said that they were "unified" for the first time in history and because of, not despite, their occupation by the British, who took on responsibility for political administration (though it was not an integrated administration) of the territory as a whole. This was a unification, however, that was felt by most Somalis only in the constraints they faced as colonial subjects and not yet in their own political functioning. It was also short-lived. In 1948 the British returned the Ogaden to Ethiopia and in 1949 the United Nations decided to place the former Italian Somaliland under Italian trusteeship, envisioning independence at the end of 10 years. In 1954 the Haud, a vast area used for seasonal grazing, was also ceded to Ethiopia by the British.

This period (into which Nuruddin Farah was born in 1945), beginning with the British occupation and continuing under the postwar repartition, was a time of rapid transformation in Somali society, producing, along with certain advances, the troubled social and political conditions in which most of Farah's work is set. For one thing, these events resulted in shifting borders, increased policing of those borders, and changing patterns of administrative protection extended to Somalis using the lands crossed by those borders. These factors in the colonial presence generated clan disputes over territorial claims on a scale not seen before, thereby introducing new political dimensions into clan rivalries. In another important development, Britain reversed its policy of neglect in Somalia and began programs of education intended to provide Somali cadres for the administration of the territory. These programs continued under the British northern protectorate but were developed much more strenuously under the Italian trusteeship in the south.

Several consequences are of particular relevance for our reading of Farah. One was the rapid creation of an urban intelligentsia, which would develop into the "privilegencia" of Farah's novels. This was a class of young, educated, literate, multilingual Somalis whose origins very often were not in the long-established town families but rather in nomadic families and communities from which they migrated for education (both in colonial schools and abroad) and employment, but to which they retained strong ties. Another result of the expansion of education in the 1940s and 1950s was that this urban intelligentsia became the base for the nationalist sentiment and activity that had first arisen out of religious brotherhoods. In anticipation of eventual independence, organizations such as the Somali Youth League and the Somali National League formed to press a political agenda that included education, the development of a Somali script, an end to clannishness, improvements in the status of women, and the unification of Greater Somalia as a single nation. Furthermore, the continued partition of Somalia into British and Italian Somalilands and an occupied Ogaden produced different experiences and institutions in these areas (opportunities for education and advancement in civil service, for example, were much greater under the Italians than under the British); made it impossible to separate nationalist politics from the territorial configuration of clans; and complicated communication, because English was the language of administration and education in the north, Italian served those functions in the south, and Amharic was forced on Somalis entering school in Ethiopia. This last point leads in turn to yet another consequence of colonial patterns and policies in this period: the large-scale introduction of literacy and foreign languages into public discourse. The Somali language remained unwritten, despite several attempts to fit an orthography to it, and so economic and social advancement under colonial conditions and, to a certain extent, the pursuit of nationalist political organization were dependent on languages other than Somali, languages that were the property of the occupying powers and of the urban elite.

These were the conditions, then, in which Somalia achieved independence. The British agreed to renounce control of the northern territory in time for it to unite with southern Somalia as the trusteeship ended, and on 1 July 1960 the Somali Republic came into existence. The new state, with its elected president, National Assembly, parliamentary government, multiple political parties, and continuation of the tradition of free and open political participation, had reason to be hopeful for its future. Lingering problems, however, immediately clouded the picture. One was regionalism and the older problem of clanism that it fed and exacerbated. Because of differences in Italian and British colonial policies, southern Somalis were better positioned to assume and exercise political power in the independent state. Differences in political posture between the two regions became graphically apparent in 1961 when the new constitution was approved in a nationwide referendum by a vote that was overwhelmingly favorable in the south while drawing strong opposition in the north, and when army officers in the north rebelled in an unsuccessful attempt to secede. The policy goals of the new government were largely those of the preindependence parties out of which it was formed, but it had little success in meeting them. No progress was made on the language issue, for example, and the overriding concern with unification produced only an inconclusive and somewhat costly conflict with Ethiopia over the Haud in 1964. Among the costs of that conflict were acceptance of a client-state relationship with the Soviet Union in order to secure weapons (Ethiopia at the time lying securely in the Western fold) and an accelerated military buildup that was out of balance with Somalia's economic and political circumstances. The government and National Assembly drew charges, with some justification, of corruption, clan rivalry, and nepotism.

Out of this climate of increasing stagnation erupted the event that would set the course of Somali national life to this day and produce the antagonist that would haunt Farah's fiction. On 15 October 1969 a bodyguard assassinated the country's president, Abdirashiid Ali Shermaarke, and less than a week later the army deposed the government, installing Major General Maxammad Siyad Barre as president of a new Supreme Revolutionary Council whose 25 members were all military officers. The new government announced an ideology that was at once Marxist and Islamic, but few took these commitments seriously. The SRC renamed the country the Somali Democratic Republic while suspending most democratic institutions, including the National Assembly, the constitution, and political parties. The new policy agenda in many ways resembled that of the former government, but the new regime was not hampered by the same due-process constraints and therefore made more rapid progress in some areas than its predecessor. More serious (though still limited) attempts were made to improve the status of women. Power over local government was removed from traditional clan assemblies in order to reduce "tribalism." The *diya* system was outlawed. Portions of the population were resettled for economic advantage.

By far the most impressive of the new government's accomplishments was the achievement at last of an official Somali orthography and the spread of literacy in the Somali language. Attempts to create a system of writing had been many, but none had taken official hold or come into widespread use. Arabic had played a religious function for centuries in Somalia, but no one was able to make the Arabic script accommodate the Somali vowel system. A system called Cusmaaniya was developed in the 1920s and corresponded very well to the phonetic features of Somali, but it did so only by means of an invented alphabet for which there were no typewriters or printing presses. The Latin script used in European languages lacks some of the consonants of Somali but lends itself more easily than Arabic to adaptation, and it was a system using Latin characters that was introduced in 1972 on the third anniversary of the revolution. The military government imposed the new system with great determination, eliminating other languages from official usage, initiating an intensive literacy program, and decreeing that civil servants would be expected to pass a proficiency test within three months or face dismissal. By the following year Somali had become the sole language of instruction at the elementary-school level and within 10 years Somali-language textbooks were in use in all subjects at all grade levels. There are conflicting claims as to the degree of success of this literacy campaign. In 1983 Hussein Adam, editor of the official party journal in Somalia and therefore a government spokesman, wrote, "Somalia claims today a literacy rate of over 60%."[16] A 1990 United Nations estimate, however, put Somali literacy at only 24 percent, though the rate may once have been somewhat higher than this and fallen.[17] Whatever the true figure, the efforts of the military government to standardize the Somali language, bring it into written use, and modernize it to a level of adequacy for a wide range of purposes represent a significant and lasting legacy.

As with so many others in the Somali story, however, it is a mixed legacy, one that increased the power of Somalis to communicate but that also helped Siyad Barre to consolidate his own power. Comments by two individuals involved in this effort are unintentionally telling in this regard. Adam, in the report just quoted, notes that "the implementation of written Somali in various spheres of public life gave greater content to the rudimentary notion of Somali consciousness, namely the simple feeling of solidarity, the awareness of identity, strengthening the 'we' versus 'them' attitude" (Adam, 33). B. W. Andrzejewski, a British linguist who shared responsibility for the creation of the new orthography, indicates that it was official policy to develop new vocabulary through foreign loanwords "at higher levels of specialization," such as mathematics and the natural sciences, but that "using the existing resources of the language" was preferred "at the lower levels of education and in the vocabulary designed for public use, such as political terms, [where] this principle" has among its advantages "the strengthening of patriotic feelings and self-confidence."[18] The cheerful assumption behind these statements is that the very fact of using a language involves the user in attendant ideological commitments. It is not unusual for governments to profit by this fact through various means of controlling language use. In postrevolutionary Somalia, however, the government did more than just tightly control all public use of language through patronage, censorship, and monopolization of the media. It actually created the language used by its subjects, thereby owning and controlling public discourse to a degree matched by few other governments and quite at odds with the principles of open debate at the heart of both traditional political culture in

Somalia and Farah's own vision of political life. Still, as we have seen, that culture has always known the power of language to work ill as well as good. For example, Samatar explains how *afmiishaars,* traditional orators especially skilled in the negative use of language, joined the migration to the towns where they put their talents in the service of those in power: "Freed from collective kinship accountability and protected by powerful patrons, *afmiishaars* found the impersonal society of the city a fertile field in which to exercise their dark rhymes and to ruin reputations with impunity. Patronized by politicians and powerful men, they began to derive status, influence and economic privilege from their gift of the gab, and nowhere was this more obvious than in their intimate attachment to the powerful in the politics of pre- and post-independence Somalia" (Samatar 1982, 31). What took place in the new Somali political culture then, especially after 1969, was a loss of the traditional mechanisms for balancing and bringing accountability to the excesses of political rhetoric.

Those who practiced such rhetoric on behalf of the government of Siyad Barre had much work to do to disguise the brutality and failures of an increasingly tyrannical regime. The military officers who seized power in 1969 promised to restore civilian authority but never did so. Instead, in 1976 the SRC was dissolved, the Somali Revolutionary Socialist Party organized, and government control turned over to the Supreme Council of the SRSP. Within the Council, actual power rested in the hands of a five-member committee, including Siyad Barre and his son-in-law. Although national politics had supposedly been officially cleansed of "tribalism," virtually all positions of political power and trust were held by members of just three clans, those of Siyad Barre, his mother, and his son-in-law. In 1977 Siyad Barre invoked the nationalist dream of unifying Greater Somalia by lending government support to the independent Western Somali Liberation Front, committed to reclaiming the Ogaden from Ethiopia, a move that initially strength-ened his popularity among the Ogaden clan. Military success was short-lived, for the Soviets used the occasion to switch their support to Ethiopia, whose own Marxist revolution had come in 1974. Siyad Barre immediately accepted Western patronage to replace that of the Soviet Union, but the exchange did not bring him significant military assis-tance and Ethiopia drove the Somali army out of the Ogaden in 1978. That defeat on the battlefield (the most important battlefield of all for Somali nationalists, the Ogaden), the resulting flood of refugees, and the ease with which Siyad Barre had bent his knee first to one neocolonial

superpower and then to another fed the already growing disillusionment
with the revolutionary government. In the wake of an abortive military
coup in April 1978, two opposition groups formed, significantly aligned
with two different clans who felt excluded from power.

This led to even tighter single-handed control by Siyad Barre, and
with tighter control came harsher repression. In 1982 the government
put 17 prominent politicians under arrest, and the pattern of these
arrests revealed the extent to which Siyad Barre was desperately manipulating clan loyalties to stay in power. In 1986, weakened physically by
a car accident and politically by power struggles within his party and his
clan, Siyad Barre used his elite Red Beret forces to wage brutal campaigns of repression (whose measures included rape and the destruction
of wells) against clans and regions he considered threats. His government faced further strain when the droughts of 1985 and 1986 led to
severe famine in 1987. In 1988 Siyad Barre turned the full force of his
army against dissidents in the north, bombing the city of Hargeysa and
causing 40,000 deaths—an act of suppression that only strengthened
the opposition to his regime. Armed resistance grew, and Siyad Barre
responded by provoking massacres of unarmed crowds and imprisoning
prominent citizens and sheikhs who were trying to find a peaceful resolution to this national disaster. Clan militias, many armed by the weakened government, clashed across the country, and by November of 1990
widespread fighting erupted in the capital. On 27 January 1991 Siyad
Barre fled to the countryside with the remnants of his army, leaving
Mohamed Farah "Aidid" and Ali Mahdi to struggle for control of
Mogadiscio. These final days before the fall of Siyad Barre form the
background for Farah's most recent novel, *Secrets*. The departure of
Siyad Barre brought an end to the military dictatorship but not to the
forces of political chaos that he had helped bring into being. To recount
the next stage in Somali national life, however, a stage that is still in
progress, would carry us beyond the material of Farah's books to date.

In bringing our historical account to a close, we should note, however, that Siyad Barre's consolidation and abuse of power faced resistance not only from armed opposition groups but from very traditional
cultural fronts as well, especially oral poetry. As we have seen, it is no
contradiction in speaking of Somali political poetry to say that it is part
of the tradition to be innovative, for the forms employed by oral poets
are grounded not simply in adherence to custom but in functional prac-
ticality. In the case of this urban culture of resistance, the innovations
were not only formal and stylistic but also technological. Most Somalis

in the towns had long since acquired access to radios and audiotape players in order to participate in an oral culture that continued to be vigorous despite advances in literacy. These resources were brought into play by Somali poets who resisted the regime both from within the country and from exile by means of radio transmissions from abroad and through a brisk underground commerce in smuggled audiocassettes.

Farah's fierce literary resistance to dictatorship and other forms of oppression is properly read, therefore, as continuous with a tradition of Somali political poetry that is alive and active today. In the same measure as that poetry, though in different ways, it is profoundly informed by the history and culture of the Somali nation. Farah is both a product and a close student of that history and culture and has drawn on them extensively in the composition of his novels and plays. A detailed familiarity with this frame of reference therefore is indispensable to a productive reading of Farah's work, not only because it supplies a requisite factual vocabulary but, also, just as importantly, because it illuminates the complex, subtle, and very particular struggle over the meaning of political justice and legitimacy that is at the heart of that work.

Chapter Two
The Life of a Literary Nomad

I recall standing in a flat in Rome and holding a dead telephone in my hand. I had rung my eldest brother in Mogadiscio, requesting that someone pick me up at the airport, and my brother had advised me against returning home. But the words that have stayed with me are: "Forget Somalia, consider it dead, think of it as if it no longer exists for you!" A few minutes later . . . I felt as though something live was surging up from inside: whereupon another country was fired into existence, a new country responding to another logic, . . . that of a novelist who's been denied the possibility of returning to the land of his inspiration.
—Nuruddin Farah, "Homing In on the Pigeon"

Nuruddin Farah's writing is inseparable from the history of Somalia, and yet physical separation from Somalia has been Farah's own lot for most of his adult life. Moreover, although he is a profoundly political writer, his personal mode of engagement in politics has been intensely private. Like the life of his nation, therefore, Farah's own life is marked by apparent contradictions. There is a pattern to these contradictions, however, that provides a useful model for investigating the complex and difficult relationship between the private and public spheres that develops as a major theme over the course of his work.

It is often said that Farah's life is a "nomadic" one, and so it is. He has never, however, shared the life of the traditional nomadic pastoralist, which, for all its movement, is one very much tied to a single, relatively small community. Farah's wanderings, on the contrary, have engaged him in many widely scattered communities and cultures, a dimension of his experience that comes into play in the eclectic frame of reference and range of ideas that are so characteristic of his writing. Another dimension that is of importance to an understanding of his work is the degree to which the power of words, whose force in Somali culture we have noted already, becomes for Farah an instrument of self-definition, marking his life as one centered in the mind and the imagination. These two closely related dimensions are of vital importance to Farah's literary biography from its beginning.

The connection between wandering and words, in fact, enters into the course of Farah's life even before his birth: he is the son of an interpreter for the British colonial administration whose work took him to many parts of the Horn. His father, whose own parents and siblings were scattered across several regions of Somalia, was brought up by an elder sister in Nairobi, Kenya. He married Farah's mother in the Somali town of Kismayo and continued to travel while his family grew. Nuruddin Farah was born in 1945 in the town of Baidoa, the fourth child among five boys and five girls. When Farah was two years old the family moved to Kallafo in the British-occupied Ogaden. A year later the British turned the Ogaden over to Ethiopia, and Farah's father, rather than follow the withdrawal, left the service of the British to open a retail business in Kallafo. There Farah attended both Qur'anic school and a public school that his father helped establish for the Somali community under Ethiopian authority. Because of the lack of educational materials in Ethiopia, Farah and his classmates used textbooks produced for schools in the British East Africa colonies. A Christian evangelical mission eventually opened a school in the area as well, and from all of these diverse institutions Farah drew his early education.

Farah's life with words, from an early age, was equally diverse. He soon became proficient not only in his native Somali but also in Arabic, Amharic, and English (in that order), then picking up Italian from an older brother who traveled to Mogadiscio and learning to use the invented orthography Cusmaaniya, which he has said he viewed at the time as "an underground Somali script, a symbol of Somali nationhood."[1] Two of his great-grandfathers were oral poets, as was his mother, whom he has called his "greatest influence."[2] She composed in the *buraambur* genre practiced by women and created lullaby praise songs for the children and songs for community occasions like births and weddings. He was so impressed by his mother's powers that today he feels "she would have become a major poet had she not had so many children."[3] He retains vivid early memories of his mother practicing her craft. Significantly, those he cites are not memories of public performance but of the private creative process: "[S]he used to pace up and down wherever there was some space in the courtyard, thinking about her poems, and all I could actually hear were murmurs of her own whispers to herself. And then I used to be amazed with the final result: a poem to be sung, chanted to music."[4] Quite apart from the presence of his mother, he grew up surrounded in his community by oral poetry, which he heard performed publicly, quoted in conversation, and composed for school competitions. When he was quite young, his family assumed that he would grow up to become a poet in the family tradition.

The poetic world inhabited by the young Farah soon grew, however, to include the written word, which came to him not only through his schooling but through books supplied by his brothers, who often tested him on what he had read. Theirs was a family of readers and scholars. All but two of the children eventually earned university degrees, and his sisters received educations equivalent to those of his brothers, a fact significant in Farah's developing consciousness of the condition of women. In this family setting, he recalls, "we were brought up slightly differently in the sense that, in addition to the oral literature, we were also exposed to Arabic poetry and English poetry. So it was a richer world, I think, because it gave us access simultaneously to different cultures" (Interview, 1996). The range of those cultures was apparent already in his early reading, which included Agatha Christie, *The Thousand and One Nights,* Ernest Hemingway, Bertrand Russell's *History of Western Philosophy,* and, in Arabic translation, *Crime and Punishment* and *Les Misérables.* With all of this reading, the family expectation that Farah would be an oral poet soon transformed in his own mind into an ambition to write. His professional life as a writer may, in fact, be said to have begun at an unusually young age and in a way that made its own contribution to his artistic development: "For several years I earned my pocket money by writing letters in English or Arabic on behalf of men or women who did not know how to read or write. Aside from this being a source of income for a schoolboy, the stories they told me were fascinating, and I became privy to their adult worries and secrets, . . . affording my young mind access to the tribulations of the period before I reached my teens."[5]

Farah passed his early life, then, as a colonial subject of Ethiopia. This period came to an abrupt end in 1963 when his family fled to Mogadiscio to escape the war in the Ogaden between Ethiopia and the newly independent Republic of Somalia. This was a significant change in fortunes for the family. They had been relatively comfortable in Kallafo but had to leave their property behind to move to Mogadiscio, where Farah's aging father had difficulty finding work. Sharing the new burden of supporting the family with his older brothers, Farah became a clerk-typist for the Ministry of Education. He had nearly finished the equivalent of secondary school in the Ogaden but left with no formal certificate. He therefore took a series of courses at a teacher-training college, passing the exams needed for a secondary-school diploma over the next year and a half.

During this very busy period Farah also began submitting his writing for publication. His first substantial short story, "Why Dead So Soon?," appeared in 1965 in the now-defunct English-language newspaper *Somali News.* The story met with a favorable reception and Farah enjoyed his first taste of celebrity. A second story was published in 1966, which he then showed to the Canadian writer Margaret Laurence, who was visiting Somalia and who later wrote him from England, offering to get the piece republished there if he would only cut the last paragraph. His confidence in his ability to reach print on his own terms by then was such that he refused.

In the same year Farah was offered a scholarship to the University of Wisconsin but chose instead to enroll at Punjab University in Chandigarh, India, where he studied literature and philosophy, earning his bachelor's degree in 1969. While in India, Farah wrote intensively, producing three novels in addition to more short fiction and the beginning of a play. This was a period in which he struggled with his craft and his own sense of vocation, one that began in disappointment but culminated in the breakthrough that launched his career. He submitted the first two novels for publication, but both were rejected and have never appeared in print. An editor's letter concerning the second arrived one day in 1967 as he was on his way to take an exam in a course on the English novel. It was a particularly harsh rejection, which he recalls today as having been expressed in the following terms: "Dear Mr. Farah, If your father is a farmer, please continue in that line; if your father raises chickens, please continue in that profession, because you have no talent as a writer" (Interview, 1996). Deeply discouraged, he returned home without taking the exam and decided to leave the university, changing his mind only when his eldest brother, Mohamed, called and urged him to complete his degree and not to lose confidence. Heeding this brother's advice, as he was to do later at another crucial juncture in his life, he not only stayed on but turned his hand, in the same year, to a third novel. This was *From a Crooked Rib,* which he completed in less than a month and a half and saw published by Heinemann Educational Books, in its African Writers Series, in 1970.

From a Crooked Rib laid the groundwork for an international literary reputation that today, for most readers, rests entirely on Farah's novels. Before leaving India, however, and in the midst of his fiction writing, Farah set to work on a play, *A Dagger in Vacuum,* which he finished after his return to Mogadiscio. He made extensive efforts to get the play produced and published but without success. He continued, nevertheless, to write for the theater, eventually completing three works of drama that were produced for stage and radio audiences. He made plain the degree to which he entertained a serious commitment to the theater, even at this early stage in his career, in a 1973 letter to his editor at Heinemann, James Currey: "Look I am a dramatist, not a novelist, James. I feel this from the flow of my pen."[6] The two modes of writing were in such competition for his artistic energies at the time, in fact, that he inserted stage directions into the page proofs of *From a Crooked Rib,* a device that his publisher declined to adopt.

Farah's return to Somalia coincided with the revolution that brought Siyad Barre to power. He went to work as a secondary-school teacher and lecturer at the Somali National University—duties that included a summons from the government to give personal instruction in English to Siyad Barre's son-in-law—and he continued to write. He was newly married to an Indian woman named Chitra Muliyil and in 1970 he became the father of a son, Koschin. Though this marriage ended soon after, in other respects this was a very hopeful time for Farah, who had gained a certain prominence as the first Somali citizen to have published a novel. At the time, he saw the revolution as a good thing for the nation and even lent his support to the government: "I probably wrote one or two favourable articles in around 1971, but I wasn't actually under any pressure as such: I believed in the things that I was writing. Somalia needed a revolution and therefore we all invested our hopes in it."[7] He did not, however, see himself at the time as a political actor in the conventional sense and he hoped, as a writer, to remain above the fray: "I had come from India pregnant with a novel and a play: neither had anything to do with politics. In point of fact, my favourite authors during that period were James Joyce, Samuel Beckett and Virginia Woolf—and in my naivety I thought of their writings as apolitical. . . . I began writing the sort of things which were as apolitical as I could make them."[8]

He soon changed his view both of the revolution and of the political position he occupied as a writer. Two considerations entered into this change of heart, and the first is not difficult to discover: the increasing tyranny and brutality of Siyad Barre's rule, which he observed closely and was appalled by. The second is more personal but especially relevant to an understanding of Farah's work: the restrictions the new regime placed on his own intellectual and artistic expression. His first experience of these restrictions came when his efforts to stage *A Dagger in Vacuum* in Mogadiscio were blocked by government censors, who labeled the work "scandalously un-revolutionary" ("Why I Write," 1596). The play includes a character who becomes drunk, which allegedly "would show the moral weakness of the Somali people" (Interview, 1996). Even more stinging to Farah was the government's censoring of a novel he wrote in the Somali language, the first to appear in the newly established Somali orthography. This work was accepted for serial publication in a Mogadiscio newspaper in 1973. While Farah was away from Somalia for three months, however, publication of the novel was discontinued. Its plot concerns a young man who rebels against his parents and their principles, an image of Somali social relations that once again ran afoul of the censors, who refused even to return the unpublished chapters to Farah. His illusion that his previous work had been "apolitical" was dispelled when a distinguished Marxist scholar visiting Somalia publicly "attacked *From a Crooked Rib* savagely for being a . . . bourgeois kind of novel" that concerns itself with "some stupid young woman thinking about her own freedom, and so forth, when the nation is in chains" (Interview, 1996). As a result of this attack he was called in by the authorities for questioning. It was by now clear to him that his was to be—and had been from the beginning—the life of a *political* writer, whether he wished it to be or not.

Farah continued to write prolifically, but his work has never since been published or allowed for sale in Somalia (though some of the novels have circulated clandestinely). In 1972 he submitted to Heinemann a draft of *A Naked Needle,* the novel with which he had "come from India pregnant" and which would go through extensive revisions before its publication in 1976. During his 1973 travel outside Somalia, which took him to the Soviet Union, Hungary, Greece, and Egypt, he took the opportunity to observe other dictatorial regimes in operation, and in 1974 he wrote an outline for a series of novels that would evolve into the trilogy *Variations on the Theme of an African Dictatorship.* He set to work immediately on this material, beginning a draft that eventually became *Sweet and Sour Milk.*

At the same time, Farah was looking for ways to further his training as a writer, especially as a dramatist. In 1971 he was offered a two-year scholarship by the British Council to study Anglophone African drama and admitted by the University of Leeds to a program leading to a master's degree, but he was unable to secure a release from his teaching commitments in Mogadiscio. In 1974 another opportunity came, and this time he left for England to pursue a year of postgraduate study in theater at the University of London. He then transferred to the University of Essex, where he spent a second year. There he fulfilled very nearly all of the requirements for an M.A. but left without the degree. As part of these requirements he finished a play called *The Offering*, which he had begun in Mogadiscio and which was produced at Essex. During this second year of study he was also attached to the Royal Court Theatre in London, where he sat in on rehearsals as an informal training to become a director.

While in England he continued to work on *Sweet and Sour Milk* and in March of 1975 went to Denmark to work alone in the apartment of a friend. There he wrote a completely new draft in the space of 18 days. Returning to England with the new book in hand, he at first "put it on hold on the assumption that [he] would go to Somalia and finish it in Somalia, in other words, with some authenticity" and set to work on the second novel in the trilogy, *Sardines* (Interview, 1996). He soon changed his mind about holding back *Sweet and Sour Milk*, however, as he grew increasingly worried about the consequences that his writing might have, for himself and for his family, once he returned home. There was good reason to worry. *A Naked Needle*, which had still not appeared, offered a generous view of Siyad Barre personally but was critical of his supporters and presented some of the same "problems" that the censors had objected to in his Somali-language novel, while *Sweet and Sour Milk* was ferociously critical of the regime. A memo written to Farah's editor by an assistant in August of 1975 reveals the dilemma Farah felt himself to be in: "Nuruddin came in and is very concerned about the publication date of *Naked Needle*. He hopes to send us his other ms. *Sweet and Sour* within the next month. . . . He wants to return to Somalia next July but is worried that this might be politically unsafe. He feels that his decision whether or not to return depends on the reception in Somalia to his books and he therefore wants them both out (if we accept *Sweet and Sour*) a few months before his possible return. He says that he will then be able to gauge whether his family will be safe."[9]

It would be three more years before *Sweet and Sour Milk* appeared, but *A Naked Needle* did at last reach print in 1976 and did in fact elicit indications of the attitude the government was to take toward Farah and his family. In July of that year, as he had planned, he left England to head home. While in transit in Rome he called his brother Mohamed to ask that he be met at the airport on his arrival. Mohamed occupied a highly placed position in the Somali government, which he was eventually to lose as a result of the publication of *Close Sesame*. For the present, however, that position allowed him to form a judgment as to the likely consequences for Farah were he to return. Mohamed's advice during that phone call was that he not do so, and it took the dread form that

Farah quotes in our epigraph to this chapter: "Forget Somalia, consider it dead, think of it as if it no longer exists for you."[10] Once more Farah followed his brother's counsel—not forgetting Somalia, but renouncing hope of returning any time soon to the land of his birth, which he was not to set eyes on again for 20 years.

At this point his life as a "nomad" began in earnest. He remained in Italy for the next three years, working on *Sweet and Sour Milk* and *Sardines* (which was originally set not in Mogadiscio but in Milan). Little money was coming in from the two novels in print thus far, and so, while he worked on the next two, he earned his living by teaching English, by publishing short pieces under several pen names, and by taking up his father's original profession, "translating from various languages into various languages" (Interview, 1996). There was a growing community of young, educated Somali dissidents in Italy during this period. Though Farah did not play a role in their political activities, he knew them, observed them closely, and incorporated what he observed into his own chosen form of political action, which was to write.[11] Besides the trilogy, he continued to work at drama, including a radio play, *A Spread of Butter,* which was based on material first developed in *The Offering* and broadcast by the BBC African Service in 1978. His interest in script writing, in fact, extended to cinema, and late in 1979 he moved to Los Angeles to write for the screen. He completed at least one film script, but the agreement he was working under went sour, with the result that he found himself in difficult financial straits. In 1980 *Sweet and Sour Milk,* which had been published the previous year, won the English-Speaking Union Award. This award, however, brought Farah more honor than cash and he was forced at last to seek a teaching position at the University of Bayreuth in Germany. He spent the first six months of 1981 there and during that time wrote the whole of *Close Sesame,* completing his Dictatorship Trilogy in the process.

To this point Farah had spent his exile entirely in Europe and the United States. That pattern changed definitively in October of 1981, when he went to Jos, Nigeria, to teach and write. He resolved henceforth to keep his base in Africa and, furthermore, to live and work in as many different parts of the continent as possible. This plan reflected, in part, a personal need to be where he felt at home: "The heat, the smells, the dust that comes through the screened window, the noises you hear in the early morning. All these remind me of where I come from."[12] In part, this commitment expressed a strongly held principle that, as an African writer, he should live with and share the experience of Africans, and in this he draws a sharp distinction between himself and African writers who have made different choices: "I think it is easier for me to ask relevant questions, from which I am able to come to the right conclusions, if I am living in Africa. To talk politics as some Africans do while living in Europe is an absurdity, it is a betrayal of Africans to choose to speak on their behalf while living in the West. In Africa, I suffer the same troubles, the same food shortages, the same power cuts, as Somalis, and therefore . . . the experience of Africa helps me consolidate my knowledge of the situation" (Interview, 1989, 187).

It is a plan to which he has largely adhered. He has traveled widely and spent periods of several months teaching outside Africa in locations including Berlin, Stockholm, the State University of New York at Stony Brook, Brown University, the University of Minnesota, and the University of Texas. His home address and "base of operations" since 1981, however, has remained in one part or another of the African continent. This decision coincided with a period of consolidation in Farah's career, one that confirmed his early confidence that he was to be a writer by profession. With the publication of *Sardines* in 1981 and *Close Sesame* in 1983, the Dictatorship Trilogy was before the public, his books were beginning to appear in translation in several other languages, and offers of teaching positions were coming his way unsolicited. Though he continued to live a modest lifestyle, he was never again forced by financial pressure to write what he did not want to write or to teach when it was not convenient. Indeed, by 1989 he felt able to say to an interviewer, "I am one of four so-called major writers who live by the pen: Achebe, Ngugi, and Soyinka are the other three."[13]

While a visiting reader at the University of Jos, he wrote and produced a play, *Yussuf and His Brothers,* and he wrote the first version of *Maps.* In 1984 he moved on to the Gambia, hoping to find there "time and peace" to write.[14] In the same year, in response to a request from his editor to supply the final page of *Maps,* he instead expanded the manuscript to more than twice its original length, developing it into the beginning of a second trilogy. By 1986 he had completed a draft of the second book in that trilogy, *Gifts,* before being invited by the Gambian government to leave in response to an interview in which he expressed criticism of President Dawda Jawara. As Farah tells the story, this was a fitting conclusion to a productive period of residence that had a rocky beginning: "When I first went to the Gambia I was . . . given a few days to leave the country. They suspected me of belonging to some organisation to sabotage and help in the overthrow of the Jawara regime. . . . I was given a temporary permit until it was made sure that I was not involved in sabotage activities" (Interview, 1986, 54). From the Gambia Farah went next to Sudan, which served as his home base until 1989. During this time he traveled widely, taught in Khartoum at the national university, completed *Gifts,* and began the last novel in the new trilogy, *Secrets.*

Farah was working under a fellowship in Berlin in 1990 when his mother, whom he had not seen since leaving Somalia, died in Mogadiscio, and when Somalia entered the final stages of the civil conflict that would result in the ouster of Siyad Barre. This was the beginning of a period of transition in Farah's life, both personal and artistic, that continues to the present. When he returned to Africa later that year it was to Uganda, where he met Amina Mama, a feminist scholar who has published studies in the sociology of gender. They married in 1991. In Uganda Farah took a position at Makerere University, a position he resigned the next year following public criticism by Ugandan President Yoweri Museveni. The reason for the criticism, by Farah's account, was that Farah had urged Museveni, at the time chairman of the Organization of African Unity, to use his good offices to intervene in Somalia. Characteristically Farah proposed an intervention that would be verbal rather than military: a summons to Siyad Barre and the leaders of the opposition factions to come to the Ugandan capital of Kampala and talk until they had resolved their differences. By way of response, Museveni warned Farah away from politics in much the same language an editor had once used in warning him away from literature (and with similar effect): "Maybe you are a very good novelist, maybe an outstanding professor of literature, but when it comes to politics, let me tell you, you are too naive. If you want my advice, stay away from it."[15]

He did not stay away from it, but neither did he find that he could get at it as readily through his novels as he once had, because of the uncertain direction of Somali politics following the collapse of the Siyad Barre regime. From Uganda, Farah moved his home base to Ethiopia while continuing to travel and accept appointments elsewhere. He finished a draft of *Secrets* and with it his second trilogy in Stockholm in 1992. The backdrop to the action in these three novels is one of growing civil violence and anarchy, but the fictional image of the impending collapse throughout the trilogy remains as diffuse and unresolved as the reality that inspired it. In this climate of uncertainty Farah decided to defer publication of *Secrets* and to interrupt work on a separate novel in progress that dealt directly with the subject of civil war, waiting for the

pattern of events against which these books will be read to reach its conclusion: "I like my books to be a commentary on Somalia and the history of Somalia, and I like them to follow it to a certain degree—not to
dictate, but to follow. And it was turning out that Somalia was undergo-
ing far more changes than one could explain [or] predict. . . . So I was
holding myself back, because the Siyad Barre dictatorship was easy to
find as a theme [in the first trilogy], whereas it was very difficult nowadays, you couldn't actually tell" (Interview, 1996). Although Somalia
continued to resist explanation and prediction, Farah eventually
returned to *Secrets*, made light revisions to the 1992 draft, and published
it in 1998.

In the interim he turned to a different form of "commentary," first
undertaken in a lecture at Oxford in 1991 on the plight of Somali
refugees. That lecture was the beginning of a project of research and
reflection on the historical roots and current condition of displaced
Somalis, both inside and outside the country, and on the causes of the
collapse of civil order there. The intended outcome is a nonfiction book
whose working title is *Asleep, When Awake*. Among those displaced
Somalis have numbered most of the members of Farah's family, including his father, with whom he was briefly reunited in 1991 in a refugee
camp in Kenya and who died shortly thereafter. It was only after all of
his immediate family had left, died, or disappeared that Farah himself
returned to Somalia in May of 1996, after a 22-year absence, to pursue
his research for the book in progress. Farah and his wife now make their
home in Kaduna, Nigeria, with their daughter, Abyan, and son,
Kaahiye. There, about 100 miles from the Nigerian capital of Abuja
(the home in exile, until his death in 1995, of the former Somali dictator
Siyad Barre) Farah continues to write about the political collapse of
Somalia and to imagine its possible futures.

What meaning to attach to Farah's own exile—indeed, whether even
to call it that—is a complicated matter. Its complications moreover bear
directly on themes in his work and his efforts over the years to explain
them therefore require careful attention.

His initial impetus to "take an extended leave from Somalia" was the
obvious danger to his own safety and freedom to work that his return
would have entailed.[16] Though he writes repeatedly of people who suffer
political imprisonment and torture, he himself has been spared these
experiences. No explicit threat of arrest or persecution forced his decision in 1976 not to board the plane for Mogadiscio, but his judgment

that he "would probably have spent many years in detention centres" had he attempted to live and write in Somalia is clearly well-founded.[17] Several other considerations as well have entered into his ongoing decision to prolong his exile, prominent among them an ethical refusal to compromise with the regime. In this respect, he has insisted, "I am not the one who is in exile; it is the leaderships, the dictators of Africa that are in exile. I may be absent physically, but I am not absent spiritually nor am I exiled from my own people who, to the best of my knowledge, have a high respect for the principles by which I stand, and still retain their trust in me" (Interview, 1989a, 183). A writer who stands by his principles in this way, he has said, far from being exiled *from* his people, can be "in exile *with* them, by being distant from the corrupt elites from whom he has chosen to disassociate himself."[18]

Contrary to what one might expect, however, Farah has also chosen to disassociate himself from other Somalis who have made the same political choice regarding exile. He never actively joined the Somali resistance movement in Italy and has not taken part in organized political efforts directed against any of the several dictatorial regimes under which he has lived. He explains his decisions not to become involved in collective action in two ways. One has to do with his analysis of the actual nature of the problems facing Somalis and of the proper response of the writer to these problems:

> I'm not one of those who fights a regime. If I did not make this clear I think I should have failed in my duty as a writer: that Siyad Barre was not a target for me. No dictator is born out of a vacuum. . . . And my worry is that more and more writers, and Africans in particular, concentrate on the regime that is in power and work very hard at destroying it . . . without due regard for the society from which the dictators come. . . . Siyad Barre is not the problem. The problem is Somali society. Somali society is authoritarian. (Interview, 1996)

His preference to go it alone politically, however, also has to do with his perception of the ways resistance organizations work:

> I have an aversion to joining movements, and the reason is that movements have no center to them. What happens is that, although people are working for a cause, they're also working against one another. . . . I have never been a member of any movement, because I was known to be a dissident and therefore I didn't need my presence to justify who I was.

The majority of these people [Somali dissidents in Italy] made "move-menting" into a business, because they weren't doing anything else. They were "in politics," they were fighting against the dictatorship in the only way they could. . . .
I was also against many of the things these very people were doing . . . *outside* the movement time [i.e., in their personal relations]. Because dictatorship for me is not merely that political thing. Dictatorship for me is part and parcel of the way we live. (Interview, 1996)

For these reasons, then, Farah's political life in exile has been a solitary one.

The nature of his exile is further complicated by considerations that are more particular to Farah the private individual and the artist. One of these is a personal longing for solitude itself and therefore an ironic need for distance from the very people with whom he seeks to remain "spiri-tually" present through his writing: "We Somalis are a loving lot and we are a physical people; we touch noisily, and we talk a great deal. I have a morbid dislike of crowds, I loathe coming into bodily contact with more than one person at a time. . . . In the years I lived in Somalia, I remem-ber agonising over my privacy" ("Exile," 181). Related to this "dislike of crowds" is a dislike of being crowded by the world about which he writes, a need to be able to regard it coolly and from afar. "If I lived in Somalia," Farah has said, "it would be in my eyes, my throat, my blood, my food, everywhere, and I would be so obsessed that I wouldn't be able to write."[19] Thus he has often insisted that his ability to write effectively about Somalia is not merely unimpaired but enhanced by his distance from it: "Being away has helped me write with a clearer vision. Distance distils and makes ideas worth pursuing" (Interview, 1987b, 60). Indeed, given the enormous cultural range of Farah's artistic and intellectual for-mation, there is a sense in which he would have seen a choice to remain *in* Somalia as a personal exile and an impoverishment of his resources as a writer, regardless of the regime in power: "Even if I returned, I would still be in exile because Somalia can't contain the experiences that I have been exposed to through living in so many different countries and conti-nents" (Interview, 1987b, 60–61).

The rationale by which Farah has maintained his exile, then, is a complex one, and it has often required of him an effort of will bordering on bravado to sustain: "It's certain I've made my parents unhappy . . . ; true that I've denied my son my company. But my conscience has been content. In other words, I haven't doubted for one single instant of the correctness of my actions, my decisions."[20] His doubts, however, about this most central fact of his adult life and career, his exile from family and nation, have in fact been persistent and lively, and the questions have deepened with time. In 1990, a week after his mother's death, Farah wrote, "I often ask myself what I would do and how I would behave if I had to live in Somalia today, I wonder would I be as courageous as I am now, living abroad as I do and in relative bourgeois comfort. . . . There is no running away from the tragic intimations of who I am, and what is expected of me, a son to my parents, a father to my son, a comrade to this, an arch political opponent to that and so on and so on. . . . But would I be just as brave if I were in Mogadiscio at this very moment? I am not so certain."[21] In 1992 he pondered, "Looking back on it now I wonder if I was being unreasonable in insisting, when giving interviews to the press, that I was *not* in exile, that it was Siyad Barre who *was,*"[22]; and, despite his oft-expressed confidence that he could create true-to-life Somali characters from afar, he noted, "Of late, however, I've failed in raising in them an instinct of humanity" ("Savaging," 17). Farah's exile, then, is complex both in its motivation and in the price it has exacted.

The terms in which Farah has experienced and explained his exile—refusal to compromise with injustice, insistence on the independence of the private self, pursuit of an intellectual life that freely crosses cultural boundaries—are the terms of the dilemmas he has constructed for his own characters in one novel or play after another. What separates his experience from those of his characters is that their struggles arise within the framework of nation and family and often in relation to organized political resistance, whereas Farah has lived them at a self-conscious distance from nation, family, and political movement. This relation between Farah's life and the lives of his characters is illuminating for a reading of his work, because it calls our attention to a way of understanding these social formations—family, nation, and so on—that is crucial in Farah's political thought. For Farah, such formations are not the inevitabilities, the givens, by which lives and identities are defined; rather they are instruments to be critically used, rejected, or transformed for political purposes in which each individual, *as* an individual, bears responsibility. Farah's deepening personal struggle to come to terms with his own most basic political purposes and responsibilities, therefore, is the same struggle that he rewrites and reexamines as novelist and dramatist over the course of his work to the present moment.

Chapter Three

"The Country of My Imagination": Farah's Novels and Plays

> For a little under twenty years I have dwelled in the dubious details of a territory I often refer to as the country of my imagination. . . . I have always considered countries to be no more than working hypotheses, portals opening on assumptions of allegiance to an idea. . . . At times, though, one's loyalty may be owed to another idea equally valid. . . . During the long travel out of one hypothesis to another, . . . a refugee is born, who lives in a country too amorphous to be favoured with a name but . . . whose language is imbued with the rhetoric of future visions.
>
> —Nuruddin Farah, "Homing In on the Pigeon"

Out of the material of Nuruddin Farah's personal and sociohistorical worlds, for all their contradictions and ironies, emerges a "country of the imagination" that is remarkably unified. Interrogating relentlessly all "assumptions of allegiance," Farah has constructed in his novels and plays a world in which definitions of oneself and one's relationships to others are but "working hypotheses." The body of work that contains that world is a close weave of artistic elements and intellectual concerns sustained and developed over a career of three decades.

That development reflects three significant stages in Farah's own life and in the life of independent Somalia. The first includes Farah's first two published novels, *From a Crooked Rib* and *A Naked Needle*. These were written between 1967 and 1972, during the final years of the parliamentary government and the early years after the revolution. This was the period of Farah's undergraduate study in India and his return to Somalia as a young man flush with success, the pleasures of a new family, and legitimate expectations of a bright career in Mogadiscio as a teacher and writer. It was a time of belief, for Farah, in the promises of independence, in the correctives provided by the revolution, and in the possibility of his sparing himself involvement in political turmoil. He was primarily concerned at this stage with the need to transcend those elements of tradition that he saw as barriers to social justice and intellectual openness to the world. His work during this time is characterized by a belief that such transcendence is indeed within the grasp of those bright enough to see and bold enough to seek the space and light of freedom.

The second stage in the development of this fictional world includes *Sweet and Sour Milk, Sardines,* and *Close Sesame,* a trilogy of novels collectively titled *Variations on the Theme of an African Dictatorship,* and includes also a radio play, *A Spread of Butter,* and two stage plays, *The Offering* and *Yussuf and His Brothers.* These were written between 1973 and 1983, a period that began with the government's censoring of Farah's Somali-language novel, followed soon after by his departure into exile. The corruption and despotism of the Siyad Barre regime had by now become apparent to Farah, and as he traveled and read he observed closely the similarities between this regime and patterns of dictatorship widespread throughout Africa and the rest of the world. The primary thrust of his work during this period, accordingly, centered on efforts to understand the mechanisms of dictatorship and political resistance.

The third period in the development of Farah's work includes *Maps, Gifts,* and *Secrets,* a second trilogy of novels that Farah has, "at least for the time being," titled *Blood in the Sun.*[1] These books were drafted between 1983 and 1992, that is, between the early stages of armed Somali resistance to Siyad Barre and the beginning of the state of anarchy that followed his overthrow. Farah was by now 10 years and more into exile and traveling widely in Africa, with extended periods of residence in several African countries. In this third stage he is intensely engaged in issues of personal identity, measuring the possibilities of the human persona against the social and political realities explored in the earlier work.

These stages of development—characterized not by sharp breaks but by gradually shifting emphases—mark a body of work whose elements are tied together as a single and closely integrated fictional world in some of its most basic dimensions, among them setting, plot, character, and ideology. A more detailed look at these unifying dimensions and their expression in the individual texts—the work of the present chapter—will allow us to proceed, in the chapters that remain, to an examination of the issues whose confrontation gives life and meaning, artistically and intellectually, to that imaginative world.

What most obviously connects these texts is that all are set in Somalia.[2] This is not as banal an observation as it may at first seem if we remember that they are the work of an author who has lived in exile from his country since 1974 and who is exceptionally widely traveled and cosmopolitan. The Somali setting of the novels, moreover, is thick with the names and details of actual people, places, and events. It is, however, a very particular Somalia: the world of the city and of civic culture. All of Farah's narratives are urban-centered—either located in the city itself or in movement toward the city. The physical features of setting consist overwhelmingly of the architecture and furniture of houses, towns, and cities, seen primarily from the interior. (Rooms and furniture, in fact, provide the controlling metaphor of *Sardines,* and in *Close Sesame* a third of the book has passed before the protagonist emerges from the house where he lives.) Despite the prevalence of animal and water *imagery* in Farah's prose, almost no elements of *setting* are natural. Rural life exists and is evoked, but it either is left behind (as in *From a Crooked Rib, Maps,* and *Secrets*) or lies entirely outside the world of action.

The dimension of plot further unifies this world. Beginning with the third novel, the consistent plot device and organizing principle in Farah's work is mystery. Any one of these texts, in fact, could bear the title of the last, *Secrets,* for in all of them the action is organized around the pursuit of answers to questions and solutions to puzzles. They are not simply detective stories, however, in which truth lies hidden for a time but finally yields to an orderly process of ratiocination. The mysteries that move Farah's characters to action, on the contrary, generally remain unresolved, and those that are resolved are often revealed in the process to be ultimately unimportant, distractions from deeper and more significant mysteries. What this dimension contributes to the singleness of Farah's fictional world, then, is not a unitary and closed structure of action in which characters participate but an angle of view on the world as the characters see it, one in which they struggle to emerge from their own internal uncertainties in order to initiate action.

Ultimately these are not, in fact, narratives of events but of characters, and what they narrate, from a point of view very close to their object, is not developments in larger social worlds but the consciousness of individual characters. This is an observation that could be made of many contemporary novelists. What distinguishes Farah's treatment of character and, by that treatment, contributes to the consolidation of his work into a single fictional world is that he draws characters conceptually rather than psychologically or emotionally. They are, by and large, not of interest as personalities, that is, for the ways in which individual development and response to the world are grounded in personal history and subjectivity. Rather his characters embody conditions: particular situations that locate them among complex convergences of ideas and issues and position them along a spectrum of ways of thinking about these ideas and issues. The first five novels are tied together by a set of recurring characters; but even where this is not the case, the conditions, the conceptual problems represented by characters, recur and develop as Farah's fictional world develops. His characters do not speak idiosyncratically and cannot be recognized or distinguished by their speech. Rather they share a common language that is abstract, logical, and symbolic, even in the mouths of children and of people without formal education. To enter into their world as a reader, therefore, is to enter into a discourse of ideas imagined as flesh and blood, a lived debate, one that goes on both among and within characters.

What keeps the life pulsing in this debate is a clear and identifiable ideological heart. That core, the ground of value on which Farah's world rests, is the freedom and dignity of the human person. These are enhanced by education that is wide ranging and critical, by cosmopolitan experience, and by the free play of inner resources and impulses. In contrast, these values are threatened by restrictive tradition and education, by provincialism, and by all forms of personal and collective compulsion. While the premises of this ideology may be stable, however, its implications are not. Rather it produces a tension that, in turn, generates the conditions by which Farah's protagonists are defined as characters. This is the tension between a full individual realization and enjoyment of one's freedom and dignity and the social and political responsibilities to which one commits oneself by claiming these as fundamental values. This tension repeatedly carries the focus of Farah's work into that sphere of Somali society in which he finds both the realization and the responsibilities to be most powerful: the educated elite.

Farah's first novel, *From a Crooked Rib,* opens at a great distance from that sphere but begins almost immediately to move toward it. The protagonist is Ebla, an illiterate girl of 18 whose parents are long dead and who has lived her whole life with her grandfather in a tiny pastoral community. She has never been near a town, seen a foreigner, heard of the government, or known more than 100 people in her life, and yet she is presented from the beginning as different from the people whom she does know. She "thought about things and people in her own way," "thought of many things a woman of her background would never think of," and "had been toying with the idea of leaving home for quite some time."[3] She is already of the elite, then, by her imagination if not by her education. Betrothed against her wishes to a man of 48 who is to pay for her in camels, she slips away in the night and joins a caravan traveling to the town of Belet Wene. In so doing she raises early on a question that deepens over the course of the novel (and of Farah's work in general), the question of personal freedom and its consequences: "Not once in her life had she stopped doing anything because it would harm others. But this time, it was different. . . . If she stayed, she thought, she would always be in low spirits. And if she went what would happen?" (*FCR,* 10).

Her escape, once she decides to make it, is a defining moment for Ebla, who sees it as flight not only from the "duty of women" but from "the ropes of society," from "the country and its harsh life" and its perpetual "squabbles"—indeed "her escape meant the divine emancipation of the body and soul of a human being" (*FCR,* 12–13). To attempt such a transformation, she concludes that "the only reasonable place she could go to would be a town," even though she has never seen one (*FCR,* 15). The seemingly wide-open spaces of her pastoral world are in fact closed spaces of entrapment within a fixed system of social relations. Only in an urban space, she seems to sense instinctively, are social relations and identities disrupted and remixed as they must be if she is to make good on her escape. As she enters a town for the first time in her life, however, her first recourse is to what she has just turned her back on: her kin and the "duties of women." She finds her way to the home of her cousin, Gheddi, and his pregnant wife, Aowralla, and offers them her services as a maid-servant, caring for the cows and, after it is born, the baby. She meets a widow (unnamed in the novel) who teaches her how to find her way around town and to cook the strange foods that are eaten there, and who talks to her about her own experiences as a woman with men. This is the beginning of Ebla's education to the ways of the world beyond the countryside. Gheddi, a shopkeeper, turns out also to be a smuggler and involves Ebla in an operation that goes awry, for which he unfairly blames her. Chased from Gheddi's house, she goes to the widow, turning to the society of self-sufficient women for support, as do many of Farah's female characters.

Gheddi reasserts his authority, however, and for the second time Ebla is engaged by one man to another against her will in return for payment, this time by Gheddi to a tubercular cattle broker in return for money Gheddi needs to pay his fine for smuggling. Again she escapes, this time by eliciting a proposal of marriage from Awill, who is the widow's nephew and an official in the Ministry of Education. They elope to Mogadiscio, where, on promise of a wedding, Awill persuades Ebla to have sex with him, a painful first intercourse for her because of her infibulation. He brings a sheikh to their room the next morning to perform a perfunctory marriage ceremony and a week later departs for Italy on a three-month business trip, leaving Ebla with the landlady, Asha, and making arrangements for money to be delivered for her support.

Given reason to think that Awill is consorting with white women in Italy, Ebla again takes matters with men into her own hands by scheming with Asha to enter into a secret marriage with Tiffo, a wealthy man who is himself already married. The widow from Belet Wene then pays her a visit, bringing with her Ebla's younger brother, who tells her that her grandfather died the day she took flight. Considering the awkwardness she must face on Awill's return she reveals her prior marriage to Tiffo, who promptly divorces her. While awaiting Awill, Ebla attempts, in a long and important passage, to think through the degree to which she bears responsibility for herself and the consequences of her actions for others. Though she tries to rationalize her behavior as the natural weakness of a woman or as the fault of God, she is forced to conclude, "I am responsible for my actions" and, more specifically, "I am responsible for the death of my grandfather" (*FCR,* 158–59). Whether she is correct in this last judgment is less important than the awareness to which she has come of the uneasy relationship of freedom and responsibility. Awill arrives home to an Ebla who, through this awareness, has come to understand herself for the first time as his moral equal. Her transformation as an economic agent must await a later novel—here she performs no work and achieves no independence in Mogadiscio beyond what comes to her as the wife and sexual partner of a man. What does evolve significantly is her consciousness of her own subjectivity, of her power to reconceive herself and the world: "She looked into herself and found something new about herself. She looked into herself literally—a thing which she had never done before" (*FCR,* 161). At the close of the novel Ebla and Awill promise to tell each other everything the next day and retire to bed together smiling. Just what "everything" might mean, however, remains an open question, as Ebla is now pregnant but does not know by whom.

With *From a Crooked Rib* Farah made a name for himself as a male author of unusual sensibility for his sympathetic and intimate portrayal of a young woman and, what is more, of a woman whose background could hardly be more unlike his own. His second novel, *A Naked Needle,* stands in notable contrast, featuring a protagonist who much more closely resembles some aspects of Farah's own intellectual formation and artistic temperament while exhibiting highly retrograde attitudes toward women. Of all his work, it is this novel that Farah has come closest to repudiating, as he has the state of his own thinking at the time he wrote it. Years later, recalling that early period after the revolution when he was at work on this book, he writes, "Mine was a mind in great disorder. I knew that a novel like *A Naked Needle* was not the answer to the tremendous challenge the tyrannical regime posed, but I was tired of holding my pen in mid-air—and I thought in any case that I should get it out of my way while I gave serious consideration to how best to rise to the summons" ("Why I Write," 1596). "I am pleased it is out of print," he comments elsewhere ("Exile," 181).

At the time, however, it was by no means clear to Farah that he was dealing with a "tyrannical regime," and his character, Koschin, reflects that uncertainty. Koschin recalls critically "the Dissolved National Assembly which seated, in the days of Parliament, over a hundred members of a raped land, and under the heavy weight of their maladministering the whole country [sank] into decay," and he also praises the new regime as "the most reasonable government Somalia has ever had," generously opining, "They will certainly relax. They are giving many things thought."[4] He extols the "greatest feat that has been undertaken by the Revolutionary Government," the adoption of a Somali script, "even if they have committed several crimes that they thought were minor" (*NN,* 120). He apportions responsibility for these "minor crimes" so as to spare Siyad Barre, whom he refers to affectionately as "the Old Man," and to blame others: "The Old Man is decent, honest, wishes to leave behind a name, wishes to do something for the country—whatever he did before he came to power, like when he denied his involvement with the aborted coup during the Egal-Sharmarke government. He swore you know, the Old Man swore he had nothing to do with it, but history has it he did. Now he is washing himself clean, he wishes to do something. But it is his subalterns!" (*NN,* 80). With the exception of a quote from a newspaper article in *Gifts,* in fact, *A Naked Needle* is the only work in whose pages Farah allows Siyad Barre's name to appear during the dictator's lifetime (*NN,* 16).[5] Henceforth, he is depersonalized as "the General" or alluded to by less flattering epithets. Koschin voices, then, an ill-founded optimism about the new government that is quickly superseded by the much more critical view that Farah himself developed before the book's publication in 1976. Even in *A Naked Needle,* however, Koschin's support of the revolution is contingent: "Whoever will do any good for this country and for Africa, I shall back till I die. . . . If these fail to do that [sic] they owe us, I shall declare war against them, single-handed even though I am" (*NN,* 152). That contingency unmet, Koschin indeed goes to war against the regime in later books.

Though its political analysis sets it apart from the work that follows, other features of *A Naked Needle* encourage one to read it as a kind of laboratory for the development of materials and techniques prominent in the more mature work. Farah begins, for example, to experiment with formal structure, organizing the novel not by chapters but by elements borrowed from music: a short Prelude (whose pages are unnumbered) followed by a series of Movements—"Six movements in all," Farah wrote to his editor as the work was in progress, "Beethoven's third and fifth symphonies: the influence."[6] There are shifts in narrative point of view: the Prelude is in Koschin's first-person voice and addresses the reader directly, while the remainder of the novel is in the third person, though it hovers very close to Koschin's consciousness, often lapsing into monologues addressed, both mentally and aloud, to another character who does not appear in the text until late in Movement Four. Farah also experiments with a declamatory style of dialogue that, refined and developed, becomes characteristic of his later novels and dramas of ideas. He gives early expression to an ongoing taste for alliteration and for vocabulary that stretches lexical definitions—techniques of prose in which resonate elements of Somali oral poetry. Here too he frees himself of conventional dependence on plot.

Indeed, *A Naked Needle* involves little in the way of incident, consisting instead mainly of Koschin's musings, both mental and spoken, and of the debates into which he enters. Koschin Qowdhan is an English teacher, nearly 40 years old, who lives in a squalid room in a brothel in Mogadiscio. As the book opens he is expecting the arrival of Nancy Stonegrave, a British woman whom he had met in England and promised to marry in two years if neither had married anyone else in the meantime. In anticipation of this arbitrary and apparently meaningless engagement, he proceeds to renounce various other claims on his person. An old man from his "tribe" (a word Farah often uses, with pejorative intent, in place of *clan*) comes to him seeking a contribution to a blood-compensation to be paid on a member's behalf, but Koschin sends the old man away, disavowing all tribal loyalties. He writes a letter to the secretary of education to resign his teaching position, citing his school principal's sexual involvement with a student. He writes to his lover Maryan, telling her about Nancy and ending their 10-year relationship. A friend drops in to complain that his American wife has run out on him. He then takes a taxi to his school to complete his resignation and on the way recalls a recent trip to his home town of Kismayo, which he found to be as socially blighted as Mogadiscio. From time to time he delivers himself of disparaging remarks on the Somali people in general, who, he says "cannot tolerate the pain, but want heaven on earth without toil," who are "subordinate folk, easy to govern," and who think themselves better than other Africans but are "a sick society" (*NN*, 4, 21, 107).

Like Ebla then, though with more self-conscious sophistication, Koschin sets out to remake himself by *un*making himself socially, cutting himself loose from the conventional ties of clan, profession, romantic love, and wider community. Like Ebla too, he seeks his freedom in a social world of his own choosing and in relationships constructed so as to safeguard his independence. This world and these relationships Koschin finds among Mogadiscio's jet set: an educated and mostly rich collection of powerful bureaucrats, intellectual gadflies, and foreigners. For the remainder of the book Koschin circulates randomly in this hyperurban cultural space. The American wife of his friend Mohamed happens upon him in the street and takes him to their home where, he only then discovers, Nancy has arrived and is staying. He is quite cool and distant with her but then takes her on a long walking tour of Mogadiscio, pointing out buildings, monuments, neighborhoods, and favorite hangouts and taking these as occasions for comments on the current political and social environment. They then proceed to the home of a Somali senior clerk in one of the embassies and his Russian wife, where a party is in progress. The liquor and the conversation flow freely as Koschin moves through a swirl of social acquaintances and argues a varied array of intellectual positions, none of which compromises his posture of personal detachment. His guarded allegiance to the revolution entails no commitments that would threaten that posture. In the course of this long evening he behaves rudely to Nancy but also grows more "used to" her, finally taking her home to his room. There this novel, like *From a Crooked Rib,* ends with a couple going to bed less as lovers than as wary antagonists.

The transformation in Farah's assessment of the revolution by the time he had begun writing *Sweet and Sour Milk,* his third novel, can be read in the stark transformation of Koschin from one book to the next. For the Koschin of *A Naked Needle,* as for the Ebla of *From a Crooked Rib,* personal freedom is the concern that overrides all others, and social responsibility is the insistent question that this concern raises. In *Sweet and Sour Milk* (and all of the work that follows), social responsibility is no longer merely a question but an imperative in its own right. From a position of lofty detachment, Koschin has moved to membership in a "group of ten," all drawn from the young, educated elite in Somalia, all dedicated to learning and disclosing the truth about the repressiveness and illegitimacy of the General's government. Koschin has paid for that shift in position with his personal freedom. Though he does not actually appear as a character in the narrative, his name is invoked, here and in subsequent novels, as the first of the group to go to prison for his political activity, never to reemerge.

At the center of *Sweet and Sour Milk* are two other members of this group, identical twins named Soyaan and Loyaan. In the Prologue, Soyaan, a 29-year-old government economic advisor, arrives ill at the home of his parents, where he is tended by his mother, Qumman, and sister, Ladan. There he dies, and the only person present at the moment of his death is Loyaan, a regional health officer in Baidoa. His last words are Loyaan's name, uttered three times amid a spasm of hiccups. The remainder of the book is Loyaan's first-person account of his attempts to discover the cause of Soyaan's death and to unravel the further mysteries that this puzzle engenders. Their parents have refused on religious grounds to have an autopsy performed, but several possible causes are mentioned or hinted at: poisoned food Soyaan may have eaten at the home of Beydan, his father's second wife; some action by the Minister to the Presidency, who was with him at the meal; injections he received from a Russian doctor at a military hospital to which he was taken; medicines prescribed by a friend named Dr. Ahmed-Wellie; and suicide. Though some of these theories come to seem more likely than others, Loyaan is never able to confirm any of them. His effort to get to the bottom of the story is complicated by the government's interest in rewriting that story for its own purposes. The newspaper publishes an official account of the death in which Soyaan's last words are reported to be "Labour is honour and there is no General but our General."[7] This account is publicly supported by Keynaan, the twins' father, who is a repressive family patriarch. As a police inspector in the General's security service, Keynaan was responsible for the death of a man under torture, leading to the loss of his position and his being forced to marry Beydan, the man's widow.

In investigating the circumstances of Soyaan's death, the initially apolitical Loyaan learns of the existence of the group of ten, and of his brother's participation in it from Ibrahim, who is a member. Among Soyaan's activities for the group was to coauthor with Ibrahim a memo-

randum concerning the use of oral rumor as an instrument of power by
the General's security service. It becomes increasingly clear, to Loyaan,
that Soyaan's death, however it came about, must have been murder
and that his political involvement must have been the cause, though this
speculation too is never absolutely confirmed. Ibrahim (soon to be
imprisoned himself) invites Loyaan to join the group in his brother's
place, which he agrees to do. Among the other members is Dr. Ahmed-
Wellie, whom Loyaan begins to suspect of being a government informant and complicitous both in Soyaan's death and in the torture of
political prisoners. His complicity with the government in some manner
or other remains an open question in *Sweet and Sour Milk* and is confirmed only in *Close Sesame*. Loyaan also learns that at the time of his
death Soyaan had been at work on another antigovernment memorandum, which Loyaan attempts to locate, discovering in the process that
the minister to the presidency is in search of the same document. The
memorandum turns out to have been in the keeping of Margaritta, an
Italo-Somali woman who is a former mistress of the minister and who
has borne Soyaan a child. Margaritta gives the document to Loyaan,
who grows increasingly confrontational toward the minister, Keynaan,
and other government representatives. The minister's response is to
appoint Loyaan to the post that Soyaan was to have taken just before his
death, Somali councillor in Belgrade, a kind of official exile. At the close
of the book Beydan dies giving birth to Keynaan's child, her newborn
son is addressed as Soyaan by Ladan, and there is a knock at the door,
presumably by government agents come to put Loyaan on an airplane
to exile (though this too is confirmed only in a later book).

The question of how Soyaan died remains unresolved, though it has
become a more complicated question—and in this, perhaps, lies the key
to the only answer available. When asked the cause of death early in the
book, Loyaan "improvised a response, safe, vague: 'He died of complications' " (*SSM,* 29–30). This expression is repeated several more times in
the text, and each time its irony grows. If it is true, as we are led to
believe, that Soyaan was murdered in some way, what caused him to be
killed was the complications of his own multiple involvements and commitments and the complicating of truth by its appropriation for political
purposes. (Qumman finds in her dead son's pocket the text of a Somali
law under which anyone who spreads information unfavorable to the
government is liable to death. Keynaan's explanation of his son's death
is that he "was being used by other factions. Unwittingly he got caught
in the intricacy of tribal politics which he could not understand" [*SSM,*

93].) The same effort to render truth from the complications facing him puts Loyaan's own life in danger. Indeed, on one of the occasions when he meets the query about his brother's cause of death with the response "complications," he does so because "he wouldn't openly admit a failure on his part to deal squarely with that question" (*SSM*, 42); and these complications set in motion a process by which Loyaan eventually becomes a substitute for his brother, both within the government and within the resistance to the government.

This substitution reinforces a motif of doubleness that strongly colors this text as well as much of Farah's later work. The twins are physically so similar that no one outside the family can tell them apart, and inside the family the women see no need to do so—for their sister they are "one in two," and their mother "conceived of them as she had received them, and thus had no choice but to think of them as one person" (*SSM*, 50). As they mature they seem to diverge, taking separate professional training and developing separate personalities—"Soyaan: a man of intrigue, rhetoric, polemics and politics. Loyaan: a man of melodramatic scenes, mundanities and lost tempers" (*SSM*, 14). Under the pressures of dictatorship and resistance, however, this process of differentiation collapses. The rich multiplicity of possibilities Loyaan had experienced through the close linkage of his brother's subjectivity to his own becomes instead entrapment in a false identity that increasingly is neither his nor Soyaan's but one fashioned by the political forces at work. The government newspaper reports Soyaan's death as a martyr of the revolution but substitutes Loyaan's name and photograph. A woman who comes to the house to mourn Soyaan calls him Loyaan and addresses Loyaan as Soyaan, as does Beydan's aunt. Margaritta seats Loyaan in Soyaan's chair, serves him a drink in the same manner in which she had served Soyaan, and then drives him home drunk as she had once done for Soyaan. By an accumulation of such events the play of doubles becomes a significant element in Farah's treatment of identity in *Sweet and Sour Milk* and one that undergoes more complex development in the novels and plays that follow.

Another feature of Farah's development as a writer that is striking in this novel is the increasing degree to which he calls the reader's attention to the textuality of the work, pointing to the fact that what lies open before the reader is a collection of words assembled through the intentional artistry of the writer. One of the ways in which he does this is the explicit intertextuality of the quotations that precede the Prologue and Parts Two and Three, highly varied passages from works by Mari-

anne Moore, Mary Webster, Wilhelm Reich, Philip O'Connor, Derek
Walcott, W. B. Yeats, and James Dickey. More characteristic of techniques found in later works, however, is the epigrammatic extended
similes by which he begins each chapter. Each begins with the word *like,*
but *what* exactly each image is like, what the simile alludes to in the
chapter it introduces, is never indicated. The first, by way of example, is
also the shortest—"Like a baby with a meatless bone in his mouth, a
bone given him by his mother to suck while she is in the kitchen mind-
ing the pot which has now begun to sing . . ." (*SSM,* 1, ellipsis in the
original)—while others run to substantial paragraphs. Each is an image
of powerlessness. In more than half, this is a fetus, a baby, or a young
child. In others the image is of tires bolted to a bicycle, weeds in the
wind, or a helpless animal or insect. Almost all depict vulnerability, usually unconscious vulnerability (a baby swallowing pills while his parents
are distracted, a child deciding whether to play with a scorpion). In most
the depiction of the situation is interrupted before we know whether the
potential harm comes to pass. This device, then, serves several functions: it calls attention to the fields of unequal power within which the
action of the novel proceeds and to the gap that separates the naive consciousness of the weak from the impenetrable and inhuman consciousness of the strong; it reinforces the open-endedness of this search for a
truth that always lies beyond view; and it repeatedly emphasizes the role
of the narrative imagination in directing that search.

This last element, the primary and self-conscious role of the imagination, asserts itself in the opening sentence of Farah's next novel, *Sardines:*
"She reconstructed the story from the beginning."[8] "She" is Medina, one
of the "group of ten" introduced in *Sweet and Sour Milk,* and "the story"
is her own. As in *From a Crooked Rib,* Farah places at the center of his
novel the struggle of women to "reconstruct" themselves, to rebuild
what is socially given into what is personally true and valuable. *Sardines*
is a much more ambitious and complex novel, however, for Medina is
only the most prominent of the book's several very different female consciousnesses at work on this project of self-reconstruction. Ebla of *From a
Crooked Rib,* in fact, is one of them, as is Sagal, the now adolescent
daughter with whom she was pregnant at the end of that book. In the
imaginative space between the two novels Ebla has married yet again,
been widowed, become a savvy and successful entrepreneur, and grown
into a mother who combines, in the rearing of her daughter, the open-
mindedness she once sought in the city and the practical wisdom she has
not forgotten from her own rural upbringing. Medina is of Ebla's gener-

ation but of a very different formation. Cosmopolitan, widely traveled, and highly educated, she is named editor of the only newspaper in the country, a position she immediately loses when she refuses to print government propaganda. These events have just taken place as the novel opens. Medina then leaves her husband, Samater, becoming a single mother and teacher to her own daughter, Ubax, who is eight years old, and occupying her time in the translation of European and African books into Somali. Medina and Ebla serve, often to quite different effect, as mothers, mentors, and models to a younger generation of women that includes Sagal and her friend Amina. These are part of a wider spectrum of women remaking themselves as individuals: Dulman, a Somali singer, Sandra, an Italian journalist, Atta, an African-American visitor to Somalia, and others.

The reconstructions are not only personal, however, for they all take place within the same conditions of dictatorship that dominate the world of *Sweet and Sour Milk*. Medina accepts a kind of internal exile because she refuses to become an instrument of the regime. She opens another front in her resistance to dictatorship by opposing the matriarchy of Idil, her mother-in-law, who alienates Samater from Medina by influencing him to accept a position in the government and who threatens to have Ubax circumcised against Medina's wishes. Sagal mulls several political choices: whether to bear the child of a visiting journalist whose political sympathies she wants to shape, whether to compete in an international swimming competition and then embarrass the government by defecting, whether to join in a campaign of writing political slogans on the walls of public buildings. Amina considers whether to accept the aid of her father, whose support of the General has led to her becoming the victim of a political rape. Dulman seeks ways to redeem a singing career that her public views as complicitous with the dictatorship and turn it to the purposes of resistance. All of these dilemmas are portrayed against the backdrop of the resistance of the group of ten, here called "the movement," in which Medina and Samater both play leadership roles.

Sardines is perhaps Farah's most plotless novel to date. Although many of the characters face stark and agonizing predicaments, the narrative develops these not as a web of actions and events but as a complex debate over ideas and strategies, carried on both within and among characters. As they reach decisions and make choices, the consequences are seen, not in the arena of national politics—not in revolutions, or public reprisals—but in personal commitments and in relationships between family members, friends, lovers, and mentors and pupils. Like *Sweet and Sour Milk, Sardines* is also a novel of unresolved mysteries. There are several of these, but the most tangled is the question of why Medina leaves Samater: "Many people speculated as to what had happened, others made up their own versions of what had occurred" (*Sardines*, 6). She leaves because Samater's political choice violates her own sense of loyalty to the cause; or because she wants to prevent Idil from having Ubax circumcised; or because she wants time by herself to write a book; or because she has taken a lover; or because Samater has taken a lover—at least a dozen possible explanations are offered, some more likely than others. More than once the narrator seems to place the reader in a position to read the "real" reason inside Medina's consciousness—but the answers that turn up at these junctures are not the same.

As in *Sweet and Sour Milk,* the reader must again accept that questions do not lead to definitive answers but to "versions" of the truth, to fields of possibility in which characters make and remake themselves and the worlds they find themselves in. As in that earlier novel, too, in which Soyaan's last words are rewritten to suit the General's purposes, the government enters actively into this generation of versions of the truth, circulating or suppressing accounts of Amina's rape, the political graffiti that appear overnight, and Samater's appointment to and then disappearance from political office. In these ways the image of reconstruction with which the book opens becomes a controlling metaphor for the text as a whole. Throughout the book the developing consciousness of characters is figured in images of doors and windows opening and closing, rooms changing shape, and furniture shifting position within rooms. This imagery is echoed at other narrative levels as well: Samater is an architect by profession and the position to which the government tempts him is minister of constructions; Medina, not Samater, is the legal owner of their house, as Sagal is of hers; Samater's decision ultimately to reject a complicitous role in the government is signaled by his throwing the matriarch, Idil, out of that house; nearly all of the narrative, apart from flashbacks or events indirectly reported, takes place inside the homes of the characters. Farah has said, in fact, that "if you studied the structures of the novel, you could see that you could have done it in just two rooms" (Interview, 1996). These interior settings and metaphors of constructed dwellings signal how completely this is a novel of ideas whose most significant action is the act of contemplation.

As the title *Sardines* suggests, however, these interiors are spaces not only of reconstruction but of constriction as well, and the two dimensions are, in fact, dialectically related. Medina's political action in the open, public arena causes her to be banned and her freedom restricted except within her own home, where she begins to rethink, re-create, and ultimately enlarge herself as a political being. Her initial response to enclosure is a wish to fashion "a room of one's own. . . . A room in which one was not a guest" (*S,* 4). By the end of the book she has built something larger: "Medina would supplement her intellectual activities—her translations and original writings—with these social responsibilities . . . she would nurse, medicate and do the social work she had always meant to. . . . No, she wasn't a guest any more. She was a full and active participant in the history of her country" (*Sardines,* 263).

This pattern by which Medina's political consciousness develops also shapes the experience of Deeriye, the protagonist of Farah's next novel, *Close Sesame.* Like Medina, Deeriye exchanges the life to which he was born for "the life he . . . invented for himself."[9] Doing so causes him, as a young man, to go to prison for his resistance to the Italian colonial authorities in Somalia and, much in the manner of Medina's experience, "that confinement in prison opened to Deeriye a vista of a wider, larger world: detention compelled him to think of the history and contradictions which the neo-colonial person lives in; detention . . . made it obvious to him that he was a member of the world's oppressed" (*CS,* 103).

In creating Ebla and Medina, Farah stretched his imagination in an effort to encompass female experience. In Deeriye he set himself a similar challenge to create a character quite unlike himself: elderly, asthmatic, devoutly Muslim, centrally involved in an organized movement of resistance, and deeply embroiled in clan politics. Because of Deeriye's age, the range of historical reference in *Close Sesame* is greater than in any other work of Farah's. Deeriye was born in 1912, the year in which the Sayyid achieved a famous victory in battle and celebrated that victory in what would become Deeriye's favorite poem. His own career in nationalist politics, we learn through his memories, began when a man in another clan killed an Italian officer in self-defense and took refuge in the clan of which the young Deeriye was sultan. Deeriye refused to turn over the man, and the results were that the Italians slaughtered his own clan's herds and sent Deeriye to prison. His resistance to colonialism carried over into resistance to the General and into further periods of imprisonment, 12 years in all. As the book opens, however, this figure of heroic reputation is much enfeebled, dependent on his grown children, largely confined by physical incapacity to a room in his son's home, and fearful of the rock-throwing child of a neighbor. He is under the medical care of his daughter, Zeinab, whose husband was killed in service to the West Somali Liberation Front. His son, Mursal, is a law professor at the national university and is also a member of the group of ten along with three of his friends: Mukhtaar, Jibriil Mohamed-Somali, and Mahad, who is the son of the man to whom Deeriye gave refuge many years earlier.

These last four members of the group of ten introduced over the course of the trilogy now move to the center of the reader's attention as the others recede, and the movement itself again changes character. In *Sweet and Sour Milk* the methods of this movement are research, documentation, and disclosure. In *Sardines* political resistance becomes more overtly subversive. In *Close Sesame* it turns to outright violence, and a succession of violent acts provides the events that make plot a stronger narrative element in this book than in any of Farah's other novels. Deeriye's fear of the child, Yassin, is coupled with a fear that Mursal and his friends are planning violence of which they themselves will be the victims. The two fears are realized simultaneously. Standing at the window of his room, Deeriye is struck and injured by a rock thrown by Yassin at the same moment that Mahad fails in an attempt to assassinate the General. Mukhtaar is later killed in a fight with his own father, Ibrahim, who is a supporter of the General, and Jibriil and Mursal both die in separate bomb attempts on the life of the dictator. In this series of attacks against patriarchs, then, Yassin's is the only weapon to find its mark.

The failed conspiracy against the General is complicated by a history of clan intrigue and betrayal that reaches back to Deeriye's original act of defiance. The clan's readiness on that occasion to close ranks around Deeriye's position was shaky, and one of his clansmen intercepted a message a small boy was carrying from Deeriye to Rooble, the son of the sultan of the other clan involved, and passed it to the Italians, bringing on the punishment of Deeriye and his village. It is suggested that the General, as a young officer in the colonial army, participated in similar attacks on Somalis by the Italians. Now he himself is under attack by a Somali resistance movement and fights back by manipulating clan politics in an effort to neutralize the inspirational figures of Deeriye and Rooble. The son of Deeriye's original betrayer and the boy, now grown, who was an unwilling instrument in that betrayal both play roles in this process. Despite Mursal's attempt to protect his father by withholding knowledge of the conspiracy, therefore, Deeriye is implicated personally in the attacks, and his whole life of political resistance becomes an active factor in the current movement against the General.

Acts of violence provide the framework of action in the novel, but the idea of violence provokes the debate and stimulates the contemplation that animate this work more deeply. Deeriye and Mursal, a father and son who have stood against tyranny in two successive generations, frequently engage in long arguments as to whether violence is a justifiable instrument in such resistance. Mursal, a trained legalist, argues in favor of a strategy of violence underwritten by both traditional and state-based concepts of justice, while Deeriye, a devout Muslim who has avoided open violence in his own acts of resistance to this point, is more equivocal: "[H]e would never make use of violent means to overthrow a tyrannical regime—not he, anyway. But, he had added, he could see himself justifying, intellectually speaking, any mind which moved in this general direction of violence" (*CS,* 10–11). The issue remains on his mind as he struggles to penetrate the plans and understand the fates of Mursal and the others.

The debate carried on outwardly with Mursal becomes an internal debate, but one in which Deeriye's is not the only voice, because, from the time of the attack on his village by the Italians, he has experienced visions. Some of these belong to Deeriye's religious consciousness, in which "he saw, as would a sufi, the retreating mysterious formlessness of the divine . . . , an image peace-producing as the soul's reunion with God" (*CS,* 179). At other times the voice is that of his wife, Nadiifa, who came to him in a vision while he was in detention and continues to do so now, long after her death. Hers is a loving but more pragmatic and contentious voice. Deeriye's political consciousness is strongly shaped by these visions, in which he believes utterly even though those around him do not and whose "reality" for the reader Farah leaves ambiguous. It is Nadiifa's voice that leads Deeriye at last to a resolve to "vindicate justice," to avenge Mursal's death, and to "perform a heroic deed just when everybody had written him off as a useless old man" (*CS,* 218, 228). Acting on this resolve, he goes to an appointment with the General with a gun in his pocket. As he tries to extract the gun it becomes entangled in his prayer beads and he is shot dead by the General's bodyguards. Though Deeriye reaches and acts on a decision, this entanglement of the emblems of violence and nonviolence, in which each cancels out the force of the other, leaves the larger debate as unresolved as ever.

It is the prominence of debate as a structural element in these texts that best supports, if anything can, Farah's claim early in his career that he was a dramatist at heart. The most important debates in the novels, as we have seen, are often staged within the minds of his characters.

During the period of his work on the Dictatorship Trilogy, however, he also wrote and saw produced three plays in which these contending internal voices, still quite unresolved, are externalized in dramatic speech and action.

The first of these is *The Offering,* completed and produced while Farah was a graduate student at the University of Essex. It is set in a prison cell in Ethiopia during the reign of Haile Selassie. There are only two characters in the play, a university professor named Samater, condemned to death for treason, and an officer in the imperial guards, whose name is revealed only at the end of the play: Hailu, meaning "power." Their exchanges call to mind those of Loyaan and the minister to the presidency in *Sweet and Sour Milk,* while the setting again brings to bear the force of imprisonment as an intensifier of personal and political consciousness, as in *Sardines* and *Close Sesame.* As the play opens, the officer enters Samater's cell to interrogate him, having been chosen for this task, as he explains to Samater, for a very particular reason: "The Emperor confided to my superior officer that I would be able to understand the trend of your mind, because I am of the same disposition as yours . . . from an intellectual point of view."[10] Samater has been accused of writing treasonous letters, of inciting students to riot, and of veiled attacks on the Emperor in an article critical of "conferring the title of a deity on any given personality" (*O,* 87–88). Samater expresses outrage about the treatment he has received but does little to deny the accusations. He in fact accuses the officer of having ordered a firing squad to shoot a group of freedom fighters and of complicity in the ruination of the country. He also charges that his father and uncle have suffered retribution on his account, revealing by these charges that he has been receiving information while in prison. The officer asks if Samater has a favor to ask of him before he leaves. In a moment of weakness, Samater asks for the Emperor's "paternal pardon" but then pulls himself together and withdraws the request (*O,* 90). The officer then tells Samater a story, by which they are both moved, prompting Samater to say that they would have become friends if they had met earlier. The officer concedes that this is "quite probable" but then turns to leave (*O,* 92). As he walks away. Samater draws a knife from under his prison clothes and stabs the officer to death. As the play ends, Samater is frantically looking for his shoes.

Two years after *The Offering* was published in the Egyptian literary journal *Lotus,* a new version of the same material was performed as a radio play under the title *A Spread of Butter.* In this version the two characters are unnamed, the action is set in Somalia, and the figure of the Emperor is replaced by one called the President. The first play is not simply revised in the second, however, but in significant ways both extended and inverted. The professor is accused of virtually identical crimes and the officer has come to his cell for the same purpose. In this version, however, the professor makes no personal accusations against the officer and denies those made against himself, insisting that most of what he has been blamed for was coincidental and that his article on "deification" was harmless: "an academic article addressed specifically to my anaemic set of intellectual friends."[11] The officer in this play, unlike the one in *The Offering,* repeatedly expresses contempt for the professor as a bourgeois parasite living comfortably at the expense of the working masses. Again there is the offer of a favor, one that involves a temptation for the professor, but it takes a much more complicated form. The officer tells the professor that the President has in fact been deposed, that he, the officer, is a member of the new ruling military council, and that he is there to offer the professor a position as minister in the new government. The professor suspects that this offer may be only a trick to lead him into walking away from his cell so that he can be shot while attempting to "escape." He also resists the idea of collaborating with another regime that he believes will be just like the last one, but he is clearly tempted by the offer. At the end of the play the officer leaves the cell insisting that the professor has accepted the position, while the professor insists that he has not. The audience is never certain which will be the outcome, whether the offer is indeed a trick or is genuine, whether a successful coup has in fact taken place, or whether the professor's articles and lectures were mere academic exercises as he claims or incitements to riot as the officer charges.

In this play Farah dramatizes a confrontation between opponents who are at once opposite and interchangeable, each containing in himself possibilities that relate him closely to the other. As in *The Offering,* the officer says he has been chosen for this encounter because the two share "the same disposition . . . from an intellectual point of view" (*SB,* 2). Again the professor suggests that the two of them "might have even become friends" had they met earlier, adding that such a friendship is now impossible (*SB,* 17). This time, however, the officer's response is a good deal warmer: "Who says so? . . . Everything is possible—. . . let us become friends" (*SB,* 17). The word *friends,* it turns out, describes a relationship that is more dialectical than emotional: "Friends, you and I. Life is a see-saw game and is in constant alternate motion. . . . You see in a moment what the other saw an instant back. . . . Friends in the see-saw game, you and I!" (SB, 17–18). The professor himself takes up the same language, referring soon thereafter to "the former president, if that is what he is in the see-saw alternation of roles" (SB, 19). When the professor asks why the officer pretended to interrogate him if what he had in mind was to offer him a government ministry, the response is, "We needed to know . . . what you are like underneath, . . . whether your principles would stand up to the test" (SB, 20); but it is precisely here that the play of possibilities is at its most complex and unresolved. In one sense the professor's principles appear to have "stood up to the test": he maintains his criticism of the government and refuses to compromise by accepting the job that is offered him. On the other hand, he denies involvement in the resistance, distances himself from those who died for that cause, and shows himself to be wedded to the "priviligencia" (SB, 20). What is it that is being tested and which of these contradictory actions is the "correct" response to the test in the mind of the officer? The audience has no way of resolving this uncertainty because, in the isolation and imaginative freedom of the jail cell, the opposing possibilities of constancy and betrayal, solidarity and self-interest on the part both of the officer and of the professor, are simultaneously true. That simultaneity of alternative versions is inscribed in the larger dialectic of the two plays, the professor condemning and killing the officer in the first, the officer castigating but then co-opting (possibly in order to kill) the professor in the second.

The third play Farah wrote during this period, *Yussuf and His Brothers,* brings these opposing possibilities out of isolation and into the light of day, multiplies them, and explores the turmoil they create when expressed in the world of social action. This more complex work in 10 scenes is set in British Somaliland in the decade before independence. The colonial authorities have condemned Hussen to death for bombing a bridge near the palace of the governor. Yussuf, a pious Muslim and a leader in the nationalist cause, is organizing a plot to save Hussen by arranging for his executioners to fire into the air. The whole matter is complicated by its echoes of an event four years earlier, when Yussuf devised a similar plan to save a man accused of throwing a stone that struck the British government's representative, a plan cut short when the accused committed suicide. On that occasion Yussuf sent his wife away and married the dead man's widow, Aynaba, becoming stepfather to her son, Raageh, who is now 12 years old and devoted to Yussuf and his cause, and brother-in-law to Kulmie, a government informant.

Several problems arise in this doubling of an earlier event in the dramatic present. One is that Aynaba, who feels excluded from Yussuf's relationship with Raageh, fears that he plans to put her aside and marry Hussen's wife. Another and deeper problem has to do with the political implications of these executions. Yussuf considers the suicide of Aynaba's first husband a betrayal of the nationalist cause and, determined that this not happen again, arranges for the jailed Hussen to be denied materials he could use to kill himself. Hussen's execution is indeed aborted and he escapes, but only thanks to the compromising intervention of Kulmie. Hussen then decides to give himself up and allow himself to be executed, citing several motives, most importantly his wish to regain control of his own identity. The question of identity emerges as the audience gradually becomes aware that Hussen did not actually plant the bomb, as he is accused of doing, but has been made into a nationalist hero by Yussuf, who proclaims that the nation is one and that it does not matter who commits any given act in the cause. The indications mount throughout the play that it was in fact Yussuf himself who threw the stone and planted the bomb, though this is never absolutely confirmed. To quell the rebellion that is now raging, the government brings in an African of uncertain origin named Banana. He turns out to be the man who saved Yussuf from drowning in a shipwreck 12 years earlier and to be operating with a double so that he can assist in the nationalist cause. In the final scene Raageh reads a letter from Yussuf, who has gone into hiding with his nationalist "brothers" to plan further actions.

The debate that is staged here is, once again, a debate between the claims of personal freedom and those of social engagement, each expressed in several different and shifting voices, and the stage itself is the nationalist struggle. Yussuf frames the issue in stark terms: "My brothers are currently wrapped up in their personal worries. . . . To no avail I keep telling them that we're all one person; if one of the brothers plants a bomb which blows up a bridge, the brother in question does so not as a person, but as though he were the nation."[12] The tension between individual and collective identity that can be heard in this statement, however, belongs to a motif of doubles, masks, and mirrors that runs throughout the play. Banana, for example, plays a double role as partisan and persecutor of the nationalists. Hussen, escaping death by firing squad, finds that he has "become *another,* one with *the other,*" that there is both a dead and a surviving Hussen, a discovery that tempts him to attribute "the secret thoughts of the Hussen who had been locked in a cell" to one, and "all the saintly deeds" to the other (*YB,*

64–65). Raageh dresses in imitation of Yussuf, and Yussuf masks himself to resemble Hussen and stands before a mirror in the uniform of the chief executioner. The debate, in other words, is one that can never resolve into right and wrong, one in which all claims, those of personal freedom and those of collective engagement, bear a double burden of truth and the transgression of truth. Thus Yussuf is admirable, for example, in his resistance to colonial rule and in his insistence that "children are not to be beaten—. . . that children are to be spoken to and loved" (*YB*, 25), and at the same time he is nefarious in his various ways of manipulating others in a political cause. There is no principle in the play by which these several Yussufs (or the two Hussens, despite that character's claims) can be separated.

At the end of this parade of doubles, we are left with a mystery of a sort that is growing familiar in the work of Farah: Yussuf and other characters have disappeared and conflicting "versions" of their fates are rumored. Raageh claims to have "concrete evidence" and "hard core facts" to separate the accurate versions from those that are false (*YB*, 98). This evidence, however, is only a letter from the absent Yussuf, and its message, itself a report of a debate between Yussuf and Banana, is hardly one to inspire confidence in singular truth: "[N]othing exists unless its double exists too. . . . Our lives, I've always said are like a bridge, faceless and yet multi-profiled. Which is to say that I am a man, and that I'm at one and the same time a woman and a child rolled into one" (*YB*, 99–100). Thus the interchangeability of opposites that seems so uncontrollable in the isolation of the imagination in *A Spread of Butter* grows more unstable still in the "real world" of social relations in *Yussuf and His Brothers*. At the same time, the obligation to imagine and construct an ethically workable equilibrium among these uncertainties grows more imperative.

Nothing in the character of Yussuf would lead an audience to take his claim that he is a man, a woman, and a child rolled into one as anything other than a metaphor for the complexity of his consciousness. This particular metaphor likely occurred to Farah, however, because he was already, at the time he was writing these lines, at work on *Maps*, in which he entertains much more literally the idea of a single character who is at once male and female, adult and child, who is many kinds of person in one. Indeed the doubling, self-reconstruction, and internal debate that are increasingly central to character development in the earlier works become in *Maps* the structural principles of the book as a whole. In the process, narrative becomes not merely the medium but the very subject of the novel.

The protagonists in this narrative are Askar and his adoptive mother Misra, and the telling of Askar's story is itself the story—and the problem—of the novel from its opening page: "You are a question to yourself. It is true. You've become a question to all those who meet you, those who know you, those who have any dealings with you. You doubt, at times, if you exist outside your own thoughts, outside your own head, Misra's or your own. It appears as though you were a creature given birth to by notions formulated in heads, a creature brought into being by ideas" (M, 3). The second-person narration of this passage changes in the next chapter to first-person, and in the next to third-person, and continues to change throughout the novel. As these voices shift they often directly interrogate, challenge, and even contradict each other. All, however, are Askar's voice in a narrative that offers the sharpest and most explicit internal debate of Farah's work thus far: "You began debating with the egos of which you were compounded, and, detaching itself from the other selves, there stood before you, substantial as a shadow, the self (in you) which did not at all approve. . . . For a long time, your selves argued with one another, each offering counterarguments to the suggestions already submitted by the others" (M, 58). This debate sharpens further by the final paragraph of the novel to become something more like an internal judicial inquiry: "And that was how it began—the story of (Misra . . . and) Askar. First, he told it plainly and without embellishment, answering the police officer's questions; then he told it to men in gowns. . . . In the process, he became the defendant. He was, at one and the same time, the plaintiff and the juror. Finally, allowing for his different personae to act as judge, as audience and as witness, Askar told it to himself" (M, 246). The account produced by these voices is further complicated by a nonlinear narrative structure that begins and ends at approximately the same moment in time and moves frequently back and forth among various points in Askar's life. Moreover, it incorporates dreams of Askar's, stories from Misra's past, and vignettes that bear uncertain relationships to the characters and events of the narrative in which they are embedded. All of this is contained within a formal apparatus of parts, chapters, and chapter sections whose 75 separate pieces, ranging from a single sentence to eight pages, rarely have any direct link, one to the next. *Maps* is, in a word, of all Farah's books, the most demanding on the reader.

Askar's life begins in Farah's own home town of Kallafo.[13] Askar's father has already died in prison as a martyr in the struggle to liberate the Ogaden from Ethiopia. His mother gives birth in hiding and the two of them—Askar alive and his mother dead—are discovered by Misra, an Ethiopian woman who works as a servant in this Somali community. Misra at first cares for the infant in secret and then reveals that secret to Askar's paternal uncle Qorrax, who takes formal responsibility for Askar while leaving the role of surrogate mother to Misra. The relationship between these two immediately becomes preternaturally close and interdependent and transforms them both: "[Y]ou determined what Misra's life would be like the moment you took it over" (*M*, 8); "[Y]ou shared a bed . . . and she smelled of your urine precisely in the same way you smelled of her sweat" (*M*, 9); "[I]n the secrecy of the night's darkness, you could afford to allow the adult in you to emerge and express adult thoughts, just as Misra could permit the child in her to express its mind" (*M*, 14); "Misra . . . tucked me into the oozy warmth between her breasts . . . so much so I became a third breast . . . and I would find myself somewhere between her opened legs . . . as though I was a third leg" (*M*, 24); "I existed the second she touched me" (*M*, 24).

In this entwining of their selves Askar enters at several levels into Misra's identity as a female. Biologically, he participates in her menstruation—he envies her cleansing flow, expresses the wish to share it so as to ease her suffering, and both of them believe that her period begins under the powerful force of his stare and that he himself menstruates on one occasion. Sexually, their physical closeness is often suggestive of incest and Askar intrudes between Misra and her lovers, Qorrax and the Qur'anic teacher Aw-Adan, whom she nonetheless continues to entertain so that Askar will not be removed from her care. Socially, as Askar grows he suffers the patriarchal domination of Qorrax and Aw-Adan, whose authority permits them the punishment of his body as it does the sexual use of Misra's. Imaginatively, the course of Askar's development as a person echoes elements of Misra's own story, a story of mysterious origins, forced separation from her parents, adoption by an older man, incestuous marriage to her adoptive father, and her murder of this man who "alienated her . . . from herself" (*M*, 69), an enactment of Askar's own fantasy of killing Misra in order to free his identity.

It is Askar's perception, then, which Misra shares, that they exist in and because of each other and, at the same time, that neither can live fully and freely in the overwhelming presence of the other. This tension drives Askar's development toward manhood as he learns the power of written language, moves out into the society of other boys, becomes an accomplished teller of stories and leader of games, undergoes the pain of circumcision, and, at the age of eight, throws himself into the "ecstasy of madness that struck the town of Kallafo" in preparation for war: "What mattered, he told himself, was that now he was at last a man, that he was totally detached from his mother-figure Misra, and weaned. In the process of looking for a substitute, he had found another—Somalia, his mother country" (*M,* 96).

Before Askar can act in this new "manly" role, however, he is put on a truck, given the identity of "refugee," and sent off to Mogadiscio to live with his maternal uncle, Hilaal, and his aunt, Salaado, who teach at the university, while the Ogaden changes from Ethiopian to Somali hands and then back again. Hilaal, it turns out, is a "maternal" uncle in more than the genealogical sense: "Physically, you thought Hilaal was the exact replica of Misra, only he was a man" (*M,* 135). Further, Hilaal and Salaado live a reversal of gender roles quite unlike anything Askar has seen, Hilaal staying at home as much as possible, cooking the meals, playing "the contradictory roles of 'mother' to [Askar] and Salaado," while Salaado spends much of her time away, driving the car, and negotiating the world beyond the household (*M,* 149). Askar's childish attempt to substitute nation for mother in his drive to differentiate his own identity, then, yields to a new motherly presence in Hilaal, while his education begun in the dictatorial grip of Aw-Adan in Kallafo continues under the less authoritarian and more intellectual tutelage of that same presence. As he reaches the age of 18, however, the same conflict recurs, though the terms have grown more difficult to distinguish. He now finds himself facing the choice of enrolling in the university, as Hilaal urges him to do, by which he might help to "liberate" Somalia through knowledge, or of joining a freedom fighters' camp in the Ogaden, by which he might die heroically, like his father, in the cause of national liberation.

Into this quandary reerupts Misra, who has fled to Mogadiscio to escape her neighbors' accusation that she betrayed a freedom fighters' camp, causing hundreds of deaths, for an Ethiopian lover who turned out to be her half brother. She denies the charge, claiming she was raped by Somali partisans, and Askar has no evidence that she is guilty. She is powerless, however, in the face of the accusations made against her, not as Misra but as an Ethiopian and a woman, as an "enemy" and a "whore," accusations grounded in the perspectives of both the male

army Askar would join and the history of civilization he would help
write. Either of the choices by which he now seeks to define himself
denies the person on whom his own existence and identity once
depended, and his dilemma grows more agonizing: "Misra *was* my cosmos. . . . Now that cosmos has been made to disintegrate and Misra has
betrayed. What am I to do? I, who still love her! . . . Somehow, I felt I
knew I had to betray one of them. I had to betray either Misra, who had
been like a mother to me, or my mother country" (*M,* 172). Paralyzed
by these competing claims and by the implications of acting upon either
of them, he slips into a feverish illness, from which he emerges to learn
that Misra has been abducted, murdered, and mutilated. It is in connection with this event that he faces the questions of the police at the end of
the book and that he faces his own question: "Who *is* Askar?" (*M,* 245).

The book is Askar's answer but, as is usual in Farah's work, it is an
answer full of further, unresolved questions. The most important of
these have to do with the facts of his relationship to Misra and to the
mother through whom he and Misra are connected. There are conflicting versions of his birth, for example, and they come from three different sources, none of which can be considered entirely reliable: Misra,
who arrived only after the event; Askar himself, who insists that he has a
clear memory of his own birth; and his mother, who, according to
Askar, lives on inside him and occasionally speaks through him.
Depending on the version and the source, either Askar was responsible
for his mother's death or she died of another cause, either she was still
alive or she had already died by the time he appeared, either she breast-
fed him before she died or she did not, and either the ring of blood
around his neck was an effect of childbirth or she tried to strangle him.
Many explanations also attend Askar's experience of waking one morning to find that although he is a boy, he has "menstruated": Misra
smeared the blood on him during the night; it came from a urinary
infection; it was caused by the tension of war; it was his mother's menstrual blood that came at a time when she had taken control of him; his
body had responded to a dream in which he was menstruating; or he
simply menstruated, an irreducible fact with no other explanation.
Other uncertainties arise in the conflicting versions of events offered by
Askar's different narrative voices in the text. The second-person Askar,
for example, asserts, "To Misra, you existed first and foremost in the
weird stare: you were, to her, your eyes, which, once they found her,
focused on her guilt—her self!" (*M,* 6). The first-person Askar opens the
following chapter, however, by insisting, "Misra never said to me that I

existed for her only in my look. What she said was that she could see in my stare an itch of intelligence—that's all" (*M*, 23). Askar's elaborately reported dreams and his bouts of consciousness-altering pain and illness supply still other contentious voices and perspectives.

This is why Askar is "a question to himself" and why the telling of his story is itself the story in this novel. Like Medina, Deeriye, and Yussuf, Askar constructs and reconstructs himself, drawing his materials from the many-layered social world he inhabits. Among these characters, however, he is the most agonizingly aware of the fact that the other lives out of which he composes his life are, at the same time, engaged in their own projects of self-construction and are exerting on his imagination their own demands to be recognized. In that complicated world of social imagination, then, the only answer to the question "Who is Askar?" that can be true is a story that reveals its own telling and that allows all its differently inventing voices to be heard, a story like Askar's that both seeks and resists resolution.

Maps opens Farah's second trilogy of novels, to be followed by *Gifts* and concluded by *Secrets*. Midway through the writing of this sequence, Farah commented that in the first trilogy the "overall theme is 'Truth versus Untruth,'" while the second explores "the theme of Africa's upheaval and societal disorganisation" ("Why I Write," 1599). *Variations on the Theme of an African Dictatorship,* as we have seen, develops a common situation and set of characters and a single metaphorical figure, the dictator—metaphorical in the sense that, for Farah, the play of "truth and untruth" that perpetuates injustice is the product of a social system, not merely of one powerful individual. The second trilogy, unlike the first, is not composed as a series of explicit sequels. There is once again, however, a common metaphorical figure in these novels, which Farah described soon after completing *Secrets*: "[I]n all of them a baby boy is either found or lost. Now, imagine: an African Islamic society in which babies are abandoned. . . . The whole thing is apocalyptic. . . . Society is an orphaned baby, parentless, with no wise elder to guide it" (Interview, 1992, 59). In the Dictatorship Trilogy the family and the nation come in for equal scrutiny as arenas in which the play of political power, the struggle of personal freedom and social engagement, is staged. In Farah's second trilogy the larger public scene remains actively present but recedes, becoming a backdrop to the central drama of the family, a drama initiated by the problematic birth of a child. What is dramatized is a social strategy for conceiving, asserting, or resisting power in relationships, families as well as larger communities. In each that strategy is named in the title—maps, gifts, and secrets—and in each it involves characters in a struggle for freedom through the creation of stories of identity.

Maps, as we have seen, presents itself as a story told by the orphan child about himself and the world as he imagines it. *Gifts,* once again, is the story of a story being told, but here the child puts in only a brief, although pivotal, appearance. This is instead the tale of Duniya, a senior nurse in a Mogadiscio maternity hospital and a woman of complicated family relationships. As the daughter of a polygamous marriage, she has a beloved older brother, Abshir (her relationship to him resembling, in several respects, that of Medina to Nasser in *Sardines*), and an equally hated older half brother, Shiriye. When she was 17, she complied with her father's dying wish by marrying Zubair, a blind old man, to whom she bore twins, a boy named Mataan and a girl named Nasiiba, who are themselves 17 when the book opens. Widowed when the twins were infants, Duniya moved to Mogadiscio, began a career, and married Taariq, a journalist, who fathered her daughter Yarey and whom she later divorced. She now lives with the twins, whose independence of mind she encourages but frets about, in a house owned by Taariq's brother and sister-in-law, Qaasim and Muraayo. The nine-year-old Yarey lives with these two, who have no children of their own. Into this patchwork of relationships steps Bosaaso to court Duniya. Bosaaso, who works in the Ministry of Economic Planning, is a widower and a close friend of Mire, the doctor in charge of Duniya's ward at the hospital. Duniya first met Bosaaso at the birth of his son, who died soon after, along with Bosaaso's wife, in a fall from a balcony. He is a sympathetic figure to whom Duniya is drawn while at the same time resisting his attentions in order to avoid becoming dependent on him.

Their relationship develops haltingly until the day Nasiiba brings home a newborn infant that she claims to have found and insists on keeping. They name the child Magaclaawe, which means "the nameless one," and when they register him with the police they list themselves as coresponsible for his care, implying a commitment to each other that they have not yet made. No one comes forward to claim the baby. Shiriye, however, shows up to oppose Duniya's taking in a child who appears to be illegitimate. Qaasim and Muraayo arrive as well with Yarey, who now wants to live with Duniya, prompting Muraayo to insist that either Yarey be returned to her or she be given the foundling. In response, Duniya gives notice that she is leaving Qaasim's house with her family. Bosaaso supports Duniya in these conflicts, and the two of them grow closer in the process. Duniya learns that Nasiiba did not find the baby at all but brought it home to help her friend Fariida, the unmarried mother of the infant, whom she had secretly been assisting before the birth with money from the household fund and with donations of her own blood. It emerges that the father of the child is Qaasim and that Muraayo's claim to Magaclaawe, although unbeknownst to her, has some substance. The baby is found dead, however, and no explanation is given or indeed sought for its death. Instead Duniya heeds a voice in her mind that says, "The foundling has done whatever it came into this life to achieve," a suggestion that leads her to conclude, "Everybody had turned the foundling into what they thought they wanted, or lacked. In that case, she said to herself, the Nameless One has not died. He is still living on, in Bosaaso and me."[14] By her gesture . of commitment to the foundling, Duniya has at the same time brought into focus other possibilities in her life. She expands her own independence and capacities, preparing to establish a new home for herself and her family and learning to drive and to swim. At the same time, she commits herself to a relationship with Bosaaso in which she "gives herself" to him and begins more easily to accept his gifts, as she does those of her brother, Abshir, who arrives from abroad to play an uncle's role with the children and to provide a home for Duniya and Bosaaso.

The role of gift giving and receiving in these acts of self-definition is of central importance. Gifts are ways of enlarging or restricting definitions of identities and relationships in this novel, just as maps are in the previous one. Duniya says, "I resist all kinds of domination, including that of being given something. As my epitaph I would like to have the following written: 'Here lies Duniya who distrusted givers' " (*G*, 237). She feels keenly the threat of her dependence on Bosaaso, a male and a person of greater wealth, and the negotiation of giving and receiving is therefore a delicate matter between them: "[H]er reluctance to accept his gifts was making him tense, and this might, in the end, cause a strain on their relationship. But he did not insist that she receive everything he offered. . . . In any case, she reasoned to herself, she did accept gifts from him in the form of lifts, in exchange for meals which he ate at her place. Fair was fair, and he was the kind of man who was fair" (*G*, 150). The issue arises in other personal relations as well. Duniya does not allow her children to bring home food that others have given them, for example, calling it "corpse food" that she will allow them to eat only when she is dead (*G*, 24); and one of the sources of her bitterness against Shiriye is her discovery that he agreed to her first marriage only when he was secretly offered bride-gifts. The connection between the power of gifts to define relationships at the personal level and the same power at the collective level is made explicitly and repeatedly throughout the novel. When Bosaaso asks Duniya the reason for her reluctance to receive from others, she responds, "Because unasked for generosity has a way of making one feel obliged, trapped in a labyrinth of dependence. You're more knowledgeable about these matters, but haven't we in the Third World lost our self-reliance and pride because of the so-called aid we unquestioningly receive from the so-called First World?" (G, 20–21). Several chapters in the book end with newspaper excerpts that document the exercise of power relationships in international politics— and especially between Somalia and donor nations and organizations— through the giving and receiving of foreign aid.

Gifts threaten Duniya's freedom of identity just as maps threaten Askar's, and she, like Askar, reclaims that freedom through the telling of stories by which she reconceives herself and the social world she inhabits. The apparatus of storytelling is equally prominent in both books. The first part of Gifts is titled "A Story is Born," a title followed by the epigrammatic synopsis of Chapter One: "In which Duniya sees the outlines of a story emerging from the mist surrounding her, as the outside world impinges on her space and thoughts" (G, 1). Again like Askar, Duniya is aware of her own role as storyteller. At the close of the book, for example, she tries to understand the process by which events emerge and take on meaning: "She decided that her own epiphanic instant had occurred at a moment, on a morning, when a story chose to tell itself to her, through her, a story whose clarity was contained in the creative utterance, Let there be a man, and there was a story" (G, 241, emphasis in the original). Farah himself, in fact, has proposed in an interview the most literal reading possible of such lines: "Gifts has been missed by practically every reader whom I have met, not thinking, even for a moment, that . . . this is a story that a woman tells herself from the beginning to the end. It doesn't happen. It happens inside her head when she goes from home to work. She's narrating the story to herself and imagining what would happen if her luck turned" (Interview, 1996). This is a helpful insight in that it draws attention to the central-ity of Duniya's imagination in establishing the meaning and direction of her own life and encourages the reader to allow for a wider-than-normal range of logical possibilities in the narrative pattern of the text. On the other hand, it is, to borrow one of Farah's own favorite expressions, "only a version" of how that pattern might be considered.

Gifts, like *Maps,* is interesting as a story about the telling of a story precisely because different versions abound, with different voices and ways of constructing an account of identities and relationships. Bosaaso, for example, also takes up the role of narrator on occasion: "He diverted his mind by telling himself (and Duniya in her dream, of which he was part) the story of an only son of an only parent" (*G,* 40). This boy is himself and the parent is his mother, a storyteller by profession. Nasiiba is another of the self-conscious narrators in this book: "Nasiiba derived a thrill from turning half-truths into embellished fictions, making each tale into exactly the story you needed to hear" (*G,* 25). Not only are there different voices contributing tales but different modes of narration as well. Some we have mentioned already: the chapter synopses that introduce another kind of authorial voice and raise generic expectations of a different kind of narrative control, such as one finds in the eighteenth-century European novel, or the newspaper excerpts with their claims to real-world factuality and their evocation of a wider range of reference. Still other voices and forms take part in this growing chorus: Taariq's newspaper articles, including "The Story of the Cow," which begins with the words "This is a true story" and then proceeds to recount a miracle (*G,* 54–57); his telling of an Ethiopian creation myth (*G,* 127); or the stories of Juxaa, the wise-fool hero of northern African folktales, that Mataan recounts (*G,* 70–71, 113). Most striking of all are the stories that arise in dreams. Eleven of the 18 chapters in the book open with a character (usually but not always Duniya) dreaming or just waking from dreams that often transform or recombine elements of stories told or experienced by characters in their waking lives.

It is in relation to this varied collection of voices and ways of story-telling that Duniya's uncertainty at the end of the book must be read: "She was thinking that beginning the story had been easy, like extracting a milk-tooth. But how was she to end it?" (*G,* 241). Sitting at a dinner party at which all the people she cares most about are present, she knows that the question on her mind is a difficult one because there are different outcomes, all possible, but not all hers to tell: "She was asking herself if she was content that her guests could get on with the telling of their respective stories without her. And *the other* Duniya with *her* tale?" (*G,* 241–42, emphasis in the original). Like Askar, then, she finds herself at the close of the novel facing the task of telling well a story that reveals and respects the stories of which it is made: "Duniya, the chronicler, is no longer certain how to go on, and nothing short of a much longer pause will enable her to look back on the events as they took place in order for her to describe them accurately. . . . The world was an audience, ready to be given Duniya's story from the beginning" (*G*, 242). Too many voices mingle with Duniya's for the reader to conclude that the story is "only a dream" or that it is entirely hers to tell as she pleases; and these voices too often evoke a real world of pain and injustice for the reader to be content with a story that is responsible only to its own aesthetic logic. Faced with the power of gifts to create and maintain restrictive identities, Duniya makes her most important task the definition of a self that is free and that preserves the freedom of others to pursue their own work of self-definition.

In *Secrets,* Farah explores threats to self-definition emanating from yet a different quarter. Kalaman, the protagonist of Farah's most recent novel, occupies a world in which one's identity is subject to the control of others by the secrets they possess and reveal or withhold for purposes of their own, just as one's identity is shaped by the maps that others draw and redraw and by the dependency they impose through gifts in the two previous novels. Among these secrets is the significance of his own name, Kalaman, an untraditional name that his grandfather Nonno bestowed on him at birth. Other important secrets in the book are eventually revealed, but this one is not, although we find a number of clues as well as tentative but contradictory answers. One partial explanation is that this is a name designed to stand alone, without the usual links to the father and grandfather and, as we shall see, there is some reason for him to bear such a name. Another is that it has something to do with the Arabic alphabet, and it is true that its consonants follow each other in the same sequence in that alphabet. In a related suggestion, Nonno predicts (incorrectly) that, like himself, Kalaman will be an orator, which is one meaning of the word *kalaman* in Arabic. Elsewhere in the book, Nonno says that he named Kalaman in imitation of the squawk of a crow (an important bird in Somali mythology) that attended Kalaman's birth. On another occasion, he says (without further elaboration) that there is an allegory in Kalaman's naming that must be sorted out as the camel sorts its stored water from its own blood. On yet another, Kalaman observes Nonno writing the letters of his name among other mysterious words and numbers, allowing the reader to infer a possible connection between this name and the magical writing that Nonno practiced in his past.

Nonno's past is a repository of secrets as well, a shadowy tale of a young Qur'anic scholar who dabbles in mystical powers and is forced to flee his northern town of Berbera under a curse, arriving in Afgoi in the south, where he changes his name from Misbaah ("light" in Arabic) to Miftaax ("key") and becomes a successful farmer with a mysterious influence over animals. He is first called Nonno (a children's word in Italian for grandfather) at Kalaman's birth, in which his involvement goes beyond naming the infant. After a very long gestation, Kalaman is unable at birth to cry or urinate and is cured only when Nonno feeds him a tamarind seed and a drop of wild honey. (This matter of the child's critical first sustenance is a motif in the trilogy. In *Maps* Misra insists that Askar's mother lived long enough to breast-feed him and tries unsuccessfully to do so herself, and in *Gifts* the newborn Duniya is unable to suckle until she drinks a drop of milk from the finger of Abshir.) It is Nonno, furthermore, who whispers the traditional "secret wisdom" in Kalaman's ear on his fortieth day of life—his words to the infant are "Birds soar!"[15]

Next to the larger-than-life Nonno, Kalaman's parents seem at first slightly odd but unremarkable. His father, Yaqut, unlike Nonno, is inarticulate and generally silent. He is a dreamer and an artist who carves in marble and makes a living from the city as a grave-digger for those who have no one to pay for their burials. He saves all sorts of discarded objects, which he often works into the products of his art, and he is a devoted and nurturing father who pretends to breast-feed the baby Kalaman to comfort him when his mother, Damac, is absent. Damac, on the other hand, is an ambitious merchant with a reputation for being domineering. She aggressively defends her husband and son and guards from the outside world the secret that she has an extra pair of tiny breasts, at which, in Kalaman's infancy, her husband suckles while she nurses her baby. As a child, Kalaman is suspicious that his parents never intended to conceive him and urges them to prove otherwise by giving him a sibling. Both they and Nonno warn him in early life that it can be dangerous either to harbor or to discover secrets, and yet he shows a talent for doing both. The secrets in question are mainly sexual, having to do with his parents' relations, his grandfather's lusty affairs, his own precocious experience with Sholoongo, a girl a few years older than he, and the varied sex lives of her family. From the age of three Kalaman has been an accomplished voyeur, and Farah provides him a lot to watch in this, his most sexually explicit novel to date.

Kalaman is the first-person narrator of most of the novel, though other voices—Nonno's, Sholoongo's, and Damac's—account for several chapters. He is 33 years old, unmarried, and the successful owner of a company in Mogadiscio whose business is to prepare documents. This is an ironic choice of profession, because documents, forged and stolen, will turn out to have been instrumental in setting the course by which the life of Kalaman's family has developed. Sholoongo, whom he has not seen for 20 years, shows up unexpectedly in his apartment despite a locked door to which she has no key. From childhood Sholoongo has been a person of strange powers, reputed to be a shape-shifter, able to take the forms of animals at will. She announces that she has returned from the United States to have a child by Kalaman, for reasons she does not reveal. Just as she has found her way into his apartment, so has she penetrated his secrets, including a relationship he is having with a woman named Talaado, and she begins burrowing—the animal imagery is explicit—into secrets of his parents as well.

This connection between the animal and human worlds and the related role of supernatural experience in human affairs are themes that have been growing in importance throughout the second trilogy and that become dominant in this novel. In *Maps* the dreams of Askar often involve animals of symbolic portent or mythic powers, and Misra is thought to possess the ability to divine using meat and blood. In *Gifts* animals (especially birds and insects) are an even more prominent feature of the many dreams in the book, but the same animals sometimes cross over from dream to waking reality, and jinns reportedly play a large role in the earlier life of Duniya's first husband, causing his blindness. In *Secrets* the animal and supernatural realms emerge from the secondary role they play in the two previous novels and become integral to the narrative. Nonno, true to the name he has given himself, holds the "keys" to many of the secrets of Kalaman's world; he explains to him that the instinct by which animals find their way and the impulse by which humans maintain community are in fact closely related powers, and that Sholoongo, who is said to have been abandoned as an infant and raised by a lioness, is endowed with both. Fidow, a foreman on Nonno's farm, also has a special spiritual connection to animals, but, unlike Nonno and Sholoongo, he exercises a destructive and exploitative control over them, killing crocodiles for their skins and elephants for their tusks. In one of the most startling episodes in the book, an elephant (an animal not native to Somalia) marches into town, seeks out and kills Fidow, and marches away, clutching a cache of tusks that had been hidden in Fidow's house. This episode is recounted indirectly and becomes one of Farah's stories with "versions," one of which is that the elephant was in fact the shape-shifting Sholoongo. The truth of the matter is one more secret that belongs to Sholoongo, in whose person animal instinct and the power of secrets are most closely aligned. The association of these two powers is suggested as well in "Rhino," a rhinoceros-shaped drum fashioned by Yaqut in which townspeople sometimes leave secret letters.

One such letter, stolen many years earlier by Sholoongo, hidden in "Rhino," and discovered there by Nonno, is a clue to the central secret of the book. Contrary to Farah's usual practice, this secret *is* revealed—is, in fact, foreshadowed throughout much of the narrative—and it is Sholoongo, burrowing persistently into the hidden recesses of family history and identity, who forces the eventual revelation, despite Damac's threat to shoot her in order to prevent this disclosure. Kalaman, it turns out, is not in fact the biological child of Yaqut or grandchild of Nonno. He is the product, rather, of a scheme and a rape. The scheme is one by which a forger of documents tried to trap the young Damac into marrying him by means of a phony marriage certificate. When she refused to allow a forgery to turn her into what she was not, she was gang-raped by friends of the suitor. A pregnant Damac then turned to Yaqut, whom the world believed from then on to be her husband and the father of Kalaman, though they both knew that he was neither. The revelation of this secret comes as no surprise to the reader, but an unexpected plot twist is no more the point here than anywhere else in Farah's writing. The point of Kalaman's learning the "truth" of his identity—that he is illegitimate and begotten in violence—is instead that it turns out not to be the truth at all, or not a significant truth. Rather, he rejects the principle by which social identity is constructed through bloodlines—whether genuine or forged—and insists that he is indeed the child of Damac and Yaqut by virtue of the commitments they choose to make to one another. Nonno responds to the revelation in the same manner, proclaiming Kalaman his rightful heir just before his death at the end of the book.

This ultimate triumphal assertion of identity in family is achieved against a backdrop of political disintegration by which Somali national identity becomes all but empty. These two processes and the inverse relation between them are what most significantly tie together the three novels of the second trilogy. In *Maps,* written as Siyad Barre's control of the institutions of Somali society is loosening, the national backdrop to the family drama is one in which identity defined by the claims of citizenship founders with the political fortunes of "Greater Somalia" but nonetheless retains its seductive appeal. The family struggle at the center is one in which individuals, deeply entangled in these dynamics of national identity, seek survival of self at the expense of those they love. The orphan Askar consequently fails to transcend his parentless condition and in the end is paralyzed by it. In *Gifts*, written as the Siyad Barre regime is under direct assault by various Somali factions, Farah portrays a Mogadiscio in which physical structures, institutions, and public order are all crumbling. Duniya, meanwhile, whose public engagement is not with the nation but with a local and still functional institution, moves to escape the injustices of conventional family claims on identity and gropes tentatively toward new and less exploitative personal commitments. The nameless orphan dies but does so having "made life take shape" for Duniya and those she loves, "producing a *we* that had not been there before, a *we* of hybrid necessities, half real, half invented" (*G*, 132). In *Secrets*, first completed soon after Siyad Barre's ouster from power, the backdrop is one of civil breakdown and unrest verging on warfare, a chaotic scene of stray bullets and roaming militias in which the novel's characters are not engaged at any level other than as potential random victims. The novel and the trilogy end with the death of Nonno, who dies lamenting, "[M]y hopes of Somalia surviving the disasters are nil. Like me—and I am on my deathbed—she is as good as gone" (*Secrets*, 296). This is in notable contrast to the end of the first trilogy, in which Deeriye, another grandfather and unconventional patriarch, dies in an effort to defend both family and nation from dictatorship. In *Secrets*, however, the family as a sphere of identity is at last set free of constraint by the claims of the nation (and of its avatar the clan). The "orphan" Kalaman, like the nameless orphan of *Gifts*, produces "a *we* of hybrid necessities, half real, half invented," but one that does not demand his own sacrifice, one in which, on the contrary, his own life at last "takes shape" and commitment: a decision to marry Talaado, a wish to produce a child, and a determination to participate in the construction of his family as a legitimate ground of identity.

Chapter Four
The Politics of Autonomy

I see politics . . . , not as the idealized machinery in which government takes decisions that are good or bad for the people. I see politics as an area in which every individual, be it a little girl or an elderly man, can leave his or her mark. I see politics as the summing up of a people's daily lives.

—Nuruddin Farah, 1984 interview

I think that every human act is a political act. I think that when a man marries a woman that is also a political act. . . . I am interested in the functioning and the relationship between two human beings whose interests come into conflict of some sort. . . . I am interested in relationships between a parent and his child . . . a husband and his wife. . . . I am interested in a person who is deprived of that without which he, that particular person, cannot function.

—Nuruddin Farah, 1981 interview

From first to last, in fiction as in drama, Nuruddin Farah is a political writer. This is by no means a universally held view, however. For many readers, the central position of politics in Farah's writing begins—and ends—with his first trilogy of novels about resistance to dictatorship, preceded in earlier and displaced in later work by investigations of interpersonal relationships, gender, and sexuality, and by stylistic experimentation. Hilarie Kelly, for instance, writes that *"Maps* is a departure from the political focus of Nuruddin's previous trilogy" and takes him to task for his use of language and a range of reference that are unrelated to the political circumstances of "typical" Somalis.[1] Derek Wright too notes, though more positively, a shift away from politics in *Maps*: "[S]ince the Dictatorship Trilogy, Farah's work has moved into exciting, uncharted new territory for African writing. His fiction is a dynamically developing process that reveals a marked shift from political geography to psychophysiology, from powerscape to mindscape."[2] A reviewer of *Secrets* writes that the novels of the first trilogy "retain a certain clarity of political vision," but that, in his later work, Farah "overwhelms the ideological and historical premises of his books with a fabulist's imaginings."[3] Each of these readings applies the term *politics* in its conventional usage, referring to the workings of power at the level of governments.

As the epigraphs to this chapter suggest, however, that usage is too restrictive to make adequate sense of Farah's political thought. One must begin by taking him literally when he says that "every human act is a political act,"[4] that politics is a practice of "every individual," and that all relationships are political (Interview, 1984, 27). At the center of his fiction and drama is that primary social reality that is also at the center of politics: "the relationship between two human beings whose interests come into conflict." By "interests" he means that which defines the individual self, "that without which he [or she], that particular person, cannot function" (Interview, 1981b, 48). For Farah the fundamental value, the principle that must always be defended, is the vital autonomy of individuals to define these interests for themselves. This work of self-definition is political because it can take place only through negotiation with a social world shared with other individuals who possess and seek to exercise the same autonomy. At every level "of a people's daily lives," within every social formation—family, friendship, clan, religious or ideological community, nation—Farah's characters question their relationships, determining whether their own autonomy is being sustained or constrained. This understanding of politics as the negotiation of many participants, whose interests may well be in conflict, on behalf of individual autonomy, means that politics penetrates every corner of human experience and that it accounts for Farah's very particular treatments of identity, gender, and language, the subjects respectively of this and the remaining two chapters.

Individual autonomy is the freedom of every person to explore fully what Farah has called "the first and most important questions that all human beings ask themselves: 'Who am I?' 'Why am I who I am?' 'What is my place in this world?' " (Interview, 1989, 184). These questions, which permeate Farah's work, lead to the central preoccupation of all his major characters: to establish their identity on their own terms, inquiring into the conditions that have shaped them and the roles they want to play in the world. Ebla and Koschin, in the earliest novels, struggle to sever conventional social ties in order to be free to construct new opportunities, new possibilities, for themselves. Ebla wants "to break the ropes society had wrapped around her and to be free and be herself" (FCR, 12), while Koschin asserts that "a happy man is one who doesn't let others live his life for him" (NN, 143). Both want to avoid being controlled by others in order to direct their lives and choose freely their "place in this world." Sweet and Sour Milk focuses on the struggle to control who Soyaan was and who Loyaan will become. In Sardines

Medina works to imagine "a room of one's own" and "a country of one's own," which will afford greater freedom for herself and others (*Sardines,* 4). *Close Sesame* depicts the extraordinary achievement of an old man, Deeriye, who has largely succeeded in controlling his identity amid complex political dynamics but is now troubled by the difficulties facing his son's generation. In *Yussuf and His Brothers* Hussen struggles "to repossess [his] own soul" from the grip of Yussuf's insistent claim "that we're all one person" (*YB,* 69, 94). *Maps* is dedicated to the question of a young man's identity from the first chapter—"You are a question to yourself"—to the last—"I have one question. . . . Who *is* Askar?" (*M,* 3, 245). While certainty continues to elude Askar, the novel insists that he alone must bear the burden of determining his identity. Duniya, who has been the object of exchange between her father and first husband, in her maturity insists on being in control of her own person, on being the one to give herself, and on her own terms. Learning the facts of his parentage makes of Kalaman "a changed man" with "nothing of certainty linking" him to relationships in which he must now assume responsibility for defining his own identity (*Secrets,* 235-36).

This urgent wish to define the self is pervasive in Farah's fiction and drama, but it entails many pitfalls and risks and can take place freely only under certain political conditions. Every human is born into a social world that already has designs upon one's identity: expectations, roles, and norms amount to constructed identity sites, available for immediate occupation, and it is such prefabrications that autonomous individuals must vigilantly and persistently resist and transform. Nothing—not even one's parents—can be taken for granted, taken as beyond question. The numerous orphans and children whose parentage is somehow in doubt (Askar, Kalaman, the foundling in *Gifts,* and the children born to Amina, Sagal, and Ebla) are figures for the yet-to-be-determined, for the condition of openness to possibility that autonomy requires. This can be an anxious condition, however, and the temptation can be strong to abdicate responsibility for one's own identity. That desire is evident, for example, in Askar, the most deeply uncertain self in Farah's novels, who has a dream in which he says, "I am . . . ," but cannot finish the sentence. Still dreaming, he then sees people whose bodies are "tattooed with their identities: that is name, nationality and address. Some had engraved on their skins the reason why they had become who they were when living and others had printed on their foreheads or backs their national flags or insignia" (*M,* 42). The tattooing and engraving represent permanent definitions of self deeply appealing to one who is unable to finish the sentence that begins, "I am. . . ." Blood kinship, clan, nationality, and religion are conceptions that many of Farah's characters are tempted to use to fix their identity immovably in place. The twin dangers threatening genuine autonomy in Farah's writing are, on the one hand, the fantasy that one might be able simply to escape the already-given and therefore constraining social world, and on the other, the possibility that by surrendering one's self to one concept, one dimension, by becoming tattooed, swallowed up in a collectivity, one might avoid the burden of insisting on a unique, complicated self, a self that has the "fortune," as Misra says in regard to Askar, "of holding simultaneously multiple citizenships of different kingdoms" (M, 11).

Self-definition occurs within a world that must be shared with others, a world of preexisting expectations, roles, and definitions generated within social formations (such as families, clans, nations) that may possibly nurture but will very often constrain individual autonomy. Moreover, this shared social world usually constrains differentially: parents have more power than children, men more than women. Individuals desiring their own autonomy must be willing to examine all social relationships to determine what can be transformed and what must be resisted; they must be able to maintain a sense of identity that is coherent yet provisional and open to possibilities; and in order to address the power differential, they often need to develop collective strategies to effect changes that will support the autonomy of all. It is a difficult and lifelong process requiring that all relationships and identifications remain strategic even as individuals maintain their firm commitment to the value of autonomy.

In Farah's political thought, this process, involving the constant negotiation with social structures on behalf of individuals, must go on at every level. It is easiest, however, to see the dynamics of these negotiations in those instances in which conflict is writ large, in which autonomy is conspicuously and overtly threatened. Hence we consider initially the most readily identifiable form of political activity in Farah's work, resistance to state dictatorship, the subject of his first trilogy of novels and two of his plays, *The Offering* and *A Spread of Butter.* We do this primarily as a way of making visible other occasions for resistance to other kinds of oppression appearing in Farah's work. In doing so, we move as well with the direction of Farah's own political gaze over the course of his career. We have noted already Farah's stated wish for his books "to be a commentary on Somalia and the history of Somalia, and . . . to follow it to a certain degree" (Interview, 1996). They in fact follow it to a very great degree, and the manner in which he refocuses the lens of his political analysis from one novel or play to the next is a measure of how sensitive his writing is to developing conditions in Somalia. In his first two novels he begins his long investigation of the politics of autonomy by attending almost exclusively to local and personal relations. As the Siyad Barre government clamped its hold on the political life of Somalia, however, it forced Farah's attention to political relations in the public sphere where, for him too, the conflict was suddenly writ large and the threat to autonomy could not be ignored. Although his work during this period continues to examine closely political relations in the personal sphere, it does so in an atmosphere in which all such relations resonate to the struggle against state dictatorship.

If we consider the actors in these political dramas and the concerns that generate political dissent, we are immediately struck by how particular Farah's world is and how much he differs from other prominent African political writers like Ngugi wa Thiong'o of Kenya, Ousmane Sembene of Senegal, or Chinua Achebe of Nigeria. In Farah's writing, unlike that of these contemporaries, we find no peasants forced from their land, no workers brutalized through rapid industrialization, no mass movement of any sort. Those who resist are drawn from a privileged class of urban professionals, often educated abroad, widely traveled, multilingual, and materially comfortable. For some readers this choice of protagonists undermines Farah's political analysis. Barbara Turfan, for example, asks, "[T]o what extent can the intellectual and social elite seek to change and advance a society with which they have no real contact or identity?" and "[H]ow can the country's intellectuals produce a home-grown remedy if they are steeped in the ways of societies not their own?"[5] These questions, however, rest upon a simplification of the concept of identity that Farah's work opposes at every turn. Turfan assumes that Farah's characters are not authentically "Somali" because they are not sufficiently poor, uneducated, rural, or miserable— they do not, in other words, conform to the Western stereotype of an African "native." Part of the distinctive importance of Farah's work is that he draws the attention of many non-African readers, by his choice of characters, to a complexity of social experience in Africa that such stereotypes have trained them to think does not exist or is not "really African."

More to the point, in the context of Farah's politics of autonomy the central problem posed by dictatorship is not distributive or economic injustice but the abrogation of civil liberties and the curtailment of individual freedom accomplished through systematic public deception, conditions that make other forms of injustice possible. Farah knows well that his protagonists enjoy privileges that many Somalis do not, and that is why he himself repeatedly refers to them as members of the "priviligencia." It is, however, precisely their education and wide experience that make them so attentive to the issue of individual autonomy, that loosen the hold of imposed identities on their consciousnesses, and that place them thereby in a position to recognize and to disclose the lies by which dictators gain and hold power. Education of the public accordingly—extending more widely these forms of attention, consciousness, and analysis—is the goal of the resistance movement that Ibrahim describes to Loyaan in *Sweet and Sour Milk,* a group "composed of intellectuals and professionals who've taken an oath . . . to serve not the interests of any superpower but this nation's," a group that is "vigilant" and "conscious politically." That role falls to the intellectual elite, Ibrahim explains, because Somalia "hasn't a tradition of protest movements, trade unions or organised groups of any kind. There is no tradition such as there is in Egypt, Ethiopia, or Sudan, of student movements which can help form or unform governments or shape public opinion." When "people, inarticulate with fear, prefer not to speak," political responsibility therefore falls to articulate, educated individuals, rising to face the threat on an ad hoc basis, rather than to standing political organizations (*SSM,* 139). This pattern of political action may not replicate the forms of resistance portrayed by other African writers and may not even be very successful—indeed, it is the dictator who is left standing at the end of the Dictatorship Trilogy. It is, however, a pattern that has its place in traditional Somali political practices as we have described them in chapter 1 and that is consistent with Farah's own individualistic style of political engagement, a pattern that projects the principle of individual autonomy uncompromisingly into the politics of the public sphere.

To appreciate the way that this mode of resistance develops, we need to consider the forms of power that this dictator employs, beginning with the hold of the revolution itself on the imagination of a public weary of governmental corruption and unmet promises. Even Koschin, despite his worldly wise pose, holds out provisional hope for the new regime: "This is the most reasonable government Somalia has ever had. They will certainly relax. They are giving many things thought" (*NN,* 106); "Somalia very badly needed a revolution. . . . Revolution is truth, it is justice, yes. Justice. So far this revolution in Somalia . . .keep[s] alive the hope. . . . If this one doesn't remain loyal to the basic truths of a

Somali-African humanity, then it must be denied the rights to dominate the minds of the honest ones" (*NN,* 149). To a considerable extent, Koschin sees the ominous signs of such a betrayal—the "terror and horror from dawn to dusk," the widespread practice of deifying "the Old Man, sing[ing] his name to the skies"—but he fails to read in these signs the threat to freedom that they portend (*NN,* 149, 80). By *Sweet and Sour Milk,* however, it is clear that the "socialist" revolution has run amok and that Somalia has become a client state of the Soviet Union, which provides money and models for running a dictatorship: secret police, underground "superprisons" (where Koschin is held), and techniques for interrogation and indoctrination. The dictator serves "a cocktail of poisonous contradictions to the masses," mixing overt physical coercion with "the politics of mystification" (*SSM,* 14, 198). Freedom of speech, freedom of the press, and rights of assembly are abrogated. A government memorandum (found in a pocket of the dead Soyaan's clothing) reads, "Any person who spreads or takes out of the Somali Democratic Republic printed, reading, spoken or broadcast matter, or persons in the SDR who display, distribute or disseminate information aimed at damaging the sovereignty of the revolution of the Somali nation will be liable to death" (*SSM,* 48–49). News within Somalia is wholly controlled; Medina is fired within four days of being appointed editor of the national newspaper; radio Mogadiscio broadcasts the government's version of news; and the dictator's influence appears to extend to the international news media as well. Telephones are tapped, people disappear after dawn visits from the Security Service, and citizens are required to perform public service and undergo indoctrination at "Orientation Centres" under the watchful eye of the Green Guard. Taking advantage of a largely oral society, the General recruits his Security Service from "illiterates" who spy in shops and "report verbatim what they think they heard," leading to arrests that are made without written warrants and therefore leave no recorded traces (*SSM,* 137). In one of his memoranda Soyaan characterizes the fundamental strategy behind these measures—"Plant seeds of suspicion in every thinking brain and hence render it 'unthinking' "—and the climate of fear and submissiveness that it breeds—"Raise your children, but not your voice nor your head. To survive you must clown. You must hide in the convenience of a crowd and clap. . . . Listen to the knock on your neighbour's door at dawn. . . . They've taken another. When will your turn come?" (*SSM,* 34).

The General's methods vary: "He has some in prison; he appoints some as ambassadors; he bribes some with the portfolio of banana sales;

he forces some to retire; he has some of them tortured" (*SSM*, 92). What
lies at the center of it all, however, is his success in controlling the minds
of the people, in rendering "every thinking brain unthinking." As *A
Spread of Butter* demonstrates, even the highly trained, conscientized,
and militant "thinking brain" of a professor can be taught not to recognize the difference between political reality and appearance. Hence the
need for a resistance focused on producing an oppositional analysis of
the dictator's practices, an analysis that exposes again and again, at
many levels, his assault on the autonomy of individuals: a *self*-education
that counters the versions of reality disseminated by those in power.
Though the methods of those in the resistance often vary as the General's do, becoming increasingly subversive and violent, what strengthens and deepens in the course of the trilogy is these characters' inquiry
into the interplay of multiple forms of power. It is by the strength of
their analysis of political power, not the success of their attempt to overthrow that power, that the reader is invited to judge them.

    That inquiry reveals, throughout the first trilogy, the relationships
among dictatorship, patriarchy, and colonialism, which, taken together,
constitute what Medina identifies as "power as a system" (*Sardines*, 55).
Learning to appreciate the connections among these forms of power
constitutes, in effect, a political education, undergone in different ways
by the protagonists of each of the novels, Loyaan, Medina, and Deeriye,
through their debates with others. Insight into these connections develops as a pattern of research and discovery in Loyaan's mind, is most fully
theorized in Medina's, and most fully historicized in Deeriye's.

    To conduct the first stage of this developing analysis, Farah chooses a
character who is already trained in research and discovery as a scientist
but not in the subtleties of politics: Loyaan, a regional health officer in a
provincial town. Attempting to get to the truth about his brother's
death, Loyaan becomes quickly and confusingly immersed in "the politics of mystification [which] rendered rumours credible. Nothing was
ever confirmed. . . . People were kept in their separate compartments of
ignorance about what happened to other people and what became of
other things" (*SSM*, 198–99). In his perplexity Loyaan, and with him
the reader, must patch together, from flimsy and mismatched pieces, a
picture of the government, the opposition, and the dynamics of both. In
trying to understand what has happened, Loyaan frequently recalls an
early memory in which he and his brother, Soyaan, are threatened by
their father, a figure of "towering height" with a "fist of power; the
power of the patriarch," who tears apart a ball they are playing with.

Soyaan's response is to vow, "I will kill him one day, . . . I really will. When I am strong as he. When I can handle a knife, when I can carry a gun" (*SSM,* 30). The vignette suggests that the origin of Soyaan's will to resist the national dictator lies in this experience of domestic tyranny, a connection the novel goes on to develop, not in psychological terms as an oedipal struggle but in terms of comparable, indeed, mutually reinforcing systems of power. Consciously emulating the dictator, Keynaan styles himself "the Grand Patriarch [who] rules, with the iron hand of male-dominated tradition, over his covey of children and wives" (*SSM,* 50). Farah makes the connection more explicit still in an epigraph to Part Two of the book, quoting Wilhelm Reich: "In the figure of the father the authoritarian state has its representative in every family, so that the family becomes its most important instrument of power" (*SSM,* 95). In other words, patriarchy within the family prepares everyone for dictatorship in the state.

Farah develops the relationship between patriarchy and dictatorship in various ways, sometimes by dramatizing a father as the arm of the dictator against his own son. Keynaan claims the power of "life and death" over his sons and extends that power further to assert control over Soyaan's reputation after his death, cooperating with the state's interest in co-opting Soyaan's oppositional work by turning him into a hero of the Revolution (*SSM,* 94). Although Keynaan identifies himself explicitly with the General, he is actually a self-deluded tool, even a victim of the dictatorship. Loyaan comes to understand that, for all his rhetoric, his father in fact "sees himself as a miniature creature in a flat world dominated by a God-figure high and huge as any mountain anyone has seen . . . , and helpless too," and that the only compensation available to Keynaan is dominating his wives and children (*SSM,* 83). This view is confirmed as Loyaan learns that the General, in order to protect members of his own clan, has made Keynaan the public scapegoat in a scandal involving a person who died in detention after torture. Keynaan is indeed "a miniature creature . . . dominated by a God-figure" and therefore all the more eager to regain favor in the eyes of the God-General by cooperating in managing the reputation of his dissident son. In *Close Sesame* another father serves directly as the arm of the dictator when he is ordered to "take steps" to control his dissident son, Mukhtaar, which he does by killing him in a fight.

Loyaan's contribution to the developing analysis in the first trilogy, then, is to assemble, naively but doggedly, the pieces of a picture that illustrates the interdependence of patriarchy and dictatorship. Medina's role, in *Sardines,* is to theorize the meaning of that picture for individuals who would resist this assault on their autonomy. At the opening of the novel she has moved out of her house, taking her daughter, Ubax, and leaving her husband, Samatar. Throughout we are invited to speculate about her motive. Does she believe that by holding a ministerial position, Samatar is being co-opted by the dictator? Is she afraid of her mother-in-law who has threatened to circumcise Ubax? The question cannot, however, be resolved in favor of one hypothesis or the other, because the two issues are the same: Idil and the General represent two interlocking forms of power, both of which threaten individual autonomy. Medina herself manipulates this irresolvability as a means of opposition, publicly adopting one explanation, then another; and what enables her to maintain this ambiguity at a factual level is her capacity to move beyond it to a theoretical level where she places "the emphasis on power and not on the General; power as a system, power as a function" (*Sardines,* 55). Her educational task is to try to lead others to analyze power in the same manner, to see "Idil *in* the General; the personal *in* the political"; "If only Xaddia could understand that I'm fighting for the survival of the woman in me, in *her*—while demolishing 'families' like Idil's and regimes like the General's" (*Sardines,* 258–59).

Like Soyaan's, Medina's initial experience of tyranny is in a family dominated by "the typical authoritarian patriarch," her grandfather, "the cruellest man [that the women of his household] had ever known," a "monstrosity" rumored to have set fire to the house on the occasion of Medina's birth and to have driven his son-in-law to suicide (*Sardines,* 57). This firsthand knowledge of patriarchal oppression and especially her own experience of circumcision position her to recognize "the personal" as "the political," to grasp the connection between patriarchy and dictatorship. She develops this in a debate with her mother about raising children. Fatima wants them to kiss the hands of adults: "A child is an inferior being" and in her view is properly kept in doubt about the motives of the towering adult with the half-raised hand. "Neither you nor Nasser," Fatima complains, "is willing to incline head, back, and body to kiss your mother's hand. . . . But Samater is *an incliner of head, a bender of body*" (*Sardines,* 148, emphasis in the original). Knowing that Samater has indeed learned subservience at his mother's knee, Medina doubts that he will be able to resist either the General's or Idil's demands. Her moving out of the house, therefore, is in effect a complex gesture of opposition to both of them and at the same time a means of creating new terms on which she and her family can live.

Loyaan's research and Medina's theoretical analysis, then, show that patriarchy can structure familial relationships in the same way and often to the same ends that dictatorship structures civic relationships, and that when it does so it is oppressive to both men and women, sons as well as daughters and wives. Deeriye's historically informed perspective extends their understanding of "power as a system" with new emphases. First, patriarchy and state dictatorship are linked to multilayered experiences of colonialism in the Horn of Africa; second, Deeriye concentrates on clan rather than family as a social formation hospitable to patriarchy, showing that clanship, as managed by the General, is a legacy of colonialism. This further exploration is carried forward not by individuals representing the modernized "priviligencia" but by one who is himself a patriarch and who is deeply committed to his Islamic faith, in short, one who in many ways represents "tradition" even as he critiques it. In this way Deeriye becomes a model for how individuals can select from the materials of their social world those elements that they require for autonomous acts of self-definition.

Deeriye is a patriarch whose religious faith has sustained his long life of political resistance; he treats his family members with respect and affection, extending to all a full measure of regard for their dignity. This is not to say that in *Close Sesame* patriarchy is no longer a problem, for alongside Deeriye we have Ibrahim, who slays his own son in the name of clan interests and loyalty to the General. By focusing here on patriarchy within the clan, we see more sharply than ever how it penetrates interlocking social formations and operates synergistically with other forms of power, namely, state dictatorship and colonialism. Deeriye contemplates these connections as he sits in the Baar Novecento attempting to assess the multiple rumors about his son's resistance activity; he regards the elders at his table with disdain tempered by wide experience:

> You found the likes of them all over Africa, the Middle East and Asia: old men who employed the power of tradition and the trust of their own people in order to support and justify a non-traditional authoritarian head of state; the same men who served the colonial governments were now serving these dictatorships or authoritarian regimes.
> 	. . . *How on earth could a man* [like Ibrahim] *be asked for either the head of his son or his acceptance of the policies of the "Father of the Nation, the Patriarch of Patriarchs?"* Paraphrasing the ideas of a philosopher whose name eluded him . . . , he said to himself: *In the figure of the chieftain, the authoritarian state has its representative in every clan or tribe so the elders of the clan*

become its most important instrument of power. He reminded himself that
tribal chieftaincy was the invention of Egyptian viceroys who were the
absentee landlords of Somalia. As an institution, it probably could be
dated as an eighteenth-century form of rule, a delegating of power the
Egyptians themselves had learnt from the Turkish Empire days. (*CS,*
103 – 4, emphasis in the original)

The reprise of the quotation from Wilhelm Reich, first used in *Sweet and
Sour Milk,* draws our attention to the structural parallels between family
and clan, both patriarchal and both made to serve the purposes of
authoritarian regimes.

What is new here is Deeriye's insight that these "traditional" institutions of power are in fact historically the "inventions" of those whose
interests they serve, inventions that are now managed by the General
and by the "old men" in the bar to consolidate and legitimize their
power.[6] He understands the consolidation of power among elders in a
clan and the cultivation of clan loyalty to be products of colonial experience that began with Egyptian and, before that, with Turkish penetration into the Horn. Deeriye's depiction of the patriarchs and clan elders
in the Baar Novecento as men complicitous with colonial authorities
reiterates a connection made frequently in Farah's work. Medina's
grandfather, Gad Thabit, that "monstrous" family dictator, found it
convenient to work with the Italian colonial authority. The General
himself served the same colonial army that Deeriye opposed as a young
man. In *Maps* Askar's abusive Uncle Qorrax collaborates with the
Ethiopians in the Ogaden. Throughout the first trilogy patriarchs collaborate with colonizers and the General manipulates the "tradition" of
clan loyalty, just as the colonizers did, as a way of augmenting his power
and dividing the opposition. Medina describes the government as "an
incestuous circle which draws its members from the General's clan and
those related to this tribal oligarchy through marriage" (*Sardines,* 92). In
Secrets Kalaman derides the "ignorance" of "foreigners who held the view
that 'Somali politics is clan politics' " and asserts that "what makes one
kill another because [the victim's] mythical ancestor is different from
one's own . . . has little to do with blood, more with a history of the per-
version of justice" (*Secrets,* 43, 76-77). Clan is so discredited in Farah's
writing that it stands out as the one social formation that is never shown
to be recuperated by individuals to support human freedom or dignity,
never shown as anything other than a spurious claim that is always to be
resisted.

Extending the kind of historical perspective that Deeriye so values, we are reminded that in precolonial Somali pastoralist society, clan functioned differently, as a way in which groups of people made provisional alliances regarding grazing and water rights in response to changing conditions, a form of social organization in which (male) individuals, through debate, significantly influenced the nature and duration of those alliances. Neither clan membership nor the role of elders fixed power relationships or compromised autonomy to anything approaching the extent to which the colonial governments and the Siyad Barre dictatorship did. It should be noted that Farah's thinking about clan runs counter to much of the scholarship and conventional wisdom regarding Somali society. During his 1996 interview, he discussed his views on this subject.

> Now, at no time in my writing have I ever mentioned the names of clans, and the reason is because I always knew that the moment you play clan name games, you're talking about something completely different from Somalia and that you are actually talking about things in colonial terms, [or] if you want, postcolonial terms, but never, never in traditional Somali terms. . . . You see, people do not fight in the name of clan. . . . You will not have gotten anywhere nearer an understanding of who a person is by defining them according to a clan name. . . . You have two million persons sharing a clan name and any individual's ideology is obviously going to be very different from as many of the two million as possible. (Interview, 1996)

Farah makes the point that it is individuals *as* individuals who oppose dictatorship and recalls his strenuous disagreement with the practice of human rights' groups that give the clan name of victims of torture:

> Victims have no clan names. When someone is detained, tortured, dealt with rather savagely by dictatorial regimes, you do not belittle that person by giving the name of the clan from which they come. And the reason is that it is not the clan that is getting this terrible treatment, it is *this* person for *his* idea. . . . Clan is not a definer. Clan is not an organizer of people. These are a disparate group of persons who are brought together by circumstances, like a rain shower. We are all standing together under a jetty . . . and we could become friends for a few minutes because there is a thunderstorm and we are all seeking shelter under the jetty. . . . That's how clans work: for a very short period of time. When people get to know each other, they become individuals. . . . No one can represent a clan. Neither does anyone represent a nation. (Interview, 1996)

In these remarks Farah makes clear his respect for the fundamental autonomy of the individual as a political actor and his emphasis upon the properly provisional and strategic dimension of social identifications. His assertion that "no one can represent a clan [or] a nation" means, on the one hand, that the significance of individual political commitments should not be diminished, as they are if we assume that someone performs an act *because* she or he is a member of a group. On the other hand, Farah's assertion reminds us of the danger of so emphasizing identification with a group that one presumes to *become* the group, to speak for and represent it.

What we can learn from Farah's own remarks and, in a particularly developed way, from Deeriye is the need to challenge received versions of history, to be constantly aware that powerful interests invent histories in order to maintain their authority. Throughout the trilogy Farah's resisters perform this analytical work, exposing the falsifications of colonialism, patriarchy, and the General's dictatorship, and testing as well the merits of other ideologies that make claims on individuals' loyalties (Marxism and Afrocentrism among them). In *Sweet and Sour Milk* Loyaan anticipates Deeriye's more sophisticated historical analysis when he recalls that, under a colonial educational system, he and his classmates were taught that "they had no history":

> The Tower of Pisa. The Duomo of Milan. . . .They were told that Merca [a Somali town] had no history since it didn't have monumental buildings. . . . What lies! Merca had no documented history. Mogadiscio had none. Well, not until . . . here we are, hear us out (had said the teacher), not until the Arabs came. . . . Riding the powerful waves of the sea came the *Daters,* bringing with them . . . lighted visions, chanting a call of prayer. . . . The Daters. The Tyrants. The Crescent. The Cross. The Red Star of Blood and human sacrifice. (*SSM,* 132)

The last phrase allows us to associate the Soviet-style dictatorship of the General, one that makes its appeal by presenting itself as Islamic, with the much earlier conquest of the Horn by Arabs. These in turn are connected with European colonialism, and all are exercises in power that demand "human sacrifice" and that collectively amount to a sustained assault on the dignity and freedom of individual Somalis.

Other characters in Farah's work share something of Deeriye's historical understanding of the many forms of power and the many ways it can impose, erase, or falsify identities. In *Gifts,* for example, Duniya, Bosaaso, and Mire put their discussion of received world views in the context of "traders, Arab and European, wandering the African continent, propagating their faith, making gifts of their deities and beliefs (like present-day foreign aid), presents that the Africans accepted with little question" (*G*, 93). Medina understands her relationship with Sandra as a further development in a history that includes Italy's colonization of Somalia, her own grandfather's complicity with the colonizer (Sandra's grandfather), and the debate about Marxist theory as a neocolonial form of Western hegemony. When Medina and Atta, an African-American woman, argue about the history of domination, Atta invokes a form of racial consciousness, claiming special kinship with Somalis: "My race remembers sufferance. . . . One doesn't forget centuries of suffering. . . . I remember this suffering, this pain. *Therefore I am*" (*Sardines*, 195, emphasis in the original). In words that recall Farah's comment that "clan is not a definer," Medina firmly responds, "No race has memory of pain, sufferance and chains, just as no race has a monopoly on intelligence. . . . In Auschwitz it was humanity which suffered, not a particular race. . . . The same is happening in Palestine, in the US, in South Africa and other places. No race has a monopoly over pain. . . . Each . . . of us suffers in his or her own way. And when some blacks are suffering, rest assured that others are doing well. You suffer because you are a human being, . . . not *because you are black*" (*Sardines*, 195–96, emphasis in the original). Atta refuses the work of defining herself as an individual with a unique history and therefore with unique responsibilities. She simplifies and falsifies her own identity by reducing it to an invented history that she has learned from others—"My race remembers. . . . *Therefore I am*"—thereby rendering herself, as the novel demonstrates, a willing subject for the dictator.

Deeriye, of all of Farah's protagonists, best resists this damage that invented histories can inflict on individual freedom—but he does more than this, for he himself consciously practices the invention of history and tradition as an act of political liberation. "I invent histories," he says to Zeinab, "I try to create symbolic links between unrelated historical events" (*CS*, 229). Such a link he finds in the year of his birth, 1912, when "the first African party of resistance was formed . . . , known as the African National Congress; it was also in the year 1912 that the Dervish movement of the Sayyid in Somalia defeated the British imperialists" (*CS*, 13). He also links the history of Islam to his political commitments through the meanings of the names of his son and of his son's comrades: "Mursal, Mahad, Mukhtaar and now Jibriil. What a fine set of names. . . . Mukhtaar, the chosen one, leaving a message for the messenger Mursal; and Jibriil [Gabriel] wishing to bring forth the dawning of a new era by delivering the divine message to the messenger" (*CS*, 76). It is "as though they were invented as part of one's burning need to change the destiny and history of a nation. . . . All carriers of *the message*. . . . The message of the Lord; the message of the revolution" (*CS*, 153).

Deeriye's first political act was, in effect, to reconceive the links implied by clan membership, extending protection to a young Somali of another clan unjustly threatened by the colonial administration. To his own clansmen's objections he responded, "Aren't we all one clan, and aren't the Italians our enemy?" (*CS*, 38). As he spent time in prison for this act, the links multiplied in his mind and he came to see himself "as a Pan-Somalist and a Pan-Africanist" (*CS*, 13). Through these inventions he redefines various communities—religious, national, and ideological—in ways that enrich rather than restrict his freedom to define his own political being and relations. They are liberatory rather than restrictive inventions because they are his own, freely chosen and provisional. He is able to see, therefore, when the face of the tyrant has changed and when alliances must change accordingly. In 1934 Deeriye defended an individual (Mahad's father) from the Italian authorities; in the present moment he recognizes that the threat to autonomy comes from the state itself, and he supports another individual (Mahad) against the Somali authorities.

We have suggested that the Dictatorship Trilogy makes highly visible the struggle for individual autonomy by locating it at a moment when individual freedom is conspicuously threatened, when a collective struggle on behalf of individual autonomy is demanded. In the course of their struggle, Farah's protagonists recognize that their autonomy is threatened, not by a single dictator but in multiple and complex ways, and therefore that resistance along a very wide front is required. They undergo an education into the nature of power as a system and, in particular, the interconnections among dictatorship, patriarchy, and colonialism; they recognize that this system of oppression operates by taking control of available social formations (family, clan, state, religious and ideological communities) and, consequently, that these formations and indeed all social relationships must be critically examined and may need to be resisted or transformed. To insist on autonomy, to keep one's critical intelligence constantly at play, to interrogate all of one's relationships and challenge the most widely received traditions is demanding, lonely work in the most democratic of contexts; to persist in the face of brutal forms of tyranny requires great courage; and to find ways to preserve one's own autonomy within a collective struggle is an especially difficult negotiation.

Farah pays special attention to two particularly acute contradictions that bedevil resistance work at every level, taking Medina and Mursal as his case studies. *Sardines* raises the dilemma that in resisting tyranny one may become a tyrant, and *Close Sesame* explores the antithetical risk of allowing one's identity (and therefore autonomy) to become engulfed in collective struggle. Both conditions are the result of ingesting something of the tyranny one is opposing: the magnification of personality in the first case, the extinction of personality in the second. As Deeriye observes, when the struggle is not against an outsider but against tyranny inside the community, "things become unclear, priorities are confused. The enemy is within: a cankerous tumour" (*CS,* 166). For Medina and Mursal, the "enemy within" is not only the dictator within the nation; it is also the temptation to install a form of dictatorship within oneself.

As we have seen, Medina has a strong theoretical grasp of how dictatorship and patriarchy are mutually reinforcing and consequently a clear rationale for opposing the power of the domestic tyrant (Idil) and the dictator. Her analytical intelligence is demonstrated in every conversation, and she has made a courageous stand on behalf of freedom. In her efforts, however, she adopts the conduct of a tyrant herself, dictating to her child, husband, and younger companions in the resistance, trying to make all conform to her own arrangements and strategies. The narrator's first words of introduction alert us to this tendency: "Medina was as strong-minded as she was unbending in her decisions, and she guarded her secrets jealously. . . . She was as confident as a patriarch in the rightness of all her decisions" (*Sardines,* 6). In moving away from Samater, she has sought "to dwell peacefully in a notion, find a home in it, . . . a room that she could call her own . . . ; a home in which her thoughts might freely wander without inhibition, without fear; a home in which patriarchs like Gad Thabit and matriarchs like Idil . . . were not allowed to set foot" (*Sardines,* 255). She is certain that this is an essential step to protect her own and Ubax's autonomy. Her father, Barkhadle, however, has had reason already to remind her, "You must leave breathing-space in the architecture of your love; you must leave enough room for little Ubax to exercise her growing mind. You mustn't indoctrinate, mustn't brainwash her. Otherwise you become another dictator, trying to shape your child in your own image" (*Sardines,* 15–16). Her young friend Sagal also questions Medina's style of moth-

ering: "Mother-as-martyr or mother-as-the-all-knower. In the final
analysis, what is the difference between yourself, Idil and Ebla?" (*Sardines,* 55). Her brother, Nasser, uses her metaphor of homemaking (a
metaphor that, for Medina, expresses her autonomy) in order to suggest
that she "has created a habitat in which she alone can function. . . . No
room for either Samater or Ubax" (*Sardines,* 256). Rearranging the furniture of her world, Medina has "put the chair in the wrong place in the
dark. When Samater awoke, he stumbled on it and broke his neck"
(*Sardines,* 256). Xaddia, Samater's sister, directly accuses Medina of
bringing harm to others: "What was the point of the charade in which
Samater lost face and his job, my mother her son and dignity, Nasser
and Dulman their freedom? What point have you made?" (*Sardines,*
259). Finally and perhaps most tellingly, Nasser connects her tactics
with those of the General. Discussing with her brother how the dictatorship stays in power, Medina says, "The strategy has remained the
same: *starve and rule.*" Immediately Nasser associates her phrase with her
domestic situation: "Why had she left Samater? To make him see how
much in need of her he was, she would wait until he came crawling on
all fours. *Starve and rule*" (*Sardines,* 108–9, emphasis in the original).

Medina herself is aware of the danger that she may become like the
General. From the outset she is "worried . . . that an overreaction to
Idil's tyrannical behaviour could influence her adversely, make her
harsher towards herself, unfair to Samater, obsessive about Ubax" (*Sardines,* 7). She applies to herself Sagal's "theory of antinomy," in which
opposites become identical, telling Sagal that " 'the General's power and
I are like two lizards engaged in a varanian dance of death'—the
emphasis on power and not on the General; power as a system, power as
a function" (*Sardines,* 55). To this Sagal replies, "Two is a number of possible contrasts: you and Idil, on the one hand; you and . . . Sandra on the
other. . . . My theory of antinomy is concerned with the basic contradictions inherent in the elimination of one's direct rival. You are in a ring
with Idil inasmuch as you both have the same aim: to possess Samater"
(*Sardines,* 56–57). Both women appreciate that any form of power creates a contradiction for those who oppose it in the name of freedom.
Medina is then prompted to remember how urgently she and Nasser
had wanted to oppose Gad Thabit, even plotting to kill him. She
remembers too that Gad Thabit was the "grand challenger" of Sandra's
grandfather, the colonial governor, but that the two men "struck up a
friendship of sorts; in their rationale there was no conflict of interests
between them. The challenger and the defender became one, Sagal's

theory of antinomy would explain" (*Sardines,* 58). Medina can see that in their "dance of death," she and the General also could become one. Her problem, then, is how to get outside "power as a system, power as a function," how to displace the dictator and his various avatars without herself becoming another of them. It is a dilemma that she never resolves.

Tyranny threatens individual autonomy, then, not only by its direct assault on the individual but also by risks endemic to the very act of opposing it. Through the character of Medina, Farah explores one such risk, the distortion of one's identity into that of another tyrant; through Mursal he examines a second insidious form of this "enemy within," the engulfment of one's identity in what one comes to see as a "larger" cause than the autonomy one is struggling to preserve.

In an atmosphere thick with spurious appeals to loyalty orchestrated by the General in the name of religion, nationalism, and tribalism, Mursal aspires to carry on the work of his father as a guardian of individual rights, threatened now not by the colonizer but by "the enemy within," the homegrown dictatorship. More than ever, the mode of resistance is in question. The group of ten has been reduced to four, each committed to an isolated "kamikaze" act of violent retaliation. Mursal swings between a terrible sense of isolation, pushing him toward madness, and an intense desire to belong to a heroic community of resisters. As the son of a national hero, he has imbibed his father's conviction "that the history worth studying is one of resistance, not capitulation; and that all great men—Shaka Zulu, Ataturk, Nkrumah, Cabral, Garibaldi, Lenin, Cabdunnaasir, Gandhi, the Sayyid—have one thing in common: the shaping force of their lives has been resistance" (*CS,* 166). This is an intimidating roster of heroes, one that exerts a "shaping force" on the lives of Mursal's own group. If Mahad, for example, perishes in his commitment to resistance, Deeriye speculates that his "soul would perhaps live in another: if not a Somali, then perhaps a Zulu struggling against the tyranny of apartheid, a Palestinian fighting for the principles of human justice. Life was made of encounters and departures: the living dead meet the spiritually dead when both dwell in a tyrannical state" (*CS,* 117). This thought is explicitly echoed by the child Samawade (underscoring the sense of a family tradition of resistance) in language that seems troublingly to shrug off the reality of his own father's probable fate: "Some of us have to go to prison or die for a principle or a cause so that others, whether they are aware of it now or not . . . can live a decent life. . . . And who knows, [Mursal's] soul may enter and give life

to a warrior in Zululand or Palestine" (*CS,* 195 – 96). Deeriye reflects on
Samawade's pronouncement with considerable ambivalence: "It was
incredible how one could indoctrinate a child into thinking what one
liked, make a Mursal out of a Samawade; it was unbelievable how one
could burden a child with the weight of history" (*CS,* 196). Deeriye
himself has remained in control of the histories he has invented during
his life of political struggle; the "indoctrination" he hears in Samawade
and Mursal suggests that they do not share that control, that they are
the subjects rather than the inventors of histories that define them as
"living dead meeting spiritually dead," their names lost among the
names of heroes, their "souls" merged into those of nameless "warriors"
of other "principles" and "causes."

Deeriye's doubts concerning the impact of "heroism" on his son's
identity deepen once Mursal's death is confirmed, and he struggles in his
own mind to separate that impact from the provocatively parallel fate of
Soyaan's identity, a question further complicated by the historical burden that he has laid upon the shoulders of his grandchildren, all named
for legendary resistance heroes and thereby dedicated at birth to a cause
they could not yet have chosen:

> But was Mursal a hero? He was definitely different from the hero manu-
> factured to order, a hero who died under the name of Soyaan. . . . What
> if he died unmourned and unburied . . . ? Samawade, Cantar, She-
> herezade, Ataturk, Jamaal and Shaka were named, anointed thus so they
> would continue the struggle others had begun, and Mursal was there
> only to keep the flames going, keep the live coals under a bed of ashes so
> that . . . they would find the fire buried under the ground: and like one
> of those instant cameras already adjusted: click! With button pressed,
> the printed photograph would unroll: a family-portrait with a healthy
> background, grandfathers and fathers and uncles dedicated to a struggle,
> amen!, the liberation of Africa! (*CS,* 218).

This passage celebrates an honorable tradition of resistance, but its
metaphorical language betrays a tension between the mode of struggle,
which is collective action, and the value it is intended to preserve, individual autonomy: the live coal that is justified only by the flame in
which it is eventually consumed, the human images already adjusted
and generated in the press of a button by the machinery of liberation.

In Mursal are reproduced and intensified the public dimensions of the
complex negotiations of autonomy and responsibility that have been
Deeriye's life. Other dimensions, relating to the personal and domestic

spheres, take root in Deeriye's other child, Zeinab, who challenges her brother quite directly about the price in human freedom of his mode of commitment, referring to him and his comrades as "four persons bamboozled with notions of power and the weighty responsibility of restoring it to the masses at whatever cost" (*CS,* 76). She puts to Mursal the same question that Xaddia had put to Medina: What about other dimensions to one's life, other commitments and responsibilities?: "And what about Natasha, this poor foreign wife whom you'll leave behind as a widow, what will become of her . . . once you're dead or in prison?"; "Natasha. Samawade. Your father. Us. Do you care?" (*CS,* 125, 127). To these claims on his identity Mursal responds, "Each of us is doing it the lonely way, all the way, toward a healthy autonomy, Zeinab; one of self-definition or self-destruction; and away from familial (tribal) dependence" (*CS,* 127). What Mursal characterizes as "healthy autonomy"— one that balances with equanimity the alternatives of "self-definition or self-destruction"—sounds to Zeinab like "a very laborious way of justifying the madness in which we dwell, the kind of madness we've witnessed in this country and many countries in Africa, Asia and Latin America. . . . Mass madness. . . . Which is what dictatorships are, or create. Mass madness. Mass euphoria" (*CS,* 127). Madness haunts the novel in the forms of Khaliif and Mukhtaar, both of whom attempt to gain through their madness "the autonomy their families, their society, their jobs and contacts had denied them; the same autonomy [Deeriye] himself had sought thirty-odd years before" (*CS,* 123). For Zeinab, such madness is not another form of autonomy but an engulfment of identity in which the capacity for autonomous self-definition dissolves. The issue, then, that Farah explores through Mursal in *Close Sesame*—the temptation to engulfment—is no more resolved than Medina's temptation to tyranny. Farah's determined indeterminacy forces us to consider not the particular resolutions of his characters but the situations they face and the debates they engage in, internally and with others, over how to balance their own autonomy with their commitment to collective strategies for upholding the autonomy of all.

Though we have characterized both of these temptations as a form of "enemy within," in the conditions of state dictatorship that Farah explores in the first trilogy they arise entirely in response and in resistance to an external enemy: the dictator. The analysis performed by Farah's protagonists clearly reveals what Medina calls "power as a system," ramified in many forms of authoritarianism. One form, however, was predominant over the rest during this period in Farah's work. The historical reality of the Siyad Barre regime in Somalia at the time Farah conceived these novels was rather like an elephant in the drawing room: difficult to ignore—an overwhelmingly determining presence in Farah's consciousness and therefore in the imagined rooms he constructed for his characters. In such circumstances one ignores whatever else one is doing and tends to the elephant, for such a figure must be resisted. Thus the presence of the General in Farah's novels, while galvanizing the need for action, to a very considerable extent focuses his characters' primary attention not on the enemy within but on an enemy without. By 1983, however, when the trilogy was completed, the Siyad Barre regime showed signs of impending collapse. Although it was difficult to predict Somalia's future, to focus on a single dictator was no longer imperative and seemed not to be the most meaningful way to explore political life.

Freed of that imperative, Farah was able to turn his political thought more centrally to the problem of the enemy within. In *Yussuf and His Brothers* and *Maps* nationalism replaces resistance to dictatorship as the significant force in public life, but, to a greater extent than in the first trilogy, political struggle is located within the consciousnesses of the protagonists and within relationships between individuals rather than in action against an explicit and external enemy. Like resistance to dictatorship, nationalism provides a compelling opportunity for social commitment, one that demands of Farah's protagonists a degree of loyalty that threatens to overwhelm their autonomy and that also provides occasions for dominating others. The temptations to tyranny and engulfment no longer figure as separate tendencies but as intertwined desires within a self that continues to aspire to autonomy while fighting an enemy much less definable, and therefore more insidious, than the General.

This intertwining is conspicuous in Yussuf, a zealous Muslim passionately dedicated to anticolonial resistance, a man who sees himself and his brothers-in-struggle as interchangeable, their individuality lost in their commitment to throwing off the colonial yoke. He tells Gheddi, "You are me; you are *us*. Today you are the one whose choice expresses the nation's . . . , you are a symbol of the nation's will" (*YB,* 52). For Yussuf, it does not matter which individual performs an act of resistance: "[I]t could've been Hussen; it could've been Gheddi; it could've been I, . . . it could've been any Somali for that matter. Why does it matter *who* precisely did it? . . . It doesn't matter so long as we know and accept that it is *the nation* that has done it" (*YB,* 94–95, emphasis in the original).

Certainly Farah intends his audience to be impressed with Yussuf's fierce dedication to the nationalist cause; the indefiniteness of the historical setting, however, prevents us from comprehending the purposes behind Yussuf's stratagems or assessing his effectiveness as a resistance figure. Rather, the play invites us to pay attention to his personality. When we do so, we see both how completely he surrenders his identity to his collective work and how he robs others of their own identities, demanding that they bend to the will and identity of the nation. As the mastermind behind the anticolonial resistance, he orchestrates everything—indeed, he may play all the major roles himself. His comrade Hussen is arrested for an action that Yussuf, wearing a raincoat identical to Hussen's, almost certainly performed. Yussuf then stage-manages Hussen's escape, but Hussen is appalled by what Yussuf has done to him. Hussen berates his wife for attending his would-be execution: "How could you, my wife, be a member of a crowd which moved, roared with the noises of its irrationality, . . . you, and many others like you, you came to see the spectacle . . . as though it were theatre!" (*YB*, 77). Refusing to be "turned into the current and future symbol of our struggle," as Yussuf had planned, Hussen determines instead to give himself up to the authorities, announcing, "I decided to repossess my own soul. . . . It is only in self-immolation and in death, on my own terms, that I might re-claim the link with reality" (*YB*, 69). To Yussuf's certitude and total identification with his cause, Hussen opposes a lonely, uncertain, but insistent autonomy: "My actions aren't blessed with the infinite wisdom of God as your make-believe cosmos will have it. I'm a weak man. . . . My 'I' isn't the I in the 'I-am-the-nation,' a hyphenated phrase you're fond of employing; my I has no divine support" (*YB*, 68–69).

Yussuf is both willingly engulfed in the nationalist cause and tyrant to all those around him. Religious and nationalist fervor reinforce each other; not only does he "play god" with the lives of his brothers by putting them in front of firing squads but he frequently usurps the divine prerogative by presuming to sit in judgment on their spiritual destinies. Like the General (who also conflates himself with God), Yussuf tries to manage all that happens in his realm without respect for individual lives. Just as the General attempts to refashion Soyaan's identity after his death as a hero of his revolution, Yussuf looks for ways to construct a favorable reading of Hussen's refusal to play his assigned part: "We're not concerned with his life, we're interested in salvaging the image of the struggle" (*YB*, 80). Women in particular have no standing in his world view. He has married Aynaba (much as Keynaan has mar-

ried Beydan) to compensate her for the loss of her husband, for whose
death Yussuf is responsible; and she remains, as the stage directions indi-
cate, "on the periphery" of his concerns. Aynaba describes Yussuf's activities in words that evoke the world of the General: "You plot; yes! you
plot and conspire: you meet other *men,* you sell and buy secrets, you
speak in whispers with some of your male conspirators while you provide for the material needs of *the women* who survive the innocent men
who die" (*YB,* 7, emphasis in the original). To her son Raageh, Yussuf is
an idol who can do no wrong, and it seems clear that he will be wholly
assimilated into this political ethos in which he will become yet another
of Yussuf's nameless doubles and brothers. (Yussuf dreams of having one
body and two heads, his own and Raageh's.) Yussuf has the lifelong
habit of staring into a mirror, in which he sees not Hussen's kind of self,
riddled with doubt and yet autonomous, but rather the endlessly repli-
cating images of himself with which he desires to fill the world. "I'm . . .
everybody here," he proclaims near the end of the play (*YB,* 87, emphasis
in the original).

Like the General in *Sardines,* Yussuf claims to be "all of us"—and yet
he is not the General. He is a dedicated servant of the cause of Somali
liberation from colonial oppression—and at the same time he is a victim
of the twin temptations to tyranny and engulfment that lurk in the politics of resistance. For Deeriye, nationalism and religious commitment
provide opportunities that enhance the self: the opportunity to defend
individual autonomy through a collective struggle, to expand one's
sense of membership in multiple communities, to strengthen one's purpose and dedication. For Yussuf, nationalist and religious fervor diminish
autonomy, tempting him to shed the burden of individuality in a collective identification; at the same time nationalist and religious fervor fill
him with a self-justifying sense of power over others.[7]

This strongly masculinized nationalism that intoxicates Yussuf (a
muted version of which also tempts Mursal) is intensely appealing to
Askar in *Maps.* He yearns to evade the problem of defining himself by
joining with brothers who have "imbibed an ideology . . . they envisioned as their common future: warriors of a people fighting to liberate
their country from colonial oppression," in this case from Ethiopian
expansion into the Ogaden (*M,* 109). His initiation into manhood coin-
cides with rising nationalist sentiment so that he defines himself at this
moment in relation to both gender and nationalism: "What mattered,
he told himself, was that now he was at last a man, that he was totally
detached from his mother-figure Misra, and weaned. In the process of

looking for a substitute, he had found another—Somalia, his mother country. . . . [H]e held on to the milky breast of a common mother . . . , a many-breasted mother, . . . who gave plenty of herself and demanded loyalty of one, loyalty to an ideal, allegiance to an idea, the notion of a nationhood" (*M, 96*).

Askar's declaration sounds like Yussuf's passionate nationalism but it comes from the mouth of an eight-year-old boy concerned with asserting his autonomy from his foster-mother who arouses in him a sense of engulfment at once appealing and threatening. By defending his country, Askar imagines he will "wean" himself and gain independence, and yet, as his own words betray, his notion of the nation is another form of mother, who offers a comparable experience of total identification and who demands total loyalty. He thinks that by "imbibing an ideology" (becoming "indoctrinated" like Samawade) he will merge with a collectivity of "warriors" fighting for a "common future"—the temptation to engulfment, as we have been calling it, but here revealed in its earliest formation. In *Maps* Farah merges what we conventionally differentiate as psychological terrain with the realm of the political, locating in the child's relationship with its mother the same need to negotiate for autonomy that makes every relationship political. He is not writing about the personal instead of the political, but the political that is always already in the personal, where the personal is the foundation for identity issues that will later manifest themselves in the realm we conventionally understand as political. Furthermore, he finds in this male child's relationship with his mother an origin of masculine hostility that leads to the political oppression of women, a topic we return to in chapter 5. This excavation of the foundations of identity becomes possible because Farah has eliminated the General and his overwhelming assault on autonomy from his narrative stage. With his absence, different threats to autonomy can be more fully developed, new insights gained into where the political battles of everyday life must be fought.

These threats and insights in *Maps* begin with the feeling of maternal engulfment that so strongly infuses Askar's memories of his early life with Misra. He tastes in her "a motherliness which reabsorbed [him], a motherliness in whose tight, warm embrace [he] felt joyous one second, miserable the following instant" (*M, 5*). Often he feels that there is no boundary between them, that he has "remained a mere extension of Misra's body for years" (*M, 75*). At the same time and precisely because he feels so connected to her, he wants very much to be in control of his identity. He claims to recall his birth "as though I were my own midwife," vigorously contesting Misra's accounts of this event: "[T]hese encase me like a womb and I try unsuccessfully to break loose" (*M,* 24). Later this self-birthing image of the struggle for autonomy is repeated in a dream in which he is "inside a woman who remained nameless" and "trying his best to give birth to himself." As the dream develops, however, his sense of engulfment becomes more intense: he is "moving upwards, inside another woman, . . . struggling against becoming his own coffin. Then the wish to be born whole, the wish to burst forth and *be*—this wish took on a life of its own and . . . he was shouting and screaming and kicking against the ribs of the woman who had caged him inside of her" (*M,* 182–83). Askar's urgent "wish to burst forth and *be*" is frustrated, he feels, by this maternal body (both womb and tomb) against which he wants to do violence. As we have seen, his infantile fixation on the mother's body is reiterated when, as a newly circumcised boy, he considers his relationship to the nation ("a many-breasted mother") and is strongly tempted to surrender himself to the collectivity and become a martyr for Somalia.

As in *Yussuf and His Brothers,* the temptation to engulfment and the temptation to tyranny are intertwined; in *Maps* the new development is that these temptations are shown to be rooted in the infant's relationship with its mother, later ramifying in Askar's sense of identity in relationship to the nation. We have connected the temptation to engulfment with the infant's experience of union with the mother, and we can now see how the temptation to tyranny emerges at the same time in the infantile fantasy of total control in a world in which ego and other have not yet differentiated, in which the child's ego usurps the space occupied by the mother and indeed all the rest of the world. The same boundarilessness that occasions feelings of engulfment also gives rise to the infant's sense that he *is* the world, that "he is everybody." A younger version of the General or Yussuf, Askar presumes, at least at times, that he *is* Misra—that he controls her, first through his infant stare and later through his invention of a narrative in which she is erased, overwhelmed in his fantasy of her.

In a thoughtful essay on *Maps,* Rhonda Cobham notes the ambiguity of Askar's feelings about Misra and proposes that the different narrating voices—the "I," "you," and "he"—express different attitudes. An early passage in the "you" voice captures Askar's wish to dominate: "To Misra, you existed first and foremost in the weird stare . . . focused on her guilt—her self! . . . . She was sure, for instance, that you saw her the way she was: a miserable woman, with no child and no friends; a woman who . . . menstruated right in front of you, under that most powerful stare of yours" (*M,* 6). Cobham suggests that Askar's stare "establishes the imbalance of power versus powerlessness that, from the perspective of this narrator [the 'you' narrator], characterizes Askar's relationship to the servant woman. By contrast, the 'I' voice argues later in the text that it was Misra's touch rather than Askar's stare which established the bond of love between them—a bond so strong that it ultimately breaks down the ego boundaries between the boy and the woman." Although "in many ways this ['I'] voice seems to articulate Askar's female self," Cobham suggests that ultimately the novel is not really about merged identities so much as about Askar's "erasure of [Misra] as he incorporates her entire feminine identity into himself."[8] In other words, for Cobham, the temptation to engulfment becomes a way of expressing the temptation to tyranny, the appropriation of Misra's very identity into his own.

The child's struggle for autonomy is a struggle to define himself independently of the mother, but this requires that the child become an adult willing to recognize the separate reality, the autonomy, of the parent. This recognition of Misra's independent existence constantly threatens and eludes Askar. We hear in the following passage how complicated his emotions are. Having lost one mother in childbirth, Askar fears that Misra too might abandon him, but the infantile ego that controls the world, the diminutive tyrant, provides reassurance: "[W]hen all others die, she won't, I would say to myself. So long as I lived, she would too. Either in me, or she would live a life independent from mine" (*M,* 37). That she might be independent of him is unthinkable, however, and so a fantasy immediately arises to forestall that possibility: " 'I would kill you. So you would be a corpse like my mother.' . . . Of course, I wasn't going to 'kill her' because I had hated her, far from it, far from it. What I meant was, that only in death could she and I be united— only in death, her death, could she and I be related, only then would I somehow feel as though we were a mother and her son. And then, and only then, would I find myself, alone and existing and real—yes, an individual with needs of his own—no longer an extension of a maternal hand" (*M,* 37). The possibility of Misra's autonomy and his urgent wish to become an "individual with needs of his own" both give rise to the thought of killing the mother: her death is, contradictorily, the only way in which he can become free while maintaining his fantasy of union with her. The idea is repeated more insistently on a later occasion when Askar tells Misra, "When I grow up and I am a man . . . I will kill you. . . . To

live, I will have to kill you. . . . Just like I killed my mother—to live"
(*M*, 57).

Since Askar must "kill off" Misra in order to become an adult, he is
suffused with feelings of guilty betrayal, feelings that he projects onto her
by seizing upon the highly unreliable story that he hears about *her* guilty
betrayal of Somalis. The very strength of his sense of identification with
her invites this tyrannical usurpation of her identity in which his guilt
becomes hers; in his invention of history he casts her in the highly con-
ventionalized role of woman as betrayer, her individual identity completely erased in Askar's desperate bid for his own. The particular terms
in which Askar has chosen to define himself as an independent male
allow him simultaneously to kill Misra and to keep her: as soldier or
scholar in the service of Somalia, he definitively separates himself from
Misra (who is not Somali and is therefore the enemy), but at the same
time he keeps her in the form of his mother country. Askar's infantile
experience of boundarilessness between himself and Misra, which creates
in him anxiety about engulfment, is related to his craving for definition,
for a very specifically and narrowly defined identity, an unambiguous
identity that he can wear like a tattoo. Born in the Ogaden, a contested
territory of uncertain boundaries, and orphaned at birth, Askar is of mul-
tiply indeterminate identity: "You did not exist as far as many were concerned; nor did you have any identity as the country's bureaucracy
required" (*M*, 8). Precisely in reaction to such uncertainty, he wants an
"identity card" to provide him with definition and deliver him from
being what his Uncle Hilaal calls an "unperson" (*M*, 167). That definition, to be Somali and to be male, will also serve, in Askar's mind, to
draw the boundary absolutely between himself and Misra.

In Uncle Hilaal's reminder that "throughout history" men have cast
women as betrayers, we note that Askar's relationship to Misra mirrors
political dynamics as they operate in every social formation, from family
to nation (*M*, 178). Ironically, Hilaal, so willing to invent a new relationship to gender in fluid and egalitarian terms, obfuscates his own
insight into political dynamics by his construction of Somali identity as a
privileged and pure category:

> Ethiopia is the generic name of an unclassified mass of different peoples,
> professing different religions. . . . Therefore, "Ethiopia" becomes that
> generic notion, expansive, inclusive. Somali . . . is specific. That is, you
> are either a Somali or you aren't. (*M*, 148)
>   The Somali are a homogeneous people. . . . Now this is not true of the
> people who call themselves "Ethiopians," or "Sudanese" or "Eritreans," or

Nigerians or Senegalese. . . . Somali identity . . . is one shared by all Somalis, no matter how many borders divide them. . . . Which is why one might say that the soul of a Somali is a meteor, shooting towards that commonly held national identity. (*M*, 166)

Hilaal's categorical thinking ("you are either a Somali or you aren't"; national identity is what the "soul" aims toward) serves an irredentist form of nationalism bent upon reclaiming territory (the Ogaden) at the cost of erasing the Misras of this world. He effectively passes on to Askar this way of defining himself when he obtains an identity card for his nephew: "From the way he gave it to me, you would've thought he was entrusting to me a brand-new 'life' " (*M*, 163). Askar is initially troubled that there is no room on his identity papers for Misra, uncertain whether this is because she is Oromo rather than Somali or because she was his foster-mother. He acknowledges to himself, "Misra meant a lot more to me than anyone else," but for bureaucratic purposes, their relationship has no standing (*M*, 162). She remains undefinable, erased. Askar takes great satisfaction in gaining the card: "I studied the details of my new identity with . . . a tender care. . . . I confess, I did think that I was expected, from that moment onwards, to perceive myself in the identity created for me" (*M*, 165). Instead of defining himself—something that he can really do only by acknowledging his relationship with Misra and by recognizing her independence from him—Askar allows this card to provide an "identity created for me."

Askar's approach to defining himself is in sharp contrast to Misra's. Of mixed parentage, Misra is the illegitimate child of an Oromo servant and an Amharic nobleman, later raised by an Ethiopian family and finding her home with Askar in a Somali community in the Ogaden. She does not identify "my people" in terms of ethnicity or nation but in terms of her relationships with them: "For me, my people are Askar's people; my people are my former husband's people, the people I am most attached to" (*M*, 184). She recognizes that her way of defining herself is threatened by Askar's more categorical mode of self-definition: " 'One day,' she prophesied . . . 'you will identify yourself with your people and identify me out of your community. Who knows, you might even kill me to make your people's dream become a tangible reality. . . . Yes. Kill. Murder. Loot. Rape. In the name of your people. Kill' " (*M*, 95).

Where Askar insists on fixed definitions and marked boundaries, Misra is relational, hybrid, indeterminate. Where he borrows maps and identity cards constructed by others in his attempts to answer the question, "Who is Askar?," Misra ignores boundaries and chooses for herself those whom she will call family. Askar realizes that, unlike himself, Misra would not "lose herself in the eternity of a search for who she was—for she knew who she was" (*M,* 26). Moreover, what Misra knows herself to be includes Askar as he is. The problem with Askar's maps, both those he borrows and, eventually, those he draws himself, is not that they include boundaries but that those boundaries exclude Misra as she is. Increasingly, he recognizes that to define himself he must define his relationship with a Misra who actually exists, who is independent of his emotional needs. The task of becoming an autonomous person capable of choosing his future roles in society and of answering the question, "Who is Askar?," turns out to require that one be capable of respecting the autonomy of others. It requires resisting the intertwined temptations to dominate and to be engulfed. It requires responsible acts of self-definition and the rejection of exclusionary identity cards and maps; it requires learning to negotiate boundaries with others with whom one shares the world.

As we have seen, these prove to be difficult negotiations indeed in a political world where individual autonomy and relations between individuals are subject to forces generated by dictatorship or colonial occupation and by collective resistance to these. The temptations to tyranny and engulfment are not the product of these circumstances alone, but the politics of the public sphere do provide them an especially hospitable climate in the work of Farah. Still, in the discussion thus far we have seen negotiations of boundaries that are successful and acts of self-definition that are responsible, and almost always, in Farah's work, these arise in the sphere of the interpersonal and the domestic.

That so much of his work is concerned with political relations in the public sphere is, we have suggested, a result of the continual gravitational pull of Somalia's current history on Farah's writing, obliging him to widen his gaze beyond the exclusively personal and local and to engage the problem of dictatorship once the tenor of the Siyad Barre regime became clear, and then drawing him to a still wider examination of nationalism as the claims of that regime, but not yet those of the nation, appeared to be diminishing in force. Even as he was finishing *Maps,* however, the continuing hold of an official entity called Somalia on political life was already weakening, freeing Farah in his last two novels to return to the sphere of personal relationships that centrally occupied his attention in the first two. In his recent interview with us Farah spoke of the connection between these two trajectories, the one historical and the other artistic, in the period of his work from *Close Sesame* to *Secrets.* His comments are especially relevant to the point we have now reached in our discussion and so we quote them at some length:

> There are different stages in the nation's history. . . . There is still a decency at the time that Deeriye dies. . . . There is still decency because . . . there are still intellectual questions: honesty, violence, how do you solve an unresolvable crisis? But once the gentleman—and Deeriye is a gentleman, honest, truthful—dies, then after that the beginnings of the civil war, in fact, start with *Maps*. However much it's masked, it's downhill from then on. Almost everything that happens in *Maps* is a prelude to more crises, personal, existential, philosophical, historical. And then it's also the disintegration of the family as we know it. Because there is suspicion that Askar's uncle [Qorrax] did rape his mother [Arla], so there is in fact incest of the lowest degree, barbaric. And so the clan as such is dead, and the reason is because the patriarch has dishonored it.
>
> This is the beginning of the book, of *Maps*. The boy is born, and the boy then wants to fight, not for a clan, but for a nation, because he wants to start all over again. In *Maps* . . . everything is a debris and therefore you go through the enthusiasms of nationality and then the death of nationalism, because with the end of the novel the question is, is there something called Somalia? Who am I? Who is Somalia? Who is Askar? Who is Misra? And therefore *Secrets,* in fact, terminates the process with which *Maps* begins. *Secrets* ends with the internal civil war. The external combustion of the civil war [was when] Somalis invaded Ethiopia. With the defeat, when they return, there is an implosion. . . . The signs of the implosion are there already in *Gifts.* (Interview, 1996)

In this statement Farah traces a process that is at once historically negative and, surprisingly, artistically positive for his developing exploration of the politics of autonomy. The integrity of Somalia as a nation is in precipitous decline, and the statement indicates some of the ways in which this decline is registered in *Maps*. "The signs of implosion [that] are there already in *Gifts*" are marked in the text in at least two ways. One is the backdrop of power failures, shortages of commodities, lack of public transport, and general crumbling of public institutions against which the story unfolds. The other is the shift from earlier novels and plays in the way in which Farah portrays social and material privilege. He uses the term "priviligencia" to describe a class to which many characters belong in the novels and plays that precede *Gifts*. In these texts their privileged status is manifested generally in their education, access or proximity to public power, and leisure for intellectual pursuits. In *Gifts,* for the first time, characters whom Farah means us to admire make casual use of their position of privilege for their own convenience and gain: trading illicitly in foreign currencies, obtaining generally unobtainable goods as "favored customers" of a local merchant, arranging for Abshir to enter the airport through the VIP corridor so as to avoid customs, finding ways to exempt Mataan from national service. What this behavior points to is not the moral failure of these characters but the weakening of the claims of governmental order on public consciousness. This "implosion" becomes outright "civil war" in *Secrets*: heavily armed militias attacking government forces, each other, and hapless citizens caught in their undiscriminating sights. Again, all of this serves only as a backdrop to the tale Farah has to tell.

In both *Gifts* and *Secrets*, it is not a reflective backdrop but a contrastive one: in both, the tale he has to tell is a story of liberation, consolidation, and human enrichment in social relations. Let us be clear that the chaos many Somalis have endured during the period under discussion is emphatically not what Farah wants for his country. Our point, rather, is that this is a state of existence in which the concept of "the nation" has loosened its hold on the way that many Somalis conceive themselves and their relationships and, therefore, on the imaginations of Farah's characters. Moreover, this moment in the life of Somalia has brought with it what Farah calls "the disintegration of the family as we know it." His artistic response to these historical circumstances has been to bring the politics of the interpersonal and domestic sphere, which have always been of intense concern to him, back to the center of his stage, the place of prominence that it occupied at the beginning of his career, and to explore more fully than before the possibilities of the family as we *do not* know it.

Farah's first two novels, *From a Crooked Rib* and *A Naked Needle,* are both centrally concerned with the conventions of family, marriage, and other domestic relations as definers of identity. For Ebla these definers absolutely pervade the world of the *jes,* the tiny, self-contained, nomadic community of herders to which she belongs. Her identity within this group consists entirely in the lowly duties and routines that fall to her as a ward of her grandfather and as a young woman of her community: "Not that she was intending to feel idle and do nothing, nor did she feel irresponsible, but a woman's duty meant loading and unloading camels and donkeys after the destination had been reached, and that life was routine. . . . Everybody had a certain duty to keep him or her busy. . . . This was life which took place within sight of the settlement of the central family" (*FCR,* 13–14). This domestic space, "the settlement of the central family," is virtually synonymous with the social conventions by which Ebla is bound, and the only way to escape those conventions and the definition of her that they impose is to move to a different kind of social space, one not organized by the relationships that order life in the *jes*. She follows this plan, escaping "from the country to a town, and from there to Mogadiscio. . . . 'Come what may, I am going to stick to Mogadiscio, until doomsday,' she thought" (*FCR*, 123). The difference between these two social spaces is registered in the reaction of Ebla's brother to Mogadiscio when he comes to see her: "I loathe it. Half-naked women and crazy men, noisy places, men and women hand in hand, and all crazy people. . . . You know, this place is full of people like yourself, all the outcasts, all those who could not get on well with their people in the country" (*FCR*, 138). Ebla is not, of course, an outcast but has on her own initiative launched herself in search of freedom from being the self she was forced to be in the *jes*, and she finds this freedom in the more varied and fluid social order that is possible in the city.

Koschin, on the other hand, is a creature of urban spaces from the beginning, born in Kismayo and passing his adult life in various European cities and Mogadiscio. He spends much of his time in *A Naked Needle*, in fact, walking the streets of the city: encountering acquaintances, recalling significant experiences, and interpreting Mogadiscio's historical and symbolic landscape to Nancy. It is a landscape that perfectly suits his aversion to conventional relationships, an aversion he makes quite clear in an opening address to the reader on the subject of women and marriage:

> There had been plenty of women before Nancy: there was a Nigerian . . . , an Italian . . . , a West Indian, a French girl, ten to twenty Somalis, all of whom, everything considered, had made life easier for me, helped me roll on.
>
> (In parenthesis, between you and me, I find it unbearable when any woman demands of me special attention and care; when she says she can't live without me; when she tries to limit my freedom!)
>
> What if a deaf woman and a blind man married, married and lived together, and gave birth to a hunch-back: wouldn't this be the ideal union? Wouldn't society remake its mores to accommodate this ideal family, the ideal in matrimony as one understands it? (*NN*, Prelude, n.p.)

The city, as Koschin understands it, allows one to remake mores and accommodate new ideals in regard to domestic relations in these radical and even grotesque ways because it is not socially self-contained and internally structured like the *jes* but outwardly porous and inwardly pliable. Koschin reproduces these features of the cityscape in his own highly unconventional household: a room in a brothel in which his only domesticity is the barbed banter that passes between himself and his hired cook and the ephemeral intimacies that he hears just beyond his walls.

The city provides, however, at best only a partial solution for Ebla and Koschin to the problem of freeing one's self-definition from the constraining conventions of family and domestic relations. Both escape the identities constructed for them by others within those relations, but when they attempt to deploy social identities that they shape for themselves, they resort to the same conventions, living subversively within them rather than transforming or replacing them. "One should do whatever one wants to," Ebla tells herself, "that is life. That is what I love. . . . I love life, and life lies in marriage, and marriage is born out of a couple from opposite sexes" (*FCR*, 126). Though she has rejected two husbands chosen for her by others, she is unable to conceive of herself outside of marriage as she has seen it practiced and so submits to the arrangement, but learns, with the coaching of her friend Asha, to use it to her personal advantage through deception, secretiveness, and the cash potential of her sexuality. While proclaiming, "I prefer whoring to marrying," Koschin prepares to honor a marriage agreement with Nancy that he knows to be meaningless and that will only formalize an abusive relationship (*NN*, 32). Despite the apparent contrast between Farah's first two protagonists, then—the naive peasant girl and the world-weary man-about-town—both are studies in the same dilemma. Koschin insists that "a happy man is one who doesn't let others live his life for him," and Ebla embraces the same principle as a woman (*NN*, 143). Neither, however, desires or is able to live a life of solitude. (They are in no way different from Farah's other characters in this; the human being, throughout his work, is a profoundly social creature.) They must therefore negotiate social relationships that allow the autonomy they seek, and it is in this that they fail. They refuse, escape, abscond, resign, and deny but in the process secure only a blank freedom. When they attempt to write a new social self upon that blankness, they are unable to conceive new relationships in which to do so. Instead they fall back on the old conventions, which they use manipulatively, that is, in the same way that they themselves have been used or seen others used by them, thereby rendering specious the freedom they think they have won.

Farah's entire body of work calls into question the conventions of familial relationships. Indeed, nowhere in that work do we find a single conventional family that is also functional, if what we mean by conventional family (in the context of Farah's strong focus on the nuclear family) is one that includes a mother and a father who are married to each other, living together, and both Somali, and that also includes one or more of their children by birth. In Farah's work families that fit this definition (as well as many that do not) are not functional, that is, they do not allow for the freedom of all their members from exploitation within the family. Among the examples are the families of Keynaan in *Sweet and Sour Milk,* of Deeriye's friend Rooble in *Close Sesame,* or of Qorrax in *Maps.* Families whose members are more fully functional are not conventional (at least not at the moment of the action represented in the text). Medina and Samater, for example, are separated; Deeriye's wife, Nadiifa, is dead; Mursal's wife, Natasha, is not Somali; Hilaal and Salaado cannot have children. All of these examples come from the period in Farah's work that is dominated by the problem of external, macro-level threats to individual autonomy posed by state or colonial tyranny and by collective resistance to these, threats that in turn put pressure on family and domestic relationships in the ways we have seen.

In his two most recent novels, *Gifts* and *Secrets,* that pressure eases as the larger threats break up and blur, allowing a return to first principles in Farah's treatment of politics, a return to the issues that arise in the domestic sphere. In his interview with us Farah stressed the centrality of these issues to his work as a political writer:

> The problem is Somali society. Somali society is authoritarian. Let's change our ways and let's start with the family. Let's start with the father, the son, and the mother. Let's start from the man in the kitchen. . . . Politics usually means a concentrated effort on engineering society through elections, through free expression, journalism, something called democracy. This is not what I consider myself to be part of. What I am interested in is to be able to work within the family as a unit, and if there is no democracy in the house, there can certainly be no democracy in the capital. (Interview, 1996)

"The capital" having effectively disappeared as a possible site of democratic political relations, Farah turns his gaze in the last two novels more exclusively than ever before on "the family as a unit," on "the house." Although the theme of personal gifts in the first of these has its parallel in that of international aid, the parallel functions primarily on a rhetorical level to reflect attention by analogy (and often contrastive analogy) back on the problem of exchange at the personal level—the characters are in no sense actors in that larger sphere and that is not where the drama lies.

In *Secrets,* Farah often invites the reader to consider a possible causal relationship between the fate of the family and that of the nation. Speaking of the effects of Sholoongo's return, for example, Nonno says, "I doubt there is a way of explaining these incidents in isolation from the tension all around, the persistent rumors of a civil savagery about to be embarked on, and numerous other bizarre happenings in the land. They are all connected" (*Secrets,* 118). Such comments, however, are in every case speculative—at no point do any of the narrators specify what these connections might be. As in *Gifts,* the drama plays out entirely on the stage of the domestic and the interpersonal and is in no way reliant on the backdrop of civil strife. Family relations develop, for good or for ill, in ways that are unconstrained by the larger collapse of civil order.

In these last two novels we find not only a return to the settings of the first two but a reprise of their protagonists as well. Farah himself has made an explicit connection between Ebla and Duniya. In *Gifts,* he says, we are "going back to the same story as Ebla's, with only one difference, and that is, she stays with the man: . . . the same age, same kind of background, but one of them stays, the other one goes" (Interview, 1996). That is to say that Duniya, like Ebla, is given in marriage, as a naive country girl, to an old man selected by her male relatives to suit their purposes; unlike Ebla, she agrees to the marriage. The serious character interest of the novel, however, lies in Duniya at the age and stage in life of the Ebla of *Sardines:* middle-aged, once widowed, once divorced, and the single mother of strong-minded children entering early adulthood. Aspects of Koschin, too, are reprised in Kalaman, who claims, "It wasn't in my nature to be unkind to women" but enters liaisons with a number of women who, like Koschin's lovers, "make life easier" for him while he persistently sidesteps marriage (*Secrets,* 51).

Both Duniya and Kalaman struggle to establish their own autonomy against the conventions of marriage and family, though they feel the grip of these conventions in very different ways. For Duniya the prob-lem is the traditional understanding of marriage and family as structures of authority rather than as relations of equality, structures in which, as daughter, sister, and wife, she has always had to cede status to a father, brother, or husband. As a single mother she attempts to maintain a household that is not ruled by hierarchy, though she often has to fight back the instinct to do otherwise, as when she sees Nasiiba smoking for the first time: "Duniya reminded herself that theirs was a household where there was a semblance of individual freedom and problem-sharing, where there was no male authority: weren't freedoms like these to be taken?" (*G*, 187). While Duniya is largely successful in eliminating the element of authority from her family and allowing thereby "a semblance of individual freedom" for all its members, she resists expanding her life to include a permanent relationship with a man because of her often-reinforced perception that such a move would inevitably reintroduce conventional lines of authority and thereby throttle her own freedom.

In the character of Kalaman, Farah gives a new twist to the problem of individual autonomy and the politics of the domestic sphere. For Kalaman the issue is not authority but normalcy, not his shunning of convention but his yearning for it. His parents' marital intimacy excludes him—or so he believes. "I sensed deep in the flow of my blood," he laments, "that my parents had no intention of having me," and his conviction is strengthened as his repeated pleas, "Mummy, give me . . . a sibling," go unmet (*Secrets*, 79, 167). Nonno shares Kalaman's sense of distance from Damac and Yaqut, remarking that he has "often envied them their physical closeness, a man and a woman loving and trusting each other almost to the exclusion of all others" (*Secrets*, 133). Kalaman feels himself to be a particular victim of that exclusion: "It wasn't easy to grow up in a household in which your parents fall silent the moment they hear you coming" (*Secrets*, 198). As it turns out, his feeling that his parents hold him at a distance is not without foundation, but he misconstrues their reason for doing so. Their failure to produce a sibling for Kalaman "wasn't for lack of trying," and their silence has quite a different explanation, as Yaqut eventually explains to his son: "We're truly sorry if we locked you out, but then we had no choice but to exclude everybody from knowing our secrets. Can you imagine a man and a woman living in sin, as they say, in a traditionally Muslim society such as ours? We would have been stoned to death" (*Secrets*, 168, 260).

Until those secrets are revealed, their marital relations and his acceptance as their child into the center of the family appear to him to be incompatible. He sees these family dynamics greatly magnified in Sholoongo's family, in which every form of sexuality imaginable is practiced, including incest and bestiality, and in which the rejection of the child from the center of the family has taken a correspondingly extreme form: Sholoongo's abandonment as an infant in the wilderness to be raised by animals. It is a very different experience of the world from

Duniya's, one that leads him to distrust families as he knows them, not because they are bound by convention but because they do not bind their members—do not bind him—securely enough. His response as an adult is to distance himself from his parents, to disdain his father in particular, to withhold commitment in his relationships with women, to be wary of human society in general, and to suspect that ultimately it is he who is beyond loving. In a rare moment of candor with Damac, before learning the truth about his parentage, he pleads with her, "Open your mind and your heart to me, Mother. I am your one and only son," and he accuses her of lacking "healthy maternal sentiment": "Starving a child of knowing the loving side of its parents is . . . cruel. . . . You feed the child on self-mistrust. . . . Distrustful of humans, I sought the company of pets. . . . Unloved, I fed on unhealthy diets of self-hate, when I came in and you fell silent" (*Secrets*, 153).

Duniya and Kalaman, then, face more complex versions of the same problem that confronts Ebla and Koschin: the difficulty of conceiving domestic relationships that promote one's own freedom of self-definition and at the same time allow other parties to the relationship the same freedom. Unlike Ebla and Koschin, however, they do not merely subvert the conventions of family and marriage but transform them and build domestic relations that are newly conceived and self-defined. That transformation becomes possible through what Sallie Hirsch, in a reading of *Gifts,* calls the "permeability" of the home. "Duniya's house," she notes, "is a center of freely moving natural activity. . . . Dragon-flies, butterflies and birds easily roam into and out of the house. Similarly, Bosaaso and the community at large find Duniya's residence open to their visits."[9] We may think of this permeability as the boundarilessness that we have noted in Misra's personal identity applied to domestic relationships. Such relationships are, like the city in which they are set, outwardly porous to the comings and goings of members who freely enter or leave and inwardly pliable in the roles those members occupy relative to each other.

The domestic space of Duniya's home is indeed permeable, and not necessarily because she wants it that way. The birds and insects enter her house as they do her dreams, uninvited. The only way to keep them out—of both her house and her consciousness—would be to shut the windows and doors (which are recurrent images in this novel), to control the space within entirely, as Medina does. To do so, however, would be to run the risk of tyranny that Medina incurs, and Duniya is determined not to deform her children's autonomy by claiming and asserting authority in a home that is as much theirs as hers. The local wildlife comes and goes, therefore, as do the neighbors—and as do Bosaaso and the foundling. Bosaaso first slips very much uninvited through an opening in Duniya's life, his face appearing in a rearview mirror in which she had expected to see that of a taxicab driver. He has no conventional claim upon her—he is neither a clansman, nor a relative, nor a suitor who has paid a clansman or relative for her hand—but seeks to enter her life by the osmosis of his gifts: a ride to work, a sack of sugar, a driving lesson. Though she distrusts these, she finds them hard to keep out, so she resists dependency through reciprocity: a meal, a conversation, gifts of her own by which her sphere of domestic relations grows still more permeable. The problem for Duniya, then, becomes not how to exclude Bosaaso but how to define their relationship so as to preserve the individual freedom that she has been at such pains to establish for herself.

This redefinition comes about through yet another uninvited entry: that of the foundling. Like Bosaaso's gifts, this child cannot be excluded from Duniya's home, but like those gifts, he also poses a threat to her autonomy, a threat in which we hear echoes of *Maps*. The foundling cries "as if possessed, dominating Duniya's consciousness as no other baby had ever done before" and as Askar dominates Misra's consciousness (*G*, 66). "For Bosaaso the foundling served as an excellent pretext to call at Duniya's place whenever he pleased," a pretext not unlike the one Qorrax uses to take sexual advantage of Misra (*G*, 72). Most importantly, the foundling, like Askar, requires identity papers, a formalization of the child's identity that impinges on Duniya's own identity, as it does on Misra's. In Duniya's case, officialdom requires that a man register as co-guardian, a role that Bosaaso steps forward to fill, reimposing on Duniya, if only on paper, a conventional family relationship with a man.

On the other hand, the presence of the foundling makes Duniya's home a more permeable domestic space, the very opposite of the self-contained relationships between Askar and Misra; and the baby's death frees and at the same time compels Duniya to consider the possibilities of the virtual relationship it has created for her: "When the baby had been alive neither Duniya nor Bosaaso had thought of inventing things to occupy them: he had made life take shape around them. And people came, visitors arrived in hordes, to play cards, to consume tea, to tell each other stories and to become friends. Duniya couldn't help taking account of the fact that the foundling's death imposed a compulsory set of grammatical alterations on their way of speaking, producing a *we* that had not been there before, a *we* of hybrid necessities, half real, half invented" (*G,* 132, emphasis in the original).

As she mulls the "we" she shares with Bosaaso, other relationships come in for redefinition as well, most notably her relationship to her daughter, Nasiiba. Nasiiba is in a sense a mother to the foundling, for it was she who introduced the baby into the family, an act through which she is the "mother" of the changes the baby has introduced in Duniya's life. This figurative reversal of roles between mother and daughter is made explicit as Duniya seeks Nasiiba's help in preparing for her first serious evening out with Bosaaso. She acknowledges "the need to put herself in her daughter's hands," speaks to her "not unlike a very young girl trying on her mother's high-heel shoes," submits to Nasiiba's shocking demand that her mother undress in front of her as if she were her daughter, and allows Nasiiba to behave "like a mother readying her daughter for a children's party" (*G,* 134–35). The reassessment of her relationship with Bosaaso that this evening out inaugurates leads to her acting on "a deep-seated wish to give herself to him, a wish that had taken days to mature" (*G,* 202). The scene of lovemaking that ensues resolves the tension between the two themes of autonomy and permeability that has characterized this developing relationship in particular and Duniya's developing politics of the interpersonal more generally. Both maintain strong separate identities while making love (rather than dissolving into a single self, as the sexual act is often depicted), passing control back and forth from one to the other: first "she lay on top of him, the mistress conducting the speed and flow of the river of their common love" while "he followed the rhythmic dictates of her orchestrated movements"; then "they altered positions" and "he was on top now"; and again "they swapped positions," their separate thoughts being reported all the while (*G,* 207). At the same time, the imagery of windows and doors once again evokes the permeability of the relationship, its openness both to the outside and to the shifting roles within: "The moon entered"; "he opened a window"; "Bosaaso approached Duniya's body as if it were a door"; "she let him in"; "and then the doors of her body opened wider" (*G,* 206–7).

This is a triumphal moment, and the triumph is not sentimental but political. The achievement, in other words, is not the consummation of a love affair or the union of two people as a heterosexual couple, and the book is not an endorsement of marriage—the details of people's choices in such matters, Farah has said, are "none of my business" (Interview,

1996). The triumph is in the manner in which the consummation, the union, has been accomplished, one in which the individual autonomy of both parties is preserved, in which indeed the relationship is shaped in such a way that its primary purpose is to promote and expand that autonomy. The relationship becomes in this way not a convention to which the parties have fit themselves but an original social arrangement that they have freely created and affirmed together. It is an authentic product of democracy in the domestic sphere, and that *is* Farah's business as a political writer.

Because the protagonists of Farah's earliest novels negotiate only escapes and not authentically new forms of relationship and because most of the rest of his work is dominated by political negotiations in the public sphere, *Gifts* is the first work in which Farah places such a triumph at the center of his stage. He does so again, however, in his most recent novel, *Secrets*. In *Gifts* the primary relationship in question is between lovers, its development resonating in the relationship between parents and children. In *Secrets* that priority is reversed, with primary focus falling on the relationship between Kalaman and his parents. Again it is the permeability of the relationship that permits it at last to develop successfully, and that permeability is even more uninvited than it is in *Gifts*. The doors and windows of Kalaman's family are, in fact, shut tightly, both to the outside and among its members. The challenges to this state of enclosure come from two sources, and the imagery of birds and other animals is again at play in both. One is Nonno, "who was more open with me," Kalaman tells his mother, "than either of you" (*Secrets*, 153). Magically in touch with birds and animals through his early (and forbidden) studies, Nonno is the apparent channel by which a crow and other birds enter the human social space of Kalaman's birth. Nonno himself penetrates that space still more deeply, with the life-giving tamarind seed and wild honey, when he learns that the newborn is unable to cry or urinate.

> Again Nonno intervened . . . to make an unorthodox request: to go into the room where Damac had given birth. Traditionally men are not allowed to enter such a room for all of the forty days of the woman's confinement. But because of the special circumstances, Nonno was granted his request.
> . . . He forged forward alone, and into Damac's room, . . . his lips ashiver with the totemic powers of the crow, to whom we prayed long ago as our sky-god. (*Secrets*, 162)

As Kalaman grows, Nonno's home continues for him to be a place of openness to birds and animals and to their special powers to intervene in human affairs.

The other, and more telling, source of penetration into the tightly closed home and family of Kalaman is Sholoongo, the shape-shifter, the burrowing animal, who arrives to pry open and probe the secrets of this family's origin. As the light is let into these secrets, Kalaman and Nonno must put aside the family history they had assumed to be correct and replace it with a very different and painful tale. As a young woman, Kalaman's mother, Damac, was pursued by a suitor whom she refused, the suitor presented a false marriage certificate and was still refused, a gang of thugs used the same document to attempt to blackmail her and raped her when the attempt failed, resulting in the conception of Kalaman; Yaqut then committed himself in love to Damac and to Kalaman though he and Damac never married, concealing these facts to avoid public opprobrium for themselves and Kalaman. The role that Sholoongo plays in penetrating the recesses of this family is much more equivocal than Nonno's. One reason that she is in a position to disclose these secrets is that she has had a hand in manipulating them, having stolen evidence of the crimes that were committed against Damac. She has shadowy designs of her own on the family, including sexual designs on three generations of its men: as a younger woman she seduced Yaqut and aborted his child; she returns to Somalia in order to become pregnant by Kalaman; failing in that plan, she carries out a "simulated rape" of Nonno in Kalaman's bed, asserting, on the supposed authority of the Prophet, that the resulting child "would be the child of Kalaman, not its putative biological parent, namely Nonno" (*Secrets*, 268, 266). In her own narrative voice, she says, "I couldn't care an owl's hoot if [Nonno] had died [in the act of intercourse], or what became of Yaqut, Damac, the lot. From Nonno I got what I was after, the correct amount of sperm" (*Secrets*, 274). Taking in the full extent of Sholoongo's assault on his family puts Kalaman "in a state of delirium, . . . wondering what his blood relationship would have been to Sholoongo's children if she had had one each with Nonno and Yaqut, and one his own? Curse the blood that binds!" (*Secrets*, 201). Damac has always suspected Sholoongo of undermining her family and she curses her as vehemently as she does her own rapists (*Secrets*, 181). Sholoongo's invasion of this family has the potential, then, to tear it still further apart. Her effect instead is to compel Kalaman and Nonno to share responsibility in the secrets that have held it together. "I think of her," Kalaman says at the end of the book, "as a woman who has made each of us inquire into the meaning of truth, . . . as the shaman who has come not to heal but to dispossess us of our secret ill wills" (*Secrets*, 293-94).

Their inquiry reveals that Damac and Yaqut have for years resisted the tyranny of bloodlines—marriage defined by official certificates, parentage defined by biological force—and created a family on their own terms. Kalaman comes to understand that he has not been excluded from his parents' love and from his role in the conventions of family but, on the contrary, has received (even while rejecting) their love by virtue of their resistance to the manipulation and falsification of these conventions. Damac's faith in the solidity of this family, she says to Kalaman, is all the stronger for being "sealed . . . with a sacred trust—the fact that Yaqut and I have never married, and aren't planning to. The sacred trust of a family secret" (*Secrets*, 265). Participating fully in this secret, for Kalaman, is "like learning a new language in which the words 'father' and 'grandfather' had a charged quality about them, in which 'mother' was imbued with other significances" (*Secrets*, 262). Only now does Kalaman come to feel the family "certainties" for which he has always yearned: "I was very glad I was still [Nonno's] grandson. . . . Nonno was a certainty" (*Secrets*, 245); "In place of sperm, I thought it was the river of [Yaqut's] humanity which flowed into my blood, a more precious thing, everlasting in my memory. . . . How I loved him, the certainty that was Yaqut!" (*Secrets*, 254); "No one ever felt a love so pure in its pristine primitivity as [Damac and I] did" (*Secrets*, 263). This is the family that Nonno chooses at the end of the novel in reaffirming Kalaman as his grandson and that Kalaman embraces in proposing marriage and children to Talaado. Like Duniya—but collectively—these characters have created a form of family relationship that permits individuals to flourish. In the process they have engaged in acts of resistance to those who would threaten that freedom—to their rapists and blackmailers—by which their relationship as family members becomes "weighty, with moral as well as political responsibility bearing on it, notions [one] might not have linked to the relationship between a biological son and father" (*Secrets*, 255).

This fictional reinvention of family represents a significant culmination of Farah's lifelong effort to resolve artistically, in reference to at least one sphere of human existence, the fundamental political problem of reconciling the demands of individual autonomy and social responsibility. For a reader of Farah's work as a whole, therefore, this most recent novel creates a satisfying sense of having come full circle, of having watched a career unfold and reach full flower. It is far too early, however, to declare Farah's career complete or his goals as a writer accomplished. He is, at the present writing, a man at midlife. Somalia remains embroiled in a chaotic civil war whose outcome is utterly unforseeable. Nonno suggests at several points that Kalaman's story must be connected to the civil strife in Somalia: "[O]ur nation's predicament is our own predicament too, collectively and individually, each of us an accomplice in its ruin." The narrator concurs: "Our challenge is to locate the metaphor for the collapse of the collective, following that of the individual" (*Secrets*, 190-91). In *Secrets*, however, and at this particular moment in Somalia's history, the metaphorical connection between private and public life remains elusive for Farah. Another novel, dealing more directly with the current conflict, is, according to Farah, on indefinite hold and, indeed, Farah's fictional and dramatic writing in general lies in abeyance as he pursues other forms of reflection on the human toll of political strife in the Horn of Africa. Two realities confront each other at the current juncture: the constancy of his artistic engagement with the politics of autonomy and the particular *in*constancy of political life at this moment in the history of Somalia. How he will resolve this confrontation is beyond the power of any reader or critic to predict. What can be predicted with some confidence, however, given the remarkable development of Farah's work to date, is that the circle is far from closed and that his political vision will continue to probe human realms and relations into which few other African writers have ventured.

Chapter Five
Writing about Women

For politics, wherever you look, has become the world's male-dominated ideas. It is only through the male that this great design . . . makes sense to the viewer, that it makes sense to the dreamer. And women are excluded from contributing but little to the grand design: if at all, they do so as mothers, as wives, as mistresses, as voters, as sycophants. The politician, being male, cannot help himself: he sees only himself duplicated in the *others* he has surrounded himself with, who are also male, *others* who are his rivals, are his stronghold. And women are barred from the fortress of real political power. In Africa and everywhere else.

A writer, however, is in a sense everybody: he is a woman, he is a man: he is as many other selves as those whose shadows reflect his ghostly images; he is as many other selves as the ones whose tongues he employs to articulate his thoughts; he is as many other selves as there are minds and hearts he dwells in.

— Nuruddin Farah, "The Creative Writer and the Politician"

"The politician, being male," Farah writes, dreams the world in his own image. He dreams of a "great design," a political order of which he is the center, all-powerful. In his dream women are assigned to roles "as mothers, as wives, as mistresses," objects of his control and his desire. Like Yussuf, when the politician looks into a mirror he sees only his own image, multiplied into brothers, rivals, doubles. Politicians do not dream of women dreaming. The writer does.

Of course, women who dream can become politicians, which is to say that they can negotiate on behalf of their own "design," their invention of the world and of themselves in it. The task of the writer, in Farah's view, is to imagine a world in which politics is expanded to include just such negotiations.

Among male African writers, Nuruddin Farah is deservedly recognized for the kind of attention he has paid to women's experiences. From his first published novel, wholly centered on a young woman's bid for freedom, Farah has put women at the center of numerous works, exploring a wide range of characters from traditional matriarchs to seductresses of power to resisting feminists and their insurgent daughters. What makes these characters memorable is not so much their psychological as their ideological complexity when they reflect on their lives from various positions within patriarchal structures of power. Juliet

123

Okonkwo suggests this unusual range of representation when she
describes Farah as "the African writer who has done the greatest justice
to female existence in his writing, in the number of female characters he
projects and the variety of roles accorded them as well as in the diversi-
fied attitudes toward life represented."[1]

While all of Farah's women characters inhabit a male-dominated
world, their stories are by no means all the same: some are complicit
with patriarchy, others are violently coerced into submission; some resist
by using the weapons of the master, and others by imagining alternative
possibilities. To represent this variety within women's experience is to
participate in breaking the silence that in itself has constituted an
important mechanism for women's exclusion. For this reason, and
because Farah has from his earliest work written about women's experiences of oppression, we do not hesitate to describe him as a male feminist. Although we devote a separate chapter to his writing about
women, it is important to stress that for Farah women are not segre-
gated into an essentialized category distinct from men. Ideologically at
least (for we explore at the end of this chapter some complicating
metaphorical language that might betray ambiguity on this point),
Farah is not interested in a separate sphere of women, in women's ways
of knowing, or indeed in any generalizations about women. All his characters enjoy the same fundamental interests and rights in the mind of
their creator: "My preoccupations have remained the same. I'm interested in an individual who has been denied what are his or her rights.
Sometimes these happen to be women characters and sometimes they
happen to be men characters. But I'm interested in the struggle and in
the relationships which form after that struggle."[2]

As with family, clan, religion, and nationality, in Farah's writing gender is a social formation that his protagonists resist and transform in
their efforts to define themselves. Women's struggles against patriarchy
are not essentially different from the struggles of women and men
against state dictatorship or against any other form of power that
diminishes individual autonomy. It is fair to say, however, that Farah has
been particularly engaged by the situation of women under patriarchy,
in part because patriarchy is such an entrenched and pervasive form of
power, bearing down so unequally on women, and in part because it is a
particularly complicated instance of "the enemy within." Women who
resist patriarchy must struggle with their fathers, brothers, and sons and
with male imaginings of women; such imaginings are often internalized

and reproduced by both men and women so that the male imagination of woman becomes quite literally "the enemy within."

A prevailing male construction of women is revealed in the assertions of Farah's most closely observed family tyrant, Keynaan: "Women are for sleeping with, for giving birth to and bringing up children; they are not good for any other thing. . . . They can serve the purposes Allah created them for originally, and no more" (*SSM*, 82). According to Keynaan, female anatomy determines women's destiny and their breeding function is divinely authorized. A virtual litany of such pronouncements resounds throughout Farah's work. Another patriarch, Gad Thabit, for example, distorts religious doctrine in order to emphasize women's secondary status: " 'a woman needs a man to intercede for her and present her to Allah; a woman's God is her husband,' he would go as far as misquoting the Koran" (*Sardines*, 57). Gad Thabit rules over his household exactly like a dictator: "A woman, like any other inferior being, must be kept guessing, mustn't be given reason to believe that she is certain about anything" (*Sardines*, 144). Ebla, coming of age under patriarchy, has been schooled in how men value women: "I am a woman, and because my blood-money is half that of a man, it is apparent that I am an inferior being to him" (*FCR*, 155). Shiriye shares this general estimate of women and patronizingly reassures Duniya, "A woman needs a man by her side, for people to take her seriously and for the world's doors to open so she may enter with her head raised and her person respected" (*G*, 80). Sagal has been taught the same lessons as her mother: "[T]he Islamic concept of *cawra* [informs] the canon laws which decree that to nobody other than her own husband . . . should a woman expose any part of her body save her feet, face and hands. . . . A man isn't burdened with the weight of his body, every cell in a man is not an instigator of sin in another being. A woman's body is tempting sin and Satan dwells in it. . . . A woman's body estranges man from his Creator" (*Sardines*, 35). Koschin, neurotically fearful of any relationship with a woman, asserts that "women are the primary cause of man's doom, man's downfall" (*NN*, 54). He invokes doctrinal notions that "every woman is Eve, breathes the wickedness of Eve, the mother of destruction. Every narrative I think of concerns them" (*NN*, 143). Hilaal reminds Askar just how many narratives depict women as the evil undoers of men: "Women as whores, women as witches, women as traitors of their blood, women as lovers of men from the enemy camp—through history, men have blamed women for the ill luck they themselves have

brought on their heads. Women are blamed for every misfortune which
has befallen man from the first day of creation, including *his* fall from
heaven. *Woman* is said to have betrayed *man* at the first opportunity.
Throughout history, Askar" (*M,* 178).

In this sampling we can discern a number of the persistent features in
the ideological construction of women within patriarchy. The female
body is taken to determine women's purpose: to breed and to give males
pleasure. Religion is invoked, sometimes inaccurately, to confirm
women's secondary status: "woman" is not independently created but is a
secondary product of the creation of man—and a defective one at that:
she was fashioned "from a crooked rib," according to a Somali variation
of the Qur'anic creation story.[3] Men see themselves as superior to women
and divinely appointed to govern them and, in particular, to control their
sexuality through marriage and through religious taboos and cultural
practices relating to women's bodies. Legally and economically, women
are understood to be worth less than men. Patriarchs claim the power of
life and death over their children, exercise total authority over their
wives, and assume the prerogative of giving their daughters in marriage.
Women who live outside the protection of fathers, brothers, or husbands
are understood to have left themselves open to rape. Finally, men tell stories in which women bear responsibility for the ills of the world.

This, then, is the climate in which Farah's female characters must
somehow function, either by fitting themselves to the dominant ideology or by challenging it, asserting their right to direct their own lives, to
narrate their own stories, and to imagine the world as it might be
dreamt by a woman. Even those women who are most conformist, who
live entirely "inside the whale . . . weighed down with the contradictions
of tradition," are portrayed sympathetically and with attention to their
individual differences (*Sardines,* 8). Qumman and Beydan in *Sweet and
Sour Milk* and Fatima bint Thabit and Idil in *Sardines* accept without
question the traditional roles for women; although each has suffered
directly at the hands of men and more generally from the constrictions
deemed appropriate for women, they do not challenge their place in
society. Among these, Beydan is the most passive, marrying the man
who tortured her husband, becoming pregnant, and finally dying in
childbirth. Her whole life has been a preparation for that abject lot:
"Beydan as a child, as a girl, was never given a globe to illustrate nor a
world to dream. She was offered broken claypots to play with and bones
to dress as dolls. She was bound leg and foot to a choice not her own.
Her hand was exchanged for cash delivered. She was somebody's prop-

erty. She was nobody" (*SSM*, 152). Indeed, she is so much "nobody" that, near the end of her life, she is no longer able even to see herself in her own dream, being eclipsed by the male child for which she is merely a vessel; she tells Loyaan, "I wasn't there in my own dream. But I dreamt it all the same. I dreamt I had a boy. But unlike in dreams I usually have, I wasn't its centre-point, I wasn't even there" (*SSM*, 220).

Qumman, married to the same husband as Beydan and deserted for this younger woman, is nevertheless a more forceful personality, assertive even as she insists on a clearly limited understanding of the world. She is inclined to believe that Beydan, her rival, has poisoned her son, Soyaan; she refuses, for religious reasons, to have an autopsy performed; she has hired a master witch to interfere with Beydan's pregnancy and is convinced that Margaritta, Soyaan's half-Italian companion, is falsely claiming that Marco is Soyaan's son; she cannot fathom why Loyaan does not want the government to honor Soyaan. The world as men imagine it makes sense to Qumman and she stands by what she feels to be "her" views. Like Beydan, she has endured Keynaan's beatings and too many pregnancies; she looks forward to the day when her sons will provide for and protect her:

> Whenever some superior officer humiliated him, he came and was aggressive to the twins and his wife. He would flog them . . . . She would wait until the twins grew up, she confided to a neighbour. She would wait. Patience, patience. A third pregnancy which resulted in Ladan. And a near-fatal fourth. Society . . . required women to be tolerant, to be receptive, to be receiving—and forgiving. "Does one notice the small insects which die a suffering death under the eyeless heels of one's feet? Keynaan and his generation have never known women. Women are simply a generally generalised-about human species more mysterious than Martians," Soyaan would argue. (*SSM*, 84–85)

Farah's portrait of Qumman allows the reader to see her as she has never been seen by "Keynaan and his generation." The details of her domestic circumstances enable the reader to sympathize with her, while Soyaan's comment explicitly underscores the injustices endured by women, crushed like insects under men's "eyeless heels" without ever being recognized as fully human.

Farah is especially alert to the complexity and human drama of the women's complicity in patriarchy portrayed in Qumman, and developed in *Sardines* in Medina's mother and mother-in-law. As matriarchs, these women believe that children should learn to "bend the knee" in the

home and accept the authority of patriarchy; they extend this habit of
unquestioning obedience into civil society, to the clan and to the General. As we suggested in chapter 4, their acceptance of patriarchal
authority helps to sustain the state dictatorship. Just as Beydan was
"bound hand and foot," Fatima, in accordance with her Yemeni background, is "chained ankle and wrist and foot to the permanence of her
homestead." Initially this tightly restricted world ("she seldom came out
of her house unless it was absolutely necessary") seems to contrast with
Idil's nomadic, pastoralist life, "on the whole a lot less rigid than the
Arabic tradition of institutionalized mannerisms. She had never learned
what it was to be strangled with the strings of purdah. . . . She had a
profession, she supported her own Samater and Xaddia by making
maize-cakes on commission from a restaurant" (*Sardines*, 8). We soon
realize that both women are in their different ways controlled by men.
When Idil complains to her son of his neglect, we learn more about the
poverty she endured as a widow with a frail child, his

> nose running a stream of mucus round the clock. . . . They were so poor
> that he shared the edge of her robe when she carried him and was naked
> when on the ground, eating mouthfuls of dirt. Then she obtained a com-
> mission to bake *canjeera* and maize-cakes for a restaurant owned by a
> man who—the truth must be told—had easy access to her. . . . When
> they were slightly better off, when she had earned enough money from
> the baking ventures, the dead husband's brother demanded the right of
> *dumaal.* . . . Xaddia, the only issue of that union, was born. (*Sardines*,
> 81–82)

It is no surprise, then, that having sold her body and scrimped to provide clothes and schooling so that her son could bring home "a monthly
stipend" as a clerk, Idil now wants Samater to keep his position (and his
salary) as a government minister. Rather like Keynaan, she makes up for
her years of impotence by ruling the domestic sphere "with the iron fist
of a dictator . . . the self-proclaimed protector of tradition and religion"
(*Sardines*, 104). It is as a matriarchal dictator defending her culture that
she presses to have Ubax circumcised. Fatima sizes up the situation she
shares with Idil: "The tradition of my people encages me in a four-
walled prison and makes me the exclusive property of a man. The same
tradition . . . exempts me from being circumcised. . . . One is always a
prisoner of one thing or another" (*Sardines*, 144, 152).

Whatever the differences in their traditions, these women share a
common situation of oppression in which women's bodies are conspicu-

ously controlled by men in one way or another. They accept this situation as legitimate because they see themselves entirely in the terms of the male imagination of women. Fatima's resignation, Idil's self-righteousness, and Qumman's assertiveness, nevertheless, convey distinctive personalities that allow us to respond to them as individuals even as we also are moved by their common suffering. They feel themselves to be, as Idil says, "the product of a tradition with a given coherence and solidity" (*Sardines,* 83). Beydan, it is true, has been so reduced in the male construction of a woman as "property," as "nothing," as "an insect" that she cannot even place herself in her own dream, much less determine its content, but the other three women define themselves with a certain confidence that makes them memorable to the reader. The possibilities upon which they draw in order to define themselves, however, are severely limited to the terms offered by the patriarchal culture in which they live. They force their understanding to fit the procrustean bed of the male imagination.

Ebla, in *From a Crooked Rib,* initially resents the limitations on women in her pastoralist culture: "[G]oats for girls and camels for boys got on her nerves. . . . This allotment of assignments denoted the status of a woman, that she was lower in status than a man, and that she was weak. . . . She loathed this discrimination between the sexes: the idea that boys lift up the prestige of the family and keep the family's name alive. Even a moron-male cost twice as much as two women in terms of blood-compensation" (*FCR,* 13). Experience teaches her how difficult it is for a woman to challenge the prevailing views or to enjoy, for herself, the greater autonomy of a man. At the end of the novel, her impulse to resist patriarchal ideology falters: "He, the Almighty God, is the one who has fixed the status of human beings. He made me cost half of a man, and He must have had a good reason for doing so" (*FCR,* 155). Finding herself pregnant, she accepts a biological determination of who she is: "[T]his was a woman's role, and one has to play one's role. 'Why should I grumble if I am giving life to another person? . . . This bodily torture is what I inherited from my mother. She was a woman too' " (*FCR,* 168). The Ebla of *Sardines,* some twenty years older, positions herself between the extremes of rebellion and submission; she is a cautious pragmatist who has nevertheless passed on to her daughter, Sagal, her youthful aspiration to live in a freer, fairer world.

In *Sardines* Farah introduces several female characters who dream of lives lived outside the confines of the male imagination of women. The intensely oppressive atmosphere created by the dictatorship has helped to sharpen their analysis of the forces constraining them and has strengthened their determination to resist. The center of this group is Medina, who articulates the connection between dictators in the home and in the government. Idil and the General represent a common enemy that threatens "the survival of the woman in [her]" (*Sardines,* 259). By mentoring a group of young women whom she exposes to feminist ideas and by creating a liberal domestic environment for her daughter, Ubax, Medina hopes to enhance the opportunities of these young women to determine their own direction and to lead fuller, richer lives than their mothers. She recalls her own miserable early childhood spent with "an unchallengeable patriarch who decreed what was to be done, when and by whom. 'I want Ubax to be free of all that. . . . I want her to live her life like a dream. I want her to decide when to wake up, how to interpret her dreams' " (*Sardines,* 17). She thinks of her protégé, Sagal, as a "bridge to an unbuilt future" and wants her to learn how to build both the bridge and the future for herself (*Sardines,* 48).

These women in *Sardines,* along with Duniya in *Gifts,* are foremost among Farah's characters who reflect critically on women's experiences and develop a feminist analysis of patriarchy. While they are represented by the author as flawed, imperfect humans, their efforts to envision a world in which women enjoy autonomy fully engage Farah's sympathies. In virtually every text, he invites the reader to attend to women's oppression, focusing in particular on three ways in which women are controlled directly or indirectly by men: female circumcision, male prerogatives with respect to marriage, and rape. For many of his women characters, these are the issues around which they become conscientized, issues that provoke them to resist patriarchal authority and to conceive of alternative social structures that will support women's autonomy.

Farah was the first creative writer from Africa, male or female, to focus on the trauma of female circumcision; in his first novel, *From a Crooked Rib,* published in 1970, he provides a strikingly detailed picture of infibulation through the eyes of Ebla:

> Ebla . . . saw one of the female tenants coming out of a room, carrying a small girl in her arms. The girl had her eyes closed, Ebla could see, and there were some blood spots on the dress of the woman who carried her. . . . "Oh, my God. What a painful thing it was," she recalled. There were only two times that she wished she had not been born, and one of them was when she was circumcised. It was not only painful but a barbarous act, she thought. . . . She recalled everything. They had sliced out her clitoris and stitched the lips together, thus blocking the passageway,

but also leaving a small inlet for urinating through. They had tied her legs together, and she had been laid flat on the ground without any mattress or anything underneath her, for she would bleed on it. They had beaten drums when the girls cried, so that the beating of the drums would drown the crying. If a girl cried too much, they tucked a piece of cloth into her mouth. The wound would not heal, they had said, if a boy saw it or a woman who had just committed adultery. So the girls had been confined in a hut for a period of between ten and twelve days.

She also recalled that other night of pain—the first time she had ever had sexual contact. It was with Awill, and it was very painful, indescribably painful. She had bled and he rejoiced seeing her blood, as his manhood depended upon breaking her chastity. (*FCR,* 149–50)

Part of this passage serves as an almost clinical description of the practice of infibulation, but its effectiveness derives from being located in Ebla's consciousness. Seeing the small girl and the blood on the woman's dress sparks a moment of sympathetic identification in which Ebla conjoins this moment in the life of this girl with her own circumcision and with that of other girls alongside whom she underwent the operation: their bodies assaulted and their minds full of taboos that define gender roles for both sexes. These reflections lead, finally, to her more recent past in which Awill's moment of triumph requires her painful and bloody deflowering. Farah repeatedly represents female circumcision as an excruciatingly painful practice that has serious repercussions throughout women's lives and as an ideological inscription upon women's bodies, practiced by women in the service of the male construction of women as a way of controlling female sexuality.

This view of circumcision emerges again, for example, in *Sardines,* where Medina's strenuous rejection of infibulation is as important as her opposition to the General. The custom has deeply alienated her from her tradition-minded mother-in-law, who wants to bind her offspring to the past, whereas Medina wants to open up new futures. Idil haunts Medina's and Ubax's waking and sleeping thoughts, a knife-wielding figure threatening "to purify her innocent grandchild" (*Sardines,* 208). Medina vividly recalls the pain of her own circumcision and the complications it created for childbirth: "I fear the descending knives which re-trace the scarred wound, and it hurts every instant I think about it. . . . If they mutilate you at eight or nine, they open you up with a rusty knife the night they marry you off; then you are cut open and re-stitched. Life for a circumcised woman is a series of de-flowering pains, delivery pains and re-stitching pains. I want to spare my daughter these and many other pains. She will not be circumcised. Over my dead body" (*Sardines,* 62–63). The feminist analysis of the policing of women's bodies is extended in Medina's reaction to news of a brutal circumcision performed on a 16-year-old Somali-American girl, an act orchestrated as part of the state's harassment of her dissident parents. The generational struggle over this issue is registered again in *Gifts,* where Duniya remembers her own circumcision with anguish and seeks Taariq's "assurances that Yarey would not be made to undergo the torture of infibulation. . . . Only that morning Hibo had brought to the hospital her youngest daughter who had been circumcised without her knowledge by her visiting mother-in-law" (*G,* 115).

Men's prerogatives in marriage and the consequences for women are, like circumcision, of concern throughout Farah's writing. Older men benefit from the practice of polygamy by taking young wives while older women experience both economic and psychological harm. Deeriye is the exception among his peers in his fidelity to Nadiifa; Qorrax is more typical in his taking and casting aside so many wives that Askar cannot keep track of them. Widows like Beydan and Aynaba are disposed of by being married off to men who were responsible for their first husbands' deaths. Idil is preyed on by a brother-in-law who insists upon the right of *dumaal,* that is, the right (sometimes the obligation) for a brother to accept into his home and bed the surviving widow of a dead brother. This custom lies behind the possibility that so disturbs Askar, namely, that Qorrax may have raped Arla (his sister-in-law). Anxiously, he questions Hilaal, "Did he rape my mother? . . . Did he want to marry her when news about my father's death came?" (*M,* 140). Young girls like Ebla and Duniya are offered by male family members to men old enough to be their fathers. Ebla runs from this only to find herself victimized in other ways: after blaming Ebla for his bad luck when he is caught smuggling, her cousin tries to marry her to a tubercular associate in order to pay his debt. When she again escapes, her lover Awill arranges a suspiciously hasty marriage ceremony and then goes abroad, leaving Ebla to fend for herself by taking Tiffo as a second husband. Trying to regain some control over her situation by turning polygamy on its head, she tells Tiffo, "You have another wife and I have another husband. We are even: you are a man and I am a woman, so we are equal. You need me and I need you. We are equal." Tiffo quickly puts her in her place: "We are not equal. You are a woman and you are inferior to me. And if you have another husband, you are a harlot" (*FCR,* 145). He then announces, "You are divorced," and walks away, leaving Ebla to ponder whether she has become a prostitute (*FCR*, 152). Ebla is victimized by men who first take advantage of her vulnerability and then label her a harlot. She tries to puzzle out this double bind: " 'A man or a woman—who cheats who?' she asked herself. 'Maybe I should put these questions to other people' " (*FCR*, 165). Since no one else is there, Ebla converses with her alter ego in the mirror whom she imagines as a man; not surprisingly, she is unable to define herself in any terms other than those proposed in the male imagination of women.

The extent to which women are pawns in systems of exchange like marriage is further developed in *Gifts*. Like Ebla, Duniya recognizes how much she has been controlled by men throughout her life:

> It was when she thought of herself as a woman and thought about the female gender in the general context of "home" that Duniya felt depressed. The landmarks of her journey through life from infancy to adulthood were marked by various "stations," all of them owned by men, run and dominated by men. Did she not move from her father's home directly into Zubair's? Did she not flee Zubair's right into Shiriye's? There was a parenthesis of time, a brief period when she was her own mistress . . . as a free tenant of Taariq's, only for this to cease when they became husband and wife. Meanwhile, her elder brother Abshir's omnipresent, benevolent, well-meaning shadow fell on every ramshackle structure she built, . . . Abshir being another station, another man. (*G*, 170–71)

Throughout her life, men have sought to constrain Duniya with gifts. As a child of 4 enticed by Zubair's fine horse, she playfully agrees to marry him. At 16, she is pledged by her dying father to his old friend, and her detested half brother, Shiriye, accepts gifts from Zubair to clinch the deal. Her beloved brother, Abshir, showers her with gifts to compensate her for the injustice she has experienced as a woman, but in his benevolence he sometimes seems to her to be just one more controlling male. Recognizing the patterns in her past, Duniya now insists on avoiding any sense of dependency in her new relationship with Bosaaso, declining many of his overtures "because unasked-for generosity has a way of making one feel obliged, trapped in a labyrinth of dependence" (*G*, 20). Having freed herself to a significant degree from male control, Duniya is trying to imagine new terms for a relationship between a man and a woman, and any new partner will have to respect the self she has defined: "To know how I am . . . you must understand why I resist all kinds of domination, including that of being given something" (*G*, 237).

Female circumcision and traditional marriage are forms through which men legitimize their control of female bodies. Efforts to resist this control, to refuse the "gift" of male protection, leave women all the more vulnerable to punitive male violence. With her fellow nurses, Duniya discusses the vulnerability of working women in a city where public transport is no longer available: "Petrol shortages, power failures or the unavailability of public transport can only be defined as a double curse for women. . . . On the one hand these give unheard-of advantages to men harbouring wicked intentions towards us; on the other, by refusing to be seduced with lifts, a woman exposes herself to the perils of being raped in a dark alley" (G, 18). Accepting a ride implies that a woman is sexually indebted to a man; refusing it makes her a justifiable target of attack: a double curse indeed. Women are in fact expected to trade on their sexuality and then blamed whether they do so or not, something the naive Ebla recognizes when Tiffo calls her a harlot and Idil experiences at first hand when she has to sell herself in order to sell her maize cakes. Rape is the most extreme form of violence that men use to control women, and brutal gang rapes occur in three of Farah's novels as reminders of this constant threat to women. In *Maps,* Misra spends her entire life as a victim of male abuse, her defiled body becoming emblematic of multiple forms of violence directed against women. Her mother was a concubine of a nobleman, "none of whose other wives gave him a male child" (M, 70). When Misra is born, both mother and child are discarded. At seven she is abducted as "loot" in a raid and left with an older man whom she learns to call "Father" until he insists on marrying her. "In the end . . . she murdered him during an excessive orgy of copulation" (M, 69). She escapes but must seek the protection of another man, by whom she is later divorced. To remain with Askar, she submits to sexual relations with his male relatives. The childless Misra experiences miscarriages, stillbirth, and abortion. Accused of betraying Somali freedom-fighters, she is raped by "a dozen young men" in her village, who then put about the story that they saved her from baboons who "smelt her traitor's identity . . . and went for it again and again" (M, 186). Alone in a hospital in Mogadiscio, emotionally abandoned by Askar, she undergoes a mastectomy and is finally ritually murdered and fed to sharks.

In *Sardines* the rape of Amina becomes a story of women's resistance. Amina is attacked by young men who, ironically enough, oppose the state dictatorship. Because her father belongs to the ruling group surrounding the General, the youths rape her by way of punishing her father. In the midst of the rape they tell her "we're doing this not to you but your father . . . *Not you. Your father*" (*Sardines,* 126, emphasis in the original). The horror of her situation is thus magnified by the fact that she is merely an instrument in a quarrel between men and by the rapists' grotesque notion that they are fighting against one form of domination by exercising another. The details of the assault associate circumcision and rape as paired occasions in which male domination is literally inscribed on women's bodies: "[T]he cut, the knives, the blood on her thighs . . . her lips trembled as she saw the men unbutton their trousers . . . what pain, what pain, what pain! She had been a virgin, she had been circumcised" (*Sardines,* 126).

Amina is found by a group of male village elders, who refuse her care on the grounds that her father has punished members of their clan; the wives of the elders, however, disobey their husbands' instructions and offer Amina food and shelter, saying, "The pain is ours, the fat and wealth and power is the men's" (*Sardines,* 126). In the aftermath of the rape Amina works to reclaim control of her body and her identity. Her father and the General want to cover up the politically motivated rape and allow her attackers to flee the country; her father offers her a ticket anywhere in the world so that she can "leave behind the unfortunate disgrace" (*Sardines,* 128). Amina refuses: "I accept nothing short of your bringing all three rapists here for a public trial. . . . I want every Somali to see the political significance. I want everybody to know that every rape is political; that the powerful rape the weak" (*Sardines,* 129). Throughout this experience, Amina is supported in crucial ways by women, starting with the compassionate villagers. Sagal, Ebla, and Medina offer the idea of a new kind of female-centered family and encourage her decision to bear the child conceived in this rape: "During this period they went about together . . . with Amina in the middle, and on occasion with Ubax holding on to her little finger. There rippled through the expectant mother bubbles of delight. . . . Evening walks. The pleasure of company. A life made meaningful. Medina: books and gifts; Sagal: the warmth of welcome and friendship; Ebla: the mother of understanding. . . . No doubt Sagal, Medina and Ebla had built a motorway of possibilities for her" (*Sardines,* 129).

The strength in collective resistance and in communities of women is underscored in several ways in *Sardines* and in others of Farah's novels. Here Amina's friends are able to build "a motorway of possibilities for her" through their discussions, their reading, and their active support. The diversity of their reading is emphasized, the texts ranging from

Susan Brownmiller's *Against Our Will* to works by Frantz Fanon, Bertolt
Brecht, Anne Sexton, and a number of others specifically mentioned.
Similar supportive women's communities exist in *Gifts,* including the
nurses at Duniya's hospital, the neighbors Maryam and Marilyn who
come into her home to help with the foundling, and her daughter's circle of friends, including Fariida, the girl Nasiiba helps through her
unplanned pregnancy and childbirth. As early as in *From a Crooked Rib,*
Ebla receives support from an unnamed widow and from Asha, who
then has to protect Ebla from what is, in effect, a comic variation on
women's support groups, a gang organized by Tiffo's wife, Ardo, in
order to keep wandering husbands in line.

The rapes of Misra and Amina are explicitly politically motivated, in
the broader sense we have been using (as Amina says, "every rape is
political") and in the narrower sense of being linked to nationalist politics. In *Secrets* the gang rape of Damac reveals everyday gender politics
in extremis—the state of affairs in which, to quote Amina again, it is
business as usual when "the powerful . . . rape the weak" (*Secrets,* 129).
At eighteen Damac attracts the unwanted attentions of a "pesterer"
who refuses to be "discouraged by her rebuffs" (*Secrets,* 230). Eventually
he forces the issue by forging a certificate of marriage. Since Muslim law
permits a marriage to be performed without the bride in attendance as
long as there are two male witnesses, the "pesterer" has no difficulty in
persuading Damac's aunt that the certificate is valid. Cast out of her
home, Damac manages to establish herself in business, but in the meantime her "pesterer" loses the forged certificate in a card game to some
"riffraff," who then proceed to blackmail Damac. The extortion note
reads: "we will . . . come to make our claim, our fair dividend from having been your husband as stated in the document in my possession [the
forged certificate]. We are delighted that you are doing well in your
bead business. We're not asking for much, only a third of your monthly
take, that's all. . . . What if you don't pay up . . .? We'll intercept you
on your way home [and] humiliate you bodily. . . . Remember you are a
woman! Remember that you are responsible for what happens, should it
occur to you to refuse to cooperate with us" (*Secrets,* 261-62).

The thugs make good on their threat, and Damac becomes pregnant
as a result of a gang rape. Her support comes not from women but from
a male acquaintance, Yaqut, who learns to love her when he hears what
she has suffered. Together they quietly reject the Islamic and legal conventions of marriage which so injured Damac but commit to raising the
child of this rape as their son. After Sholoongo digs up enough of the

family secrets, Yaqut finally explains to Kalaman how, for Damac, her child was initially a source of "overwhelming neurosis," a reminder of "the humiliation of the rape. . . . At first she could not even bear the thought of holding you to her breast. Only after seeing more and more of me in you, and less and less of any of the rapists, could she relax in your presence. . . . Your mother used to be on the perilously jagged precipice of a nervous breakdown. I am glad that we have survived the suicide attempts. We've been through a great deal together, your mother and I, sharing insomnia as long as a year of sleepless nights" (*Secrets*, 260).

Yaqut's words bring home the years of damage inflicted by this rape, and yet we also become aware of the strength of will both he and Damac show in bending the tragedy forced on them into the shape of a loving family. Eventually, Kalaman is able to see his unorthodox situation as a courageous refusal to be defined by blood and lineage, that is, by the terms of patriarchy. The family he intends to start with Talaado at the end of the novel will draw upon the model that Damac and Yaqut have provided. Repeatedly in his work Farah shows how some of the most coercive and damaging forms of male domination—circumcision, control of marriage, and rape—lead his characters to reject the legitimacy of patriarchal authority, to resist male domination, and to envision new possibilities for themselves.

We discussed in chapter 4 the development of alternative families as political acts that enhance the autonomy of all members, male and female. Because women are so powerfully controlled in so many ways within the patriarchal family, transformation of the family is an especially important aspect of women's resistance. Mothers are particularly eager to create different environments for their daughters, a central concern in both *Sardines* and *Gifts*. Medina, Ebla, and Duniya foster a new kind of relationship with their daughters that is nurturing and intimate rather than threatening and distant, one that encourages independent thought. Ubax and Sagal, Nasiiba and Yarey are outspoken children who dare to question their mothers and mentors. Because Medina herself was raised in the home of a "tyrant parent towering above a trembling child, hand half-raised in such a way the child doesn't know whether" the parent is "about to hit or give or just want[s] to offer a pat on the head," she takes "a perverse pleasure in hearing her daughter's refusals, her well-articulated challenges stated in the frankest language and without fear, her defiances uttered plain as truth and her angry 'No' " (*Sardines,* 147–48, 16). "Traditionalists would describe Duniya's offspring as *hooyo-koris,* children growing up in a household with a woman as head," but Duniya is pleased to think that "theirs was a household where there was a semblance of individual freedom and problem-sharing, where there was no male authority" (*G,* 30, 187). In consequence, her children exhibit independent spirits and also a desire for relationship on new terms. Nasiiba tells her mother, "we your children know precious little about your past and you know next to nothing about our present. Don't you think it's time we got to know each other better?" (*G,* 26). Yarey calls Duniya by her first name and bargains vigorously, in her own interests, to return to her mother's home. Nasiiba acts independently to support her friend Fariida, pregnant with Qaasim's child, knowing that her mother will not press her to reveal her secret before she is ready and that the "foundling" will be invited into their home when it appears. Sagal and Ebla enjoy a particularly intimate mother-daughter relationship, which, like Duniya's and Nasiiba's, allows for independence. Sagal confides in her mother "the future she had invented for herself. A future without obstacles, . . . what she dreamt of doing and what was going to happen to give meaning to all that she held close to her heart" (*Sardines,* 41). Ebla in turn "hoped one day Sagal would be able to narrate her own life in capital letters of joy" (*Sardines,* 36). They go for walks arm-in-arm, "affectionate as pigeons" but recognizing their differences. Ebla thinks, "Each of us speaks for a generation, each of us is like a clock keeping its own time. . . . What my daughter does not have, I have. But we are two persons with two different backgrounds and two separate minds" (*Sardines,* 38–39).

All three mothers want most of all for their daughters to have the opportunity to dream, to imagine their lives for themselves rather than living within the bounds of the female roles prescribed by patriarchy. This is what Ebla means when she says she wants Sagal to "narrate her own life," what Medina means when she thinks of her as "an unbuilt bridge to the future." Well-tutored by these women, Sagal explicitly contrasts herself with Beydan: "Medina told me that Beydan before she died saw a dream in which she wasn't the central focus, and therefore she died. The focal point of the dream is always myself. I'm not Beydan. . . . The dialectics of my dream are such that I see the contradiction in the future I invent and what life's reality has in store for me" (*Sardines,* 43). Sagal is full of contradictory dreams and impulses about how to achieve her own autonomy and how effectively to resist the state dictatorship—and even about which of these is her priority. Appropriately she is associated with water, fluid and ever-changing. Her dreams run

into "life's reality" when she finds herself possibly pregnant after a single
night spent with a young man. As she considers her options, Farah captures her adolescent floundering: she is checked but still exhilarated
with her possibilities, uncertain and yet affirming that she will be the
one to determine her future:

> The wind of her imagination began to shake things so wildly she felt as
> though she were merely a branch of a tree. There: the wild fields of a
> future emerged from behind the greener courts of others. And in this
> future of futures, she was with a child. . . . Her mind scattered the seeds
> further afield and . . . harvested a future of delight. . . . What about her
> future as a swimmer? . . . Would she defy nature, her ambition, her
> wants? . . . Now her future, it seemed, chose to separate itself from the
> rest; it stood out, giant as ambition, large as a dreamt wish, but like
> promised goods not yet delivered. She was telling herself the story—*her
> story!* A woman, without taking the necessary precautions, one night
> made love to a man she had not met before that evening. And then? A
> hesitant pause came after this. Had the well of her imagination run dry?
> Why didn't she continue? Her double told her other double that she
> shouldn't *judge* but that she should *narrate.* (*Sardines,* 123, emphasis in
> the original)

The importance of women's learning to narrate their own stories, to
dream themselves at the center of a reordered world, is signaled in the
opening lines of *Sardines* as Medina "reconstruct[s] the story from the
beginning," as she "superimpose[s] a tapestry of patterns she herself had
developed, none of which, to the best of her knowledge, had known
precedents. This she believed would enable her to introduce fresh turns
and curves in the rebuilding of this large structure . . . : her life!" (*Sardines,* 3). Medina imagines "a room of one's own. A country of one's
own" (*Sardines,* 4), space in which women can move freely as "full and
active participant[s]" (*Sardines,* 263). She is "telling herself the story—
her story" of her efforts to rebuild a home for Ubax, herself, and Samater.
Storytelling is Medina's métier: she spends her days translating, telling,
and retelling stories to Ubax: "For two months, for three months, day in
and day out, the two were together from morning till evening . . . and
they would wait for Samater and celebrate his homecoming with the
retelling of what they had done, which stories they had told each other,
who had come to visit them" (*Sardines,* 5). As Medina spins for her
daughter "a tale of a million and one nights and spread[s] out its fabric,
a tale of silk originality," she wonders whether Scheherazade (and

implicitly whether she herself) "in any way gain[ed] expressive articulable humanity in the telling of the story nightly?" (*Sardines*, 25). The answer to her question is certainly yes. Precisely what one gains, in Farah's world, by telling one's own story is "expressive, articulable humanity," just what is denied to Beydan, just the opportunity that must be extended to all women. *Sardines* concludes by emphasizing the vital activities of narration and imaginative reconstruction as Medina, Samater, and Ubax retreat to "tell one another what had happened [and] to put their house in some order" (*Sardines*, 263).

The activities of narrating and reordering are again conspicuous in *Gifts*. Like Medina, Duniya wants to feel that she is in control of the domestic space she inhabits with her children, and she too moves out of her house when a relative threatens to interfere with them. Storytelling is thematized in the title to Part I, "A Story is Born," and throughout the novel right up to the final paragraphs, where Duniya "was thinking that beginning the story had been easy, like extracting a milk-tooth. But how was she to end it?" (*G*, 241). Duniya's situation and language recall Sagal, who also has difficulty seeing her way to the end of her story. The shift in verb tense, as *Gifts* comes to an end, is a further reminder of how much the story is an activity of Duniya's: "Duniya, the chronicler, is no longer certain how to go on" (*G*, 242). As narrators of their own lives, Duniya and Sagal both feel oddly split, as if they have a double. Sagal's "double told her other double that she shouldn't *judge*," and Duniya feels that it is some "other Duniya" who has ordered her dinner and wonders if "*the other* Duniya with *her* tale" has taken her place at the table (*G*, 241–42, emphasis in the original). Their uneasy self-consciousness in the course of self-invention makes them similar to Askar, divided (as Sagal reminds herself not to be) between narrating and judging activities conducted by the three aspects of himself represented in the three pronouns he uses—a parallel underscoring that in Farah's work women and men share the same desire to control the narratives of their lives.

Thus far we have focused on women's experiences as conveyed through women characters, many of whom are consciously resisting patriarchal ideology, narrating their own stories and dreaming of new political structures. Several of Farah's male characters might also be called feminists and many are sympathetic to the suffering of women. Their reflections contribute to Farah's representation of women's oppression in patriarchy. For instance, the sight of his mother being beaten by her husband provokes in Soyaan a murderous wrath, and he recognizes that his father's peers treat all women as nothing more than insects under their "eyeless heels" (*SSM,* 84). Bosaaso is almost an idealized feminist man; in fact, as we have noted, Farah has suggested that he may be a creature of Duniya's imagination—her "dream" of a man who will respect her autonomy. He understands her concern not to become dependent upon him for transport or anything else, and he works with her to keep parity in their relationship, often willing to be "more of a recipient than a giver" (*G,* 236). Bosaaso also shares Duniya's view that "men have assigned to themselves all the sacred, powerful, spaces, forbidding women from being visible or present in such places as mosques or at meetings of a council of men reaching decisions which affect the whole community, including women" (*G,* 217). Like Medina and Duniya, Bosaaso is interested in reorganizing domestic space, electing to "commemorate" his mother by building "a mausoleum of a kitchen in tribute to her." He explains to Duniya that "in a world in which derogatory terms like Nigger, Woman and Native have become badges of honour, I believe that a woman like my mother afforded me the opportunity to take an appreciative look at the world" (*G,* 216). Bosaaso recuperates a room hitherto associated with women's circumscribed role and makes it the center of his house. He is equally ready to make adjustments in his life to include Duniya and is prepared to sell the house so that when she is ready, they can make a new home on equal terms.

Abshir's acts, like Bosaaso's, are also guided by his understanding that women have suffered unjustly at the hands of men. He explains his generosity to Duniya in this way: "If you were a boy, you wouldn't have been married off to a man as old as your grandfather in the first place, and in the second, you might have got a scholarship to a university of your choice, because you were brilliant and ambitious. An injustice had been done. It has been my intention to right the wrong as best I could. I am sorry" (*G,* 238). Although Deeriye does not consciously use the language of women's rights, he views contemptuously the "ninety-nine per cent of his peers [who] remarry when their wives die or age" as "materialists" who use wives as a sign of status and virility (*CS,* 24). Unlike all his friends, he is loyal to one wife to whose words he attends even after her death. He shows courtesy, respect, and affection to his feminist daughter, Zeinab, and to his daughter-in-law Natasha. After Mursal is killed, he kneels before Natasha, supplicating her to believe that she still has a place in their family. His oldest friend reflects that none of Deeriye's peers "would do anything as saintly as that; that no one among them was humble enough to bow and 'hold the knees' of a woman, let alone seek forgiveness of a woman—who was white and a Jew at that" (*CS*, 209–10).

A number of male characters show Deeriye's quiet sensitivity and tenderness in their treatment of others, especially women, and some intentionally choose nontraditional family arrangements that afford women greater autonomy. Among these are Soyaan, Mursal, Medina's father Barkhadle, Yaqut, Samater, and Hilaal. These last three have in various ways reversed traditional gender roles with their wives. Yaqut is a quiet artisan who works at home, raising Kalaman and sometimes allowing him the pretense of breast-feeding at his father's chest, while the enterprising Damac manages a shop. Samater lives in a home owned by his wife where "not only did he cook meals for Medina and Ubax, he was also the official dishwasher of the household when the maid was not there," driving his mother Idil to remark that "Medina has larger testicles than you. Just as I had bigger ones than your father" (*Sardines*, 74, 83). Hilaal cooks and does housework while Salaado teaches at the university, drives their car, and manages all banking and legal affairs (*M*, 18). Hilaal has taken the further step of having a vasectomy after he and Salaado learned that she could not bear children, thereby challenging the stigma attached to female infertility. Physically, Hilaal reminds Askar of Misra because of his "natural body odour" and the fact that he "liked to make bodily contact, just like Misra!" (*M*, 18).

In his exploration of gender, Farah takes us beyond characters who want to change social relations between men and women to characters who imaginatively identify with or project themselves into the body or voice of the opposite sex. Such a capacity to experience the world as either sex suggests that humans may attain, through such imagining, more complex and inclusive perspectives on the world, perspectives based on a shared common humanity. As indicated in the epigraph to this chapter, Farah reckons this an important potential within the creative writer, who "is in a sense everybody: he is a woman, he is a man." Sometimes, however, gender crossings are undertaken by male characters who feel engulfed by women. We need, therefore, to consider the possibility that such exercises of the imagination might also express hostility and the desire to dominate.

When Farah's female characters imagine themselves as men, they typically explore how the world might appear from a position of power. In *From a Crooked Rib* Ebla, recognizing that she is pregnant, looks at an unfamiliar image of herself in the mirror and begins a dialogue with herself in which a female voice first interrogates a masculine voice, and then vice versa, as they debate which sex controls a relationship (*FCR,* 165 – 66). In *Sweet and Sour Milk* Ladan and Loyaan conduct a brief conversation in which both mimic the voices of both their parents (*SSM,* 225). Medina at first sees herself "engaged in a varanian dance of death" with the General but later recognizes that she and he might exchange places, she the challenger becoming the defender, the oppressed woman becoming the tyrant in the house (*Sardines,* 55). When Idil boasts that both she and Medina have bigger testicles than their husbands, she expresses the wish to have that which is needed to exercise power within patriarchy. In *Gifts,* as Nasiiba helps her mother dress for a date, Duniya, feeling unaccustomedly vulnerable, thinks that her daughter, who is controlling her mother's body, has suddenly taken the role of a man: "Was Duniya now seeing Nasiiba as 'male'? Had she not stripped her, as men had, had she not rendered her powerless as men had? 'What are you doing to me, Nasiiba?' she asked" (*G,* 137). In *Secrets,* Sholoongo the shape-shifter takes to the furthest extent the imaginative projection of the self into other forms, animal as well as human. One possibility at play in this novel is that Sholoongo transforms into an elephant seeking revenge on a poacher. In a comparably aggressive style, Sholoongo arrives in Mogadiscio, invades Kalaman's apartment, and insists that he impregnate her. As a child, she demonstrated the same force of character (perhaps the influence of her lioness foster-mother), encouraging Kalaman to drink her menstrual blood and to have sex with her so that she could give him a sibling. Barely a teenager, she slipped into Yaqut's bed and seduced him; subsequently she tried to seduce Nonno, while he bathed in the river, and got a kick in the chops for her trouble. The motif of sexual role reversal, with Sholoongo the eager initiator, is emphasized at the end of the novel where she is at last successful in seducing a sleepy Nonno, mimicking a form of male rape known as *daba-gur.* Nonno is not altogether unwilling; he later explains to Kalaman that "we met and made love in the world of pretend, the world of simulated rape in reverse" (*Secrets,* 294). Domineering Sholoongo is explicitly associated with Carraweelo, the mythic Somali queen whose tyrannical matriarchal rule was overthrown by men. Although Damac hates Sholoongo for the "nympholepsy" she induces in men, she is in certain respects like her. It is Damac who notes that Sholoongo's name refers to "an ancient precapitalist form of banking among women," an arrangement that once permitted women to enjoy the kind of economic independence that Damac herself pursues, a status now conventionally reserved for men (*Secrets,* 171).

Numerous male characters in Farah's works are sympathetic to the vulnerability of women and respond by imaginatively identifying with women's roles and bodies so strongly that they seek some kind of transformation or merger. After Salaado has one of her ovaries removed, Hilaal wants to share her physical and mental pain: "My beautiful wife had suffered, I said. I too must. So I took myself off to the hospital. And had a vasectomy done. If she couldn't—well, so I couldn't" (*M,* 152). As a child, Askar shares Hilaal's empathy for women's suffering when he wishes he could share Misra's menstrual pain: "If I had some of it, then Misra will have less of it, yes?" he asks Karin (*M,* 49). Abshir in *Gifts* and Nonno in *Secrets* both act as nurses to newborns who refuse the breast. Abshir reminds Duniya, "When you were less than an hour old . . . and you refused to breast-feed and our mother was too unwell to take care of you, it was I who fed you the first drop of milk, a gift you wouldn't take from anyone else" (*G,* 236). Similarly, Nonno is the only one who can get Kalaman to accept his first drink from his finger, the magical tamarind juice. In a more striking cross-gender identification, Kalaman's father, Yaqut, occasionally pretends to breast-feed his child as well as nursing along with the infant at Damac's second set of breasts. Kalaman as a child often expresses the wish to become pregnant and to that end drinks Sholoongo's menstrual blood. When these characters wish to take on a woman's role, it frequently indicates their empathy or desire to nurture or, as in the case of Kalaman, to possess women's procreativity.

Other moments of identification and merger on the part of male characters appear to arise from more conflicted feelings about women and identity. Whenever Samater recalls first making love to Medina, he can never tell the story quite the same way, but in every version "Medina was the heroine . . . , Medina was the one who decided what to do and when" (*Sardines,* 191). He hears her voice inside his own head and "would do anything at her command" (*Sardines,* 186). His evident admiration suggests that he enjoys being dominated by her. A dream is recounted (the identity of the dreamer unspecified) in which Samater and Medina are swimming and come upon "Idil, large as a monster and bosomy, with her large milkless breasts flat on her mound of a chest" (*Sardines,* 207). When she announces that she has come to circumcise Ubax, Samater strikes her dead in the water.

> Her corpse floated huge like a whale. Samater pulled her further and further into the deep zones of the ocean and buried her in the secret womb

of the sea. When he swam back . . . Medina was horny and hot with lust and they began to make love energetically. "Come, come now, come into me, let me fold you inside me, my leaf," she said. The sea, dark and green and black, opened up and swallowed them whole, greedy as love. And Samater dove in and read the contours of her womanhood, his lust enlarged her sex like a speculum. (*Sardines,* 208)

In this dream Samater is repelled by the huge but "milkless" breasts of his mother and wants to kill her (or to act on Medina's wish to kill her—or perhaps this is, in fact, Medina's dream). The imagery explores involuted mergers as Samater pulls his whalelike mother into the "secret womb" of the ocean and is himself folded into Medina's body, and then both of them are "swallowed whole" in a sea of sexual desire. We have indicated previously that such engulfment can also be understood as a kind of male appropriation of the woman's body; here Samater controls by "read[ing]" Medina's "womanhood" and widening her vagina with the instrument of his penile "speculum."

Such identifications with women expressed in the imagery of transformation, incorporation, and engulfment are significantly extended in Askar's consciousness. More than any other character, he projects his imagination into other bodies, starting in infancy when he feels himself to be part of Misra's physical self: "I seem to have remained a mere extension of Misra's body for years. . . . I was her extended self" (*M,* 75). At times he feels as if he is Misra, as if she is his "missing half," or as if she is "a creature of his own invention" (*M,* 42, 178, 107). On several occasions Askar dreams that he changes places with or is transformed into a girl, and he explains to Hilaal that he has the "strange feeling that there is *another* in me, one older than I—a woman" (*M,* 151). For all this, Askar's identification with women leads him to feel revulsion and hostility. When he discovers blood on his groin, as if his strong sense of identification with Misra had actually transformed his body into that of a menstruating woman, he is frightened and disgusted (*M,* 105). On the one hand, he remembers wishing he never had to separate from Misra and grow up as a man. When he is five years old, he remembers Misra saying, "You are on your own!" and his response is first to try to become her by wrapping "her *shamma*-shawl round his shoulders, looking very much like a woman" (*M,* 56). His feelings quickly shift, however, as he allows the shawl to fall to the ground, announcing that when he grows up, he will kill Misra. His imaginative identifications of himself with women do not lead Askar to act empathically or in ways that respect women's autonomy. Like Samater, he loses a sense of his own identity in his imaginative projections of himself in a woman's body, giving rise to the wish to kill the engulfing mother figure.

Maps works both as a cautionary tale about men's imagination of women and as an exploration of the permeability of gender boundaries. It is, after all, a novel written by a man who imagines a woman character and a male protagonist who identifies with her while failing to imagine her existing autonomously outside male categories. Clearly Farah pays attention to the ambiguities that attend any writer's efforts to project himself or herself into experiences of the opposite sex. Implicitly, he invites readers to consider his own work in this light. We therefore turn to Farah's use of figurative language in order to assess how successful and how consistent he has been in writing about women, in conveying a world as experienced by women, and in locating the limits of the male imagination of women even as he attempts to move beyond these limits.

In a study of Farah's metaphorical language, Jacqueline Bardolph notes that he "uses the figure of woman in its many symbolic or allegorical roles: she is Mother Somalia, the earth and the language which cannot be ignored. She is an image of perverted power, an ogress. Womanhood is also associated with humiliation, the rapes and excisions being akin to the powerlessness of the people."[4] Such a reading would seem to conflict, however, with Farah's refusal to treat women as a homogeneous class or their gender as an essential trait. It is reasonable to ask how it is possible for a writer to use "the figure of a woman" as a symbol without implying that women belong to a category that can be associated with the symbol, without denying women their individual identity.

Let us explore how Farah negotiates this dilemma. In two novels he gives central female characters names with symbolic resonance, names that associate women with nature, with that which is primal, given, and passive, rather than with agency or activity. Misra, we are told, means "foundation of the earth" and Duniya means "world" or "cosmos" (*M,* 177; *G,* 93). Other elements in *Maps,* along with Misra's name, invite allegorical readings; and Bardolph and Derek Wright, among other critics, offer interpretations of the novel based on Misra's identification with Somalia, Ethiopia, or the Ogaden and on the equation of woman with land, earth, or foundation—that which is contended for by men.[5] Wright develops one possible reading from a passage in which Misra tells Askar that "Somalia is seen by her poets as a woman—one who has made it her habit to betray her man, the Somali. . . . You know the poem in which the poet sees Somalia as a beautiful woman [who] accepts all the advances made by the other men—to be precise, the five

men who propose to her. She goes, sleeps with them, bears each a child
. . . and has a number of miscarriages" (*M*, 98). Wright observes that
"the figure in the novel whose personal history approximates closest to
the archetype in the fable is in fact Misra," who is pursued by five men
and has miscarriages that could correspond to lands once settled by
Somalis but no longer included within the national borders: the
Ogaden, northern Kenya, and Djibouti (Wright, 107). Farah sets up
such possible interpretations, however, only in order to unravel them.
As Wright observes, Misra's ethnic identity as Oromo destabilizes the
allegory, and the metaphorical association of woman with conquered
land, rather than being a vehicle for the issue of nationalism, points
instead to the issue of male domination: "Misra, as the woman Somalia,
is the abused, enslaved victim of brutal patriarchal tyranny. . . . If Misra
fails as an image of a free Somalia or a free Somali Ogaden, it is not
because she is a foreigner of mixed Oromo and Amhara descent, but
because no woman in the Horn of Africa can serve in a signifying system
which indulges in the cliched gendering of national freedom in falsely
heroic and idealized terms" (Wright, 107). Here Wright captures what
is characteristic of Farah's use of woman as a symbol. Farah himself has
described his practice this way: "Like all good Somali poets I use women
as a symbol for Somalia. Because, when the women are free, then and
only then can we talk about a free Somalia" (Interview, 1981a, 61). He
deploys a conventional metaphor equating land (Somalia) with woman
but turns it to his own political purposes, making woman a symbol in
order to argue the evils of treating woman as a symbol.

Such a practice is risky, however, because it depends upon readers'
ability to stay light on their interpretive feet, rethinking how metaphors
and symbols are working and recognizing the ironies in the uses to
which the writer puts them. Misra undeniably is, in Bardolph's language, "associated with humiliation" and "powerlessness," an overdeter-
mined figure of a victim. Indeed, Askar sees Misra in precisely this way
when he looks at her scrubbing on her hands and knees; what springs
into his mind, revealingly, is the classic image of a humiliated woman
about to be violated by "the master [who] comes from behind and he
takes her. How many films [showed] maids . . . raped by their employ-
ers . . . or a secretary by her boss? How many stories in which a slave is
raped. . . . In all of them, man was 'taker,' the woman the victim" (*M*,
52–53). Gazing on Misra, Askar concludes that "women were victims in
all the stories he could think of. Misra. Shahrawello. And even Karin.
The soul is a woman—victimized, sinned against, abused" (*M*, 52–53).

The point of the novel, however, is Askar's failure, despite his intellectual comprehension of woman's oppression, to imagine Misra in any way other than as a symbol, whether it be the divinely engulfing mother, the betraying whore, or the eternal victim. Even when Askar says "the soul is a woman," he allegorizes reductively in a way that ensures that he will never see Misra as a person. On the one hand, Farah constructs Misra in such a way as to symbolize the oppression experienced by all women. On the other, he wants his readers to notice Askar's failure to see Misra as a person. She is, ironically, no freer in Farah's imagination than in Askar's—can be no freer, if the device he is using is to work—but by pointing to Askar's limitations, Farah draws attention to the limits of the male imagination of women and to the risks attending his own strategy as a writer.

A passage from an earlier novel, *Sweet and Sour Milk,* places similar demands on readers to explicate shifting, even contradictory, uses of woman as a symbol. At one point Loyaan thinks of "power" as a "mistress of wicked ways" who had been sleeping "manless, unloved" until the arrival of the General (*SSM,* 173). This is the sort of figurative language that, in *Maps,* Hilaal deplores because it reiterates the invariable association of women with prostitution and betrayal. Nothing in the text of *Sweet and Sour Milk* alerts the reader at this point to be critical of Loyaan's metaphor. Within 10 pages, however, female figures are used metaphorically to strikingly different effect. Ladan and Qumman are summoned to sweep the streets in preparation for a procession honoring a visiting dignitary:

> They would prepare the village's roads just as a mother would a daughter on the day of marriage, skin oil-smooth, every hair in place, the dress the right colour, bride rested, happy, welcoming, receptive. Come: take this bride, our village, as yours in sacred marriage for the brief duration of your stay in Somalia, Mr Visiting President. Come: take this key, the symbol of power, and open the cleaned and shaven legs of our womanhood. . . . We've given one Belet-Weine girl to Idi, we give you another, Mr Visiting Dignitary. (*SSM,* 188)

The passage begins as if the point of view might be located within the consciousness of Ladan and Qumman, who are comparing their street cleaning to the work of a mother preparing her daughter for marriage. With the imperative "Come: take this bride," their simile is seized by a satirical voice that cannot be ascribed plausibly to either of the women. This voice uses the figure of the bride to speak of the prostitution of

Somalia to foreign influence, Somalia being compared to a village girl given to powerful figures like Idi Amin. Far from being the "mistress of power," in this passage woman symbolizes the condition of being victimized by power. Power is a phallic "key," which will be used to "open the cleaned and shaven legs of our womanhood," as if to circumcise, deflower, and rape all at once. This satirical voice appropriates the figure of a woman's body in order to make a point about national politics, drawing parallels between two victims (Somalia under the General and the village girl about to be given to Idi Amin). As the metaphor is developed, however, the vehicle begins to usurp the tenor so that the reader's attention shifts from Somalia's figurative prostitution to other states to the literal prostitution of women under patriarchy. Either reading, however, exploits the figure of the woman's body in all its vulnerability, arguably further inscribing woman in the limited tropes of the male imagination. As in *Maps*, Farah takes a considerable risk in depending upon his reader to interrogate his language and see that this male writer has complicated the use of woman as symbol.

We have argued that, to an unusual degree, Farah has made his female characters important actors in his imagined world and has often sought to present this world as seen through women's consciousness. To this end much of the descriptive and figurative language that he uses draws on women's bodily experience. Lending out his imagination in this way is among his most characteristic practices as a writer—and among his riskiest. Several passages, drawn here as examples, suggest both what Farah accomplishes by this practice and how uneven is its impact. Farah makes the central purpose of his first published novel the presentation of the world as seen through the eyes and the consciousness of a naive young woman. Naturally, Ebla inhabits a body—the very body that defines her as worth half of a man—and at a crucial moment, she takes stock of her person. Lying in bed naked and reaching beneath the sheet, she scratches her groin and chuckles, "This is my treasure, my only treasure, my bank, my money" (*FCR,* 160). She then assesses her physical self using domestic images that occur to her as she feels her breasts "as soft as butter" hanging as if they were not part of her body, then touches "her left breast, and, as if she thought that the other one would get jealous of being over-looked or something, she hurried to give it a touch. . . . She squeezed both of them like you squeeze a lemon with no juice in it. The corns inside the breasts were smaller in size" (*FCR,* 161). This passage permits readers to gaze at the female body through the female eyes and to feel it with the female hands that Farah has imagined. While the passage represents a woman possessing and enjoying her body in an ordinary way, it draws attention to a woman's body in graphic, sensory detail.

In a comparable passage in *Sardines,* readers see the nubile Sagal through her mother's eyes: "Through the see-through pyjamas, Ebla could see her daughter's pubic hair, wild as a safari, untrimmed-curly and unshaven and shocking (she, Ebla, like most women here did not wear hair on any part of her body other than the head). She could also see the bend of her daughter's well-seated breasts, and the nipples which insisted on pushing through" (*Sardines,* 34). Part of the point of this passage is to convey the generational differences between Sagal, eager to assert herself against many conventions, and Ebla, who "believed that a woman's body is her *pudore*: she must wear it with modesty" (*Sardines,* 34); so it is relevant to the development of this contrast that the mother feel vaguely shocked by her daughter's ungroomed pubic hair and, arguably, relevant that Sagal in her boldness might wear provocative "see-through pyjamas." Moreover, Farah's writing has been consistently bold in registering the sexual dimension of parent-child relations. Some readers will value this passage from *Sardines* for Farah's recognition of a mother's response to her daughter's visible sexuality ("the nipples which insisted on pushing through"), while others will find that its appeal is mainly prurient.

Male bodies are not represented with the same specificity although they do appear in Farah's writing. In *Sardines,* Samater feels some sexual arousal, along with anxiety, during a dinner date with Atta. *Maps* offers a sympathetic treatment of Askar's circumcision at age eight: "The sticky saliva in my mouth, the drumming of fright beating in my ears, the numbness of my body wherever I touched, felt: my legs, my hands, my thighs, my penis, what pain!" (*M,* 88). Nowhere is the male body, beyond infancy, presented with the sensuous appeal of the young Ebla or Sagal. In *Gifts* Duniya, making love with Bosaaso, feels "the marks his trouser belt had left round his waist, body marks that were as prominent as a woman's stretch marks following the delivery of a number of children. He had far too many burns and scars, even for a Somali" (*G,* 207–8). In this novel of love between mature adults written in Farah's own midlife, both male and female bodies are shown in homely familiarity.

One reason that women's bodies are a focal point in Farah's writing is his attention to the intimacy shared by mothers and infants and, beyond that, the fascination felt by a number of his male characters for all the "secrets" of the woman's body. He conveys with extraordinary tenderness the physical intimacy shared by Askar and Misra and, less intensely, by Duniya and Yarey and by Ebla and Sagal. Such feelings seem important and true to human experience, but Farah's exploration has the effect of drawing attention persistently to the mother's body and breasts—in the case of Damac, her remarkable twin sets of breasts—and to the mystery of menstruation. The voyeurism of the male children Kalaman and Askar, who at a young age watch their mother or mother-surrogate make love, conveys how sexualized the mother's body is in the male child's imagination, but this also has the effect of making the mother very sexual and physical in the reader's imagination; implicitly the female body is assumed to be altogether more fascinating than the male body.

In *Gifts*, for the first time, Farah gives the role of youthful voyeur to a female child, Nasiiba: "I saw everything through the keyhole and heard everything, every single groan" (*G*, 29). In *Secrets* voyeurism is more widely practiced and male and female bodies are equally objects of the reader's gaze as a number of diverse manifestations of sexuality are explored. Kalaman interrupts his parents as they are making love to demand a sibling and watches as his grandfather and a youthful companion have energetic sex; later Nonno watches his grandson masturbating in the shower. Damac watches as Sholoongo feeds Kalaman her menses and as she attempts to seduce Nonno in the river. Kalaman witnesses his neighbor Madoobe sodomizing a cow and observes his friend Timir masturbating, having homosexual sex with Fidow, and enjoying incest with his sister Sholoongo. Near the end of the novel Sholoongo coaxes several immense erections out of the dying Nonno: "How he rose at my teasing touch! My goodness: what an erection of singular handsomeness, Nonno's. I wish the world could see what I saw, a sex of stupendous smoothness as if oiled, veined, a well-rooted body of muscles, collagen, and elastic fiber, these expanding up into a mushroom-shaped dome. At my touch, it rose to meet me, hardening with the pressures of excitement . . ." (*Secrets*, 267). While many varieties of sexuality are practiced in the novel, the male body is memorably on display.

Secrets explores the profound connection between the human and animal worlds, between human culture and nature. While the shape-shifting Sholoongo is vital in developing this connection, Farah does not, in this most recent novel, leave it solely to woman to symbolize human embeddedness in nature. Nonno is Sholoongo's double and rival in many respects, capable of transforming himself, possessed of magical knowledge, communicating with animals and birds, and, as we have just seen, he is fully as much a creature of responsive flesh as Sholoongo. In earlier novels, however, Farah employs descriptive and figurative language that proposes an uncritical association between women and the natural world, an association that reinforces the notion of woman as a less rational, more physical being than man. Numerous instances occur in *Sweet and Sour Milk*. While one might argue that the entire novel is intended to convey the oppressively limiting ways in which women are seen by men, we suggest that readers are not sufficiently cued by the text to be critical of the language associating women with nature. In the following instance, Loyaan watches Margaritta breast-feed Marco: "Then her hand fiddled with the fastening of her brassiere. Did she want to feed the child? Her chest flattened as she loosened the hooks. She undid the front, and out came long breasts which she stuffed, one at a time, like a pair of toy teats, into the savage toothlessness of hunger, the cave that was Marco's mouth" (*SSM, 65*). Here the language captures Loyaan's revulsion at what he perceives to be Margaritta's animal-like maternal manner, and one can argue that the text invites a critical perspective on this response. A few pages later, however, in one of the epigrammatic similes that open each chapter, two voices are approaching a sexual climax, followed by a woman's "shrieking hysteria" when she fails to achieve orgasm (*SSM, 82*). The image of a sexually demanding woman is succeeded by one of a sexually available female animal in the description of twilight that opens the chapter proper: the moon "collid[ing] with a herd of clouds," the sky opening up "like a cow her legs, as it accommodated the advances the moon made; it behaved like a willing cow in the company of an excited bull" (*SSM, 82*). The next paragraph introduces Keynaan instructing Loyaan about the opposite sex— "women are for sleeping with, for giving birth to and bringing up children"—a passage that perhaps is intended to associate these images with the oppressively misogynistic and sexualized world that men like Keynaan dwell in. There is, however, a lyrical element in the description of twilight at odds with such a reading, which almost seduces the reader into seeing the sky as the body of a sexually available cow-woman. In the following passage a similar metaphorical connection between women and nature is proposed, but in this instance the woman is demure, even "puritan." Night arrives as a woman "in veiled darkness like the black-scarved puritanism of a Muslim. . . . The night finally descended down the trees in Margaritta's garden like an abstract thought—vague like the sky's waistline; and uncontainable like the secrets of a woman" (*SSM*, 113). The same figurative language is repeated near the end of the novel: "Night had suddenly fallen like a veil of darkness with which a puritan Muslim woman in the Middle East might cover herself immediately she came into the view of males" (*SSM*, 241). Both passages imply a male onlooker to whom the night appears as mysterious as a woman who has "uncontainable . . . secrets" and who covers herself before "the view of males." Here again, as in the imagery of animals and clouds, the lyrical language does not signal in any obvious way that such a view of women is limiting or otherwise oppressive; once again, it invites the reader to see nature as a woman, women as part of nature.

In the following passage from *Sardines* describing Ebla and Sagal setting off arm-in-arm for a walk at night, Farah uses figurative language in a similar way. In this case the argument that the entire novel intentionally conveys the limited world of the male imagination does not obtain, so much of it being focused on women's reimagining the world:

> The two would . . . go further into the night which opened up like the teased lips of a vagina. The masked opaqueness of the hour would open like a tunnel of softness to welcome its own breed. . . . They would go together through the entrance of the night's starry doors like two feathered doves, proud in their plumage—two vessels of purity. Like egret, like cattle! They would keep pace with each other and together move in the direction of the nodal knot within the circle which their presence created: an image as fascinating as the whirlpool of a herdsman's dust. The slight wind of the night's sleazy feeling. Ebla's silky touch, Sagal's voice a sort of whisper, coming in waves of words out of which one could build a castle of meanings. . . . Sagal had by then accepted nature's patrimony; her body, like a porcupine's, shot out quills of femininity, one after another. Her body finally surrendered to the invasion of womanhood, before she even knew it. . . . Affectionate as pigeons, . . . the two trod on the hem of the retreating night. (*Sardines*, 37–39)

The intimacy of mother and daughter is punctuated throughout this passage with assertions of their differences: "But we are two persons with two different backgrounds and two separate minds. . . . But I am not you, neither are you me. . . . The two parted, each went her way" (*Sardines*, 38–39). To this extent Farah is underscoring the autonomy of each within the intimate mother-daughter relationship. The figurative language is most striking, however, in associating the two women with the dark night, envisioned as a vagina, a "tunnel of softness." While

Ebla and Sagal might be said to "take back the night" in an act of self-assertion, they are figured as part of nature, as doves, as egret, then as cattle, which soon belong to the whirlpool of dust raised by the herdsman. Sagal's body is "like a porcupine's" shooting out "quills." She is at the mercy of this natural body, bestowed upon her ironically as "patrimony," a body beyond her control, a body that "surrendered to the invasion of womanhood before she even knew it." Despite his refusals elsewhere to treat gender as an essential category of identity, here Farah suggests that women, defined by their female nature, are a special "breed" that is mysterious and invisible like the night, as a woman's sexual organs are mysteriously invisible. Moreover, the writer "teases" open this image of female night, arousing the vagina, and then (in a move reminiscent of some of Farah's male characters) ascribes to the night wind a "sleazy feeling" associated with a promiscuous night-walking woman. The association of women with nature in this passage seems to support Jacqueline Bardolph's conclusion that Farah uses women symbolically and allegorically and that in his work "women must accept their essential nature as women" (Bardolph, 444).

We do not think that such a conclusion is warranted, however, if one considers all of Farah's writing about women. As a whole, *Sardines* presents women as individuals and indeed explicitly condemns the treatment of individuals as types or categories. As Medina insists to the Afrocentrist Atta, "[N]o race has a monopoly over pain. . . . You suffer because you are a human being . . . not *because you are black*" (*Sardines,* 195–96, emphasis in the original). What is refreshingly egalitarian in Farah's writing is his recognition that women and men, white and black, all are capable of erring, of stumbling into generalizations, which it is his purpose to debunk. The highly volatile Sagal, still very much developing as a person, forms the following mental image of herself: "Sagal, in a dug-out canoe, naked and wet with tropical sweat, would in her imagination loosen the chains that tied her hand and foot to a tradition where women were commodities bought and sold, and were sexually mutilated. 'I am a river synonymous with its water. I am a woman synonymous with subjugation and oppression.' And Sagal's eyes would roll in a vague movement—like a slippery peeled onion" (*Sardines,* 62). By exercising their imaginations, women can indeed "loosen the chains" that oppress, but the youthful Sagal, in pursuing this reverie, is not so much loosening chains as indulging in old metaphors, seeing herself as a stereotypical native in a canoe and slipping into the same kind of categorical language as Atta when she asserts, "I am a woman synonymous with subjugation and oppression." The thrust of Farah's work is to make us recognize that Sagal is "synonymous" with nothing at all: she is, in principle, free to make of herself what she wants. True, Sagal is associated with water and Medina with fire but not, as Bardolph suggests, because these are elemental or natural forces, but rather because both women are associated with the capacity to transform. As we have seen, Farah uses conventional metaphorical associations in order to turn them in new directions.

Sagal is still learning how to narrate her own life and to envision her own self. Like all of Farah's characters who struggle to bring into being a new world, she trips over the old metaphors, blunders, and is uncertain of her direction. In this she is like Medina, whose rearrangements in "a room of her own" cause a number of people, herself included, to trip up. She is like Duniya, whose efforts to live on new terms often cause her to be clumsy and ungracious. A figurative language equal to the task of imagining women characters like these must almost inevitably be a language of contradictions, one that registers at once the experience of groping uncertainly toward new identities and the attraction of the tropes that have long offered a sense of certainty to the identities that these women are working to shed.

Farah has created an exceptional range of female characters who are "full and active participants" in his world. Experiences particular to women (bodily experiences such as menstruation, circumcision, infertility, childbirth, and rape, and political experiences of functioning within a climate of oppression) are given extended attention, but women's concerns are not limited to these issues. The women in Farah's novels discuss the international economic order, dependency theory, civil rights, slavery, the multiple colonizations of Africa, Islamic law, poverty, political resistance, and many other topics. These women are neither idealized nor demonized: they are clumsy, dogmatic, inconsistent, self-pitying, selfish, and hostile as well as friendly, nurturing, imaginative, and ambitious. Only minor characters are simplified, represented by one or two signature traits. Farah's most articulate feminists can be unpleasantly doctrinaire, while his hidebound traditionalists still have our sympathy. In presenting communities of women and exploring relationships among women, Farah shows their interactions sometimes as congenial and supportive but more often as informed by disagreement, debate, and searching criticism. In short, his women characters are among the most diverse and complicated of any to be found in fiction. At the heart of Farah's world are the resisters: women and men who share the need to define themselves, to narrate their own lives, to transform their world; these characters, like their author, are learning how to wrest out of what is called tradition, out of the old forms of language, out of the old metaphors and stories, new forms and new practices that will nurture the autonomy of all.

Chapter Six
Language and the Ethical Imagination

What I like to do, in telling a story, is to study the numerous facets of a tale and to allow very many different competing views to be heard, which in a sense points to the democratic drift of my writing, the drift of *tolerance*. Tolerating the views of other people and coexisting with the contradictions and not in fact considering oneself to be weak because one has accepted the views of other people means to me what democracy is. . . .

If I were to pick up my pen and pontificate in an authorial way, then naturally what I would have done would be to become . . . a priest. I am not a priest, I am in the business of intellectually analysing and debating not with myself but with ideas. . . . I don't imagine that there is any single voice, so this is why my novels are multi-voiced and, hopefully, multi-layered.

—Nuruddin Farah, 1993 interview

Language, we have argued, is the terrain on which Farah's women take their most effective stand against patriarchy. It is the instrument by which they oppose their own narrative to the patriarchal account of themselves in order to reconceive themselves as fully human subjects. For Farah, however, the act of self-narration is not simply a calculated strategy of resistance nor is it a practice only of women. It is the primary act of being human. At the core of Farah's politics, we have shown, is the principle of individual autonomy, and it is in self-narration that that autonomy expresses itself. By self-narration we mean a form of reinvention, the conscious construction in words and ideas of a story of the world, transforming the world as we find it into one in which the narrating self plays a chosen and meaningful role. When fully performed, it is a profoundly social act, one that takes place not in a vacuum but in a world that, like Farah's books, is crowded with people. To reinvent both the self and the world in which the self plays its definitional role is necessarily to reinvent others who cohabit the same world and to do so in interaction with their own narratives. The relationships created by this act of imagination, as a consequence, have the power to be either liberatory or oppressive.

In stressing the centrality of individual autonomy in Farah's work, we are in substantial agreement with Juliet Okonkwo's view, based on the first four novels, that freedom of the self is the unifying principle in Farah's thought:

> Although the main focus of action in Farah's works shifts from novel to novel, a recurrent theme binds them into a single entity. This recurrent theme is the quest of the individual for self-fulfilment, and therefore, happiness. His major characters . . . are constantly struggling to acquire a more satisfying existence for themselves based on their conceptions of a full life. Their preoccupation with freedom and the self, conforms with philosophical concepts concerning the function and place of man in society. Man's major role in life, according to the Aristotelian concept, is the attainment of the good life.[1]

Okonkwo's formulation, "the quest of the individual for self-fulfilment," indeed captures the movement of thought that binds the novels she examines as well as the rest of Farah's work into "a single entity." We argue, however, that he locates the goal of that quest not in a generalized notion of "happiness" and "the good life" but more precisely in the creative act of self-invention by which individuals transform their own identities and reshape the world to fit their own possibilities.

These transformations, whether failed or successful, are the primary centers of action in Farah's novels and dramas of consciousness. His texts are most importantly understood as narratives about narratives, stories of human beings telling themselves the stories by which they attempt to live. Acts of self-narration take many forms in the work of Farah, from public discourse to the private inventions of dream. All have the purpose of bringing the self to life by imaginatively transfiguring the world to place the meaning of the self at its center. When Beydan disappears from the center of her own dream in *Sweet and Sour Milk* therefore and says, "That I wasn't there means I must have died," she is not only predicting her future but describing her present condition (*SSM,* 221). Unable to dream herself, she has already died as a person, for, as Loyaan knows, even "beggars don't dream dreams in which they themselves do not figure. Beggars are the centre of their dreams" (*SSM,* 239–40). The connection of dreaming and other forms of self-narration to the survival of the self remains fundamental in Farah's work right up to the end of his most recent novel, *Secrets,* where Nonno offers this description of the condition of death: "All that death does is to deny you the opportunity to reinvent your life as you live it. Because dying, you cease to dream" (*Secrets,* 275).

Farah's texts are thick with the traffic of dreaming and otherwise self-inventing characters. His own narrative techniques for handling this traffic are among the most challenging aspects of his work, prompting Derek Wright, among others, to comment on "the resemblances which elements of Farah's writing bear to the standard features of postmodernist fiction. Notable among these are the novels' narrative inconclusiveness, often petering out in mid-plot; the conspicuous and ingenious play of parallelism; and the collapsing of ontological boundaries by multiple, superimposed orders of reality" (Wright, 17–18).[2] Textual elements such as these—which do indeed characterize much of Farah's work and which we examine later in this chapter—are not, however, in and of themselves postmodernist. Wright is correct in speaking only of "resemblances," for the vision that these techniques support in Farah's work is not one of unconstrained, unstable, and ungrounded postmodern subjectivity. The multiple consciousnesses that Farah dramatizes are, like the postmodern consciousness, self-aware and self-reflexive—but they are also self-critical. The foundation for such critique, the standard to which Farah holds himself and all his characters responsible, is the principle of individual autonomy whose place in Farah's politics we have developed in chapter 4. It is this principle—and specifically its insistence on each individual's accommodation of the interests and autonomy of others—that leads him to proclaim, in a most unpostmodern fashion, "the creative writer's total faith in truth and justice" ("Politician," 28). "Truth," in accordance with this principle, requires that the story one narrates of oneself and the world be free of self-deception and self-aggrandizement; "justice" further anchors and constrains self-narration by the requirement that it envision a world in which others are similarly free to enact stories of their own choosing. Not all of his characters meet these standards, of course—indeed many do not—but they are insistently present nonetheless in the very techniques by which Farah constructs his narratives.

There is much in Farah's writing to lead a reader easily into a quandary such as Wright describes: "After reading *Maps* four times, I must confess that I am still undecided whether psychological realism or postmodern experimentalism is the dominant mode of the novel" (Wright, 122). Farah's use of language in his work as a whole only makes sense, however, if we understand that its "dominant mode" is neither psychological (or any other) realism nor postmodern experimentalism but intellectual debate. His novels and plays, in the self-inventions that they depict, dramatize the formulation and engagement of ideas, primarily ideas about the nature of personal and political identity. In recent interviews Farah has described his practice as a writer in ways that help clarify this crucial point for an understanding of his work. In drawing characters, he says, "I would like to give even the people whom I disapprove of a chance for their words to be heard. It is only through a debate that we can reach an acceptable logical inclusion [sic]."[3] Though Farah most likely intended his interviewer to hear the final word of this statement as "conclusion," the debates he depicts are indeed scrupulously inclusive: "I've actually identified with almost all my characters, even the bad ones, and the reason is because one must give them fair game. One must allow them to speak something that is intrinsically truthful insofar as they're concerned, and to create such a tension between truth and untruth so that even Satan is given the power to say certain things."[4] Just as intellectual debate is his own primary mode of expression as a verbal artist, so in turn does he see it as an essential dimension of human interaction in a social world that is built, and constantly rebuilt, out of the materials of language. His entire body of work, accordingly, is an investigation of the power of language to support or suppress intellectual debate and thereby to enlarge or restrict human freedom. Moreover, he carries out this investigation simultaneously at three different levels of concern with his own practice as a writer: the representational level of fictional characters and actions, the artistic level of textual composition, and the social level of the artist's role in wider public discourses of power.

At the representational level, Farah's effort to give "fair game" in a mode of intellectual debate accounts for his approach to the development of character and voice. Some readers have been unsympathetic to Farah's narrative practice in this respect. In a review of *Close Sesame,* for example, Jim Crace writes that "the dialogue . . . lacks careful characterisation. Deeriye and his family, from 11-year-old Samawade to Mursal's American wife, converse in Farah's own ponderous narrative tones."[5] Hilarie Kelly offers the same complaint about *Maps*: "The conversational style of some of the characters appears at times to be blatantly artificial, as Nuruddin transparently puts *his* words into their mouths, be they nomad women, children, or university lecturers" (Kelly, 29). The readers who reviewed the manuscript of *Sardines* for its original publisher, Heinemann, were nearly unanimous in insisting that the character of Ubax be rewritten to sound more like a child (a recommendation that Farah resisted). These views proceed from the expectation that a novel, by definition, should deal in psychological verisimilitude, an expectation that interferes with a recognition and productive reading of the mode in which Farah's work is cast.

Writing in a mode of intellectual debate requires that each of his characters be endowed with sufficient voice to express an understanding, particular to that character, of what it means to be human and to play roles in human communities. Because they are members of the intellectual elite of their society, it is not surprising to hear many of his characters speak in such a voice. Even characters without formal education or wide cultural experience, however, use articulate and subtle language to express their analytical understanding. As a result, the voices of Farah's characters are generally distinguishable from one another only by the distinct positions they represent, not by idiosyncrasies of style, personality, or psychology, or even by the formulas and conventions of the particular cultural languages they speak. In *Sweet and Sour Milk*, for example, Keynaan surely fits the description of "Satan," from a moral standpoint, as well as any of the characters to whom Farah has given voice. Furthermore, he is illiterate and a professional thug in the service of the General's state police—psychologically, a man of brute sensibilities. Nonetheless, when Farah portrays him in conversation with Loyaan, who accuses him of dishonesty to the dead Soyaan, the language he gives him to speak is that of a man who is conscious of his position and the positions of others in a complex field of political relations and who can clearly articulate the importance of such consciousness:

> Soyaan was being used by other factions. Unwittingly he got caught in the intricacy of tribal politics which he could not understand. . . .
> I breathe life into his name [by revising the story of his death]. I make him honourable. I give him life again. A school will be named after him, perhaps a street. He will live longer than you or I. You hold me responsible for his death. I believe I am responsible for the spiritual revival of his name. . . .
> I am the father. It is my prerogative to give life and death as I find fit. I've chosen to breathe life into Soyaan. And remember one thing, Loyaan: if I decide this minute to cut you in two, I can. The law of this land invests in men of my age the power. I am the Grand Patriarch. (*SSM,* 93–94)

Ubax, Medina's daughter in *Sardines,* is another example of a character expressing her own position within a debate with a verbal efficacy that would seem to be far beyond her natural reach, in this case that of an eight-year-old girl. In the following exchange between Ubax and

Medina, it is not the immature consciousness of a child that Ubax
expresses—she in fact objects when Medina places that construction on
her words. Rather it is a mature and clear-sighted consciousness speaking from the angle of vision on human relations afforded a child by her
position among adults:

> Ubax pondered then said: "You're either afraid of Sandra or you hate
> her, I'm not sure which." . . .
> "I neither hate nor fear Sandra," [Medina] said, spacing her words
> carefully. . . .
> "You've also told me that Sagal doesn't hate or fear losing to Cadar
> and Hindiya. They are friends as well. But I've seen Sagal's face when she
> talks about them. You both look the same when you're talking about
> people you're jealous of. I can tell. Shall I draw what you look like then?
> Or when you're with Xaddia?"
> "No. It isn't the same. You don't understand. You're still a child when
> it comes to understanding these things."
> "That's what you always say to win a point. . . ." (*Sardines*, 21)

In *Maps* the illiterate Oromo maidservant Misra speaks in a voice
endowed with the analytical vocabulary required to articulate to Aw-
Adan her subtle understanding of the effect of Askar's problematic birth
on his sense of identity: "To have met death when not quite a being,
perhaps this explains why he exists primarily in the look in his eyes. Perhaps his stars have conferred upon him the fortune of holding simultaneously multiple citizenships of different kingdoms: that of the living
and that of the dead; not to mention that of being an infant and an
adult at the same time" (*M*, 4).

What these examples serve to illustrate is that these characters'
voices are not distinguishable by their language from the voices of their
interlocutors—Keynaan's from Loyaan's, Ubax's from Medina's, Misra's
from Aw-Adan's—in each case, an intellectually untrained character in
conversation with a highly educated one. What distinguishes these
voices are the concepts of identity and relationship that they serve to
articulate. By extending the power of language to his characters equally
in this fashion, Farah renders them capable of significant action (that is,
of significant acts of imagination) in the world of ideas that they inhabit.

The power of language, however, takes on more particular forms in
the work of Farah than simply the capacity to speak. Indeed, he explores
the force of language itself as closely as he does the characters who use it
to reshape themselves and each other. Several motifs in his novels and

plays function rhetorically to associate language and power, to make language, in fact, in the mind of the reader a figure for the power to transform identities and relationships. One such motif is the supernatural power of language. In traditional Somali culture (as in many cultures) the power of words to effect direct change—especially negative change—in the physical and social world through their inherent force is taken very seriously. Farah's references to this belief on the part of his characters repeatedly suggest that language is not the stuff of unconstrained play and experimentation but serious business with serious consequences. Such references abound in his work. Respect for the supernatural power of language leads a fearful Koschin, for example, to destroy an amulet that he received as a child from his mother and that contains a sheikh's prophecy (*NN*, 5–6). Because Deeriye "misread God's message and misquoted it" while in prayer, he believes his visions and visits from Nadiifa are denied him (*CS*, 132). Nonno, as a young man, was punished for a more intentional transgression: "Power-hungry, I guessed that by replacing a set of magical codes with some of my own making, I might rule the wind and the birds which ride upon it" (*Secrets*, 298). In *The Offering* and *A Spread of Butter*, a story is told of a mother who, by uttering a prayer, brings the power of language to her mute son's lips. He immediately uses that power to utter a vile obscenity, whereupon she prays again and renders him mute once more.

The strongest figuration of this form of power—and the first—in Farah's writing is the curse. His entire published work as a novelist, in fact, begins with the words "He could only curse" (*FCR*, 3). In this opening passage of *From a Crooked Rib*, Ebla's grandfather represents Ebla—to himself, to others, and to God—as a crucial support to his own life: " 'May the Lord take me away if Ebla dies before myself,' he had said several times before, in private and in public" (*FCR*, 5). When Ebla leaves rather than remain under the terms of his account of her, he gives careful thought to the question, "must he or mustn't he curse her?" before "very softly and quietly" uttering what prove to be his last words: "May the Lord disperse your plans, Ebla. May He make you the mother of many a bastard. May He give you hell on this earth as a reward" (*FCR*, 5–6). Though Ebla's brother later tells her that her grandfather died "of shock" (*FCR*, 137), the opening passage strongly associates the old man's death with the power of his own pronouncements concerning Ebla's relationship to himself. In *Maps* Askar has a long dream in which he experiences a literal loss of identity. When asked "the cause of this torment" by an old man in his dream, he answers, "My mother placed a curse on my head," to which the old man responds, "A mother's curse is by far the heaviest burden a human has carried on his head" (*M,* 61, 63). In *Secrets* Kalaman and Sholoongo, as children, take blood vows of loyalty to one another, sealing these with a curse: "May death rock the fundament of our earth, if either of us breaks this vow" (*Secrets,* 112). As adults they indeed break their vow, and their curse resonates in the death of Fidow (trampled by an elephant) and eventually of Nonno—"both the elephant and I," Nonno remarks, "were referred to, in our particular ways, as 'fundaments'" (*Secrets,* 112). In each of these examples, characters experience the supernatural power of language over human lives as quite real, a power that is invoked in connection with narratives that assert an idea of the self by positing a relationship with another.

Another motif by which Farah persistently associates language with power is the esoteric power of language, the power of inclusion and exclusion. This form of power too is closely tied to the management of identities and relationships. Its most frequent manifestation is the conspicuous recourse by a character in conversation to a language that is comprehensible to some but not to others. Koschin and Mohamed, for example, speak in Somali to exclude Mohamed's wife, Barbara (*NN,* 72–73). Ubax complains to Nasser, "Medina and Samater always talk in a foreign language when they don't want me or Idil to listen. . . . They speak Somali when they want to shut Sandra or Atta out" (*Sardines,* 102). Misra and her lover Aw-Adan speak to one another in Amharic, eliciting from Askar a similar complaint: "Misra and he had a world of their own, a language of their own, and so when they lapsed into it or chose to dwell in the secretive universe of its nuances and expressions and gestures, I felt totally excluded" (*M,* 29). Misra is herself excluded from news of her own impending mastectomy when Salaado speaks about this to Askar in her presence, but in Italian (*M,* 189). Sometimes Farah combines the esoteric and supernatural powers of language. When Misra utters curses, for example, she does so in Amharic (*M,* 10). Zubair's first wife, in *Gifts,* takes a jinn for a lover and is overheard in "conversation presumably with jinns, whom the young men couldn't see and whose language they couldn't comprehend"; and Zubair's wedding night with his second wife is interrupted by "a drone of jinns . . . speaking to one another, inside his head, in an alien language" (*G,* 34). Hilaal and Askar overhear outside their window "the voice of the master of *mingis* ceremony singing, right in the heart of Mogadiscio, in a language

. . . the spirits understand—and that language is not Somali. It is Boran" (*M, 201*).

In these ways Farah treats the esoteric power of language, like its supernatural power, as a potentially negative force—destructive in its supernatural form, divisive in its esoteric form. If esoteric language can divide, however, it also has the power to bridge divisions. Just as Farah's characters use language to restrict access to certain relationships and forms of identity, so do they extend such access by means of the same instrument. Several characters in *Secrets*—Madoobe, Fidow, and Nonno—are able to communicate by secret languages with birds and animals. In *Sardines* and *Gifts*, Medina and Mire both occupy their private hours translating books from European languages into Somali. In *Close Sesame* we find characters turning to mutually foreign but comprehensible languages in order to communicate—Natasha's American parents speak to Deeriye in Spanish, for example, and he to them in Italian—and children interpret for adults across the boundaries of language and literacy, a pattern of communication to which Farah assigns particular importance in the text: "Nadiifa had sought Mursal's assistance in reading and writing letters to [Deeriye in prison], Nadiifa a woman who did not know how to read or write but knew how to speak and Mursal who knew how to read and write and also how to understand her speech; and Natasha who could read and write but who to communicate with Deeriye had had to resort to using [her son] Samawade who spoke her language, she who didn't speak Somali well and therefore needed help. Is this not the dynamics of history?" (*Sardines, 186*). The "dynamics of history," in the world Farah represents, indeed turn on the capacity of human beings to negotiate their linguistic differences. The issue, however, is not one of communication, pure and simple. If it were, Farah could have dispensed with the cumbersome mechanics of translation in these narrative situations and allowed his characters simply to speak the same language. Rather, it is significant in Farah's political vision that the discursive world his characters occupy is multilingual, that many languages exist by which to negotiate identity through self-narration, and that control of the means to self-narration, of language, may itself become a form of power to be negotiated or contested.

The supernatural and the esoteric powers of language, then, are among the motifs by which Farah keeps his reader's attention on the potential force of language as the means by which autonomous selves build—and in many cases rebuild again and again—the social world

they inhabit in common. The function of these motifs in Farah's analysis
is figurative. The actual and instrumental force of language in the act of
self-narration, however, lies not in the supernatural or the esoteric but in
the notional power of language. It is in the exercise of this power that
the action central to Farah's novels and plays proceeds.

We take the term *notional* from an oft-quoted passage in *Maps* in
which Hilaal asks Askar, "Do you find truth in the maps you draw?"
Askar answers, "Sometimes . . . I identify *a* truth in the maps which I
draw. When I identify *this* truth, I label it as such, pickle it as though I
were to share it with you, and Salaado. I hope, as dreamers do, that the
dreamt dream will match the dreamt reality—that is, the invented
truth of one's imagination. My maps invent nothing. They copy a given
reality, they map out the roads a dreamer has walked, they identify a
notional truth" (*M,* 216). We conventionally speak of maps as projections of actual features on the surface of the planet, recording, for example, the locations of roads available to all. Askar's formulation preserves
the sense that maps "copy a given reality," but the reality they project is
an invention of his own imagination. They "invent nothing" themselves,
but have the power to "identify a notional truth," to propose to others a
reshaping of the actual world such that its roads match those invented
by a dreamer to walk upon at the center of his own dream. This
"notional truth" of Askar's maps is what we mean by the notional power
of language: the power to stand for something quite real—an inward
idea of a world shaped to fit an idea of oneself—and to project that idea
outward to meet other ideas, other notional truths. Thus the action of
Farah's novels and plays conceived in these terms plays itself out both
internally, within the individual consciousnesses of his characters, and
externally, as acts of invention projected outward into the social world;
and the articulation between these interior and exterior realms is of
increasing importance in the development of his work.

As a wholly internal event, as it sometimes occurs in the work of
Farah, the act of self-invention frees one from the resistance of the outside world, but at the same time it may serve to reinforce one's isolation
from that world. This is the dominant pattern in the two novels written
during Farah's apprenticeship period, *From a Crooked Rib* and *A Naked
Needle.* In the first, Ebla reinvents herself by closing her eyes and "wandering into nothingness and creating in her mind something which had
never existed before, and which would never exist" (*FCR,* 161). Largely
incapable (until her reappearance in *Sardines*) of living other than by
submission to men and controlling only the terms of her submission (as

in her temporary and furtive marriage to Tiffo), she takes refuge in the isolation of her own mind, exercising the power to open new spaces for herself but expressing impotence to fill that space—and both by the same acts of imagination. Like Ebla, Koschin possesses the imaginative resources to reinvent himself but lacks the clarity of vision (until his own shadowy resurfacing in the Dictatorship Trilogy) to project that self into a potentially transformative encounter with the outside world. He resigns from his teaching job, for example, and writes to the Ministry of Education about abuses at his school but insists in the letter, "I personally do not wish to filthy my hands," and says of his resignation, "That has nothing to do with my loyalty to the revolution. This was personal" (*NN,* 17, 149). His mutterings about the state of Somali society—to Nancy, his friends, and himself—are devoid of reference to any responsible role that he himself might play.

In Farah's mature work we still find instances of wholly internal self-invention, but they arise more clearly as temptations to escape or as consequences of trauma, not as the dominant pattern by which individual autonomy expresses itself. Deeriye, for example, possesses and often exercises the notional power to challenge the world as he finds it, power that remains beyond the grasp of Ebla and Koschin, but there are significant costs to such challenges. Consequently he too sometimes turns inward, to his mystical visions, as a means of intentional isolation or of escape into the illusion of an uncontested social reality: "And why visions and conjured up dreams and invented life? . . . These visions guided him through a forest of contradictory pathways, led him to a clearing in which he stood, a man above the squabbles and quagmires of inter-clan rivalries and disputes; led him away from the political amalgams of irreconcilable views; they took him to a place of quiet peace where there lived, together with him, others who were always in agreement and where there existed a loving understanding between the ruler and the ruled" (*CS,* 181). For others, like Khaliif and Mukhtaar in *Close Sesame,* escape from the pressure of social reality into an isolating self-invention takes the form of madness, of imagination no longer answerable either to the world or to the self: "What was it that made these sensible men disintegrate? Why is it that they hear *voices* from their unrecognizable selves, voices which originate from deep down in their victimized existences? A mind so overcrowded with ideas and things, a mind made into the symbol of disorder and indecision by the powers that be . . . cannot tell apart the good shadows from the bad, cannot distinguish between the virtuous and the wicked" (*CS,* 120). Askar takes similar refuge in the isolation of his mind—not in long-term madness but in the periodic delirium of illnesses induced, as Hilaal indicates, by outward events that Askar would rather not deal with: the scandalous behavior of an Adenese neighbor, the recapture of the Ogaden by Ethiopia, the report that Misra has betrayed the Western Somali cause, and the news of her death (*M, 239*). Thus Farah depicts a variety of modes in which a limited form of the essential human act of reimagining the world and one's role in it can take place, modes that range from speculative meditation to mystical vision to madness and delirium, depending on the degree of psychic pressure to which the imagining self is subject. So long as such imaginings are wholly self-contained, however, they cannot lead to a transformation of the world but can serve only as respite and refuge from the world or, at best, as a kind of laboratory for a deferred encounter with the world.

The full notional power of language arises when self-invention is brought under the control of the inventor and projected outward into social reality to engage other accounts of the world, other maps of a social terrain occupied in common. Such a map is Medina's "room of her own." Unlike the private mental refuge that Ebla creates, "which had never existed before, and which would never exist," Medina lives in a room that is originally the work of many hands besides her own and that she remakes to the measure of her own vision. The verbs in which this metaphor is developed in the opening page of *Sardines*—reconstruct, repaint, redecorate, replaster, rebuild, rework—emphasize this operation of transforming what is there already (*Sardines, 3*). This reconstruction of her own life serves as a stage from which to enter and act upon the larger world, to assert a different account of the world from the General's and from her mother-in-law's. Sagal too rescripts accounts of her political world with her own invented self in leading roles. She articulates to her mother "the future she had invented for herself . . . —what she dreamt of doing and what was going to happen to give meaning to all that she held close to her heart" and assures her that, if this future goes awry, she will invent another, and another: "I will dream again and again" (*Sardines,* 41, 43).

Medina's "room" and Sagal's "dream" are particular strategies for resolving an issue faced by many characters in this novel: the problem of where to position oneself in relation to political structures, both private and public, that one wants to change—whether to work from the inside or from the outside. In a great variety of ways, this same problem is at issue in the actions of Samater (a member of the group of ten who opts for a time to serve as a government minister), of Dulman (who sings both for the official stage and for the underground theater, before refusing to perform altogether), of Amina (who must decide whether to collaborate in the politicization of her own rape), of Atta (who places negritude before democracy in allocating her personal loyalties), of Sandra (who does the same with respect to socialism), and of a number of other characters. In each case, however, the staging, the action of the novel, is all in the invention, in the narration of one's own role. As readers, we do not see Medina attack the General or the matriarch, Samater make ministerial decisions, or Dulman perform. These actions are reported indirectly. The drama played out directly under the eyes of the reader is the clash of ideas, the lived debate of characters consciously articulating and demonstrating their positions by word and by gesture.

This world, as we see it in *Sardines,* of self-inventing characters narrating themselves by the notional power of word and gesture on a shared stage of intellectual debate is the world that Farah represents in virtually all of his mature work. To read *Close Sesame,* for example, with an eye to such a world is to see that the central drama of the book, once again, is not to be found in a specific conflict between the General and his opponents. It lies instead in a confrontation—within Deeriye's own consciousness as well as between Deeriye and other characters—of different strategies for maintaining individual identity in the face of such conflicts. As we have seen in chapter 4, this is an especially complicated challenge for Deeriye because of the complexity of the self that he has constructed over the long course of his life, encompassing, on the one hand, political commitments at many levels of relationship and, on the other, an intensely private spiritual life and longing for peace. When his counterparts in this confrontation of strategies are the other clan elders he meets in the Baar Novecento, he has little trouble measuring their choices against his own: "Deeriye was glad these men sitting here never made part of the life he had invented for himself . . . as he has invented his own history, the date of birth astraddle two important events in the history of Africa, or a future worthy of a visionary; these men existed on their own, they were real as pain" (*CS,* 103–4). More troubling to Deeriye are his debates with Mursal. Here the question of how to maintain autonomy in the face of power focuses more sharply on an ongoing consideration of the terms under which recourse to violence might serve or undermine that purpose. The outcome of these debates is Deeriye's decision, a reversal of his previous position, to make an attempt on the life of the General.

This decision brings with it a moment of new critical understanding—the culmination of Deeriye's lifelong debate with himself—in which he examines and transforms, yet again, the narrative of his own identity in relation to power. It is the ultimate dramatic moment in the novel and a profound acknowledgment, on Deeriye's part, of the notional power of language:

> Then a sudden thought came to him as he walked. . . . The thought held him hostage for a long time. It made him slow down a little and in less than a minute he was saying loudly to himself, . . . "All our lives, mortals that we are, we misname things and objects, we misdefine, we misdescribe illnesses and misuse metaphors. Why, it is not my lungs: my face! Why, this suggests the loss of face, the loss of reputation, and nothing more than that! Why, this doesn't suggest the loss of faith, the spiritual loss, the spiritual famine which envelops one—right from the moment hundreds of heads of cattle rolled. I didn't lose face: I lost faith, yes, faith, in my own capability, faith in my people. . . . Nadiifa," he said to himself silently now, "spoke of my lungs as my soul: she didn't speak of my lungs as though they were my face. Which perhaps means she believes that my soul is struggling, has been struggling to free itself and join its Creator from the day the Italians made the cattle's heads roll. Why has this never occurred to me?" (CS, 235)

This is a densely elliptical passage, but it conveys a defining moment not only in Deeriye's life but in Farah's treatment of self-narration. The great importance of this moment is that it focuses Deeriye's attention, and the reader's, on the centrality of language and ideas, rather than on events and personalities, in fashioning and assessing the meaning and coherence of one's existence. All his life, Deeriye has aspired to Farah's "total faith in truth and justice," and all his life, "mortal that he is," he has been susceptible to the self-deceptions and self-aggrandizements that undermine that faith and that register in language and ideas as "misnaming," "misdefining," "misdescribing," and the "misuse of metaphors." Reexamining critically and more strongly than ever the language in which he has narrated himself, he identifies these misuses and transforms these metaphors. His whole self-understanding changes when his "lungs" cease to be a metaphor for his bodily weakness, as he had long taken them to be, and become one for his soul, when "face" ceases to be a metaphor for his personal worth and dignity and becomes one merely for his reputation in the eyes of others. As the language in which he tells his story to himself comes into focus in a new way, so does

the story itself, and the complex life and history that he has so consciously invented and reinvented at last present themselves to him as a
coherent whole. Deeriye's subsequent failed attack on the General, like
most such events in Farah's writing, is reported only indirectly and with
few details regarding the circumstances. The true narrative climax of the
novel, however, has already taken place in this final and triumphant
piece of self-narration.[6]

In Farah's representations of social reality, then, self-narration has the
value not simply of commentary but of human action itself at its most
significant, preceding and shaping all other forms of action. Recognizing
this emphasis, we can see more clearly both the attraction that the theater has held for Farah and the dramatic dimension of his novels. In his
play *Yussuf and His Brothers,* major events like executions and rescues all
happen offstage but not for the usual reasons of stagecraft: the difficulties of representing such events in a theater. The dramatic force, rather,
lies in the tension between Yussuf's struggle to form a nationalist resistance to colonial power and his strategic invention of himself as "everyone," as the whole nation, a narrative move that we have seen made by
the General and challenged by Medina in *Sardines.* That tension is
heightened as Yussuf's self-invention clashes with Hussen's, whose quite
different formulation of the self divides it radically in two and apportions responsibility between the two selves in ways that raise new problems. The notional force of these acts of language is the force of the
drama.

This drama of self-invention grows still more complex in *Maps,* in
which Askar struggles to deploy both Yussuf's strategy and Hussen's,
imagining himself as an individual identified with the nation and, at the
same time, as a self divided among different identities and different
responsibilities. To map these "notional truths" while remaining at the
center of his own map—as Medina occupies the center of her own
"room" and Sagal the center of her own dream—requires him, as it does
Yussuf, to reinvent other lives that exist already alongside his own, especially Misra's, lives that are intertwined with his but for which he can find
no place on his evolving map of himself as Somali nationalist. As he
moves from Kallafo to Mogadiscio he redraws his map around a new center when Hilaal encourages him to tell his story. In doing so, he recruits
other lives to his own narrative purposes: "You began from the beginning, a second time and a third time. Misra was the heroine of your tale
now and you played only a minor supporting role. Which was just as
well. You needed to tell 'Misra's story,' obviously. A story has to be about

someone else even if it is about the one telling it" (*M,* 141). This version of "Misra's story" is very much about Askar. Though his uncle and aunt praise the "honesty and openheartedness with which [Askar] narrated" this story, it is a highly selective one. His own emotions and desires displace Misra's at its center, his own "stare," according to his account, discloses "her guilt," and he intentionally suppresses his knowledge of her "divining powers" so as not to "impress Hilaal and Salaado wrongly" (*M,* 141–42). The denatured Misra that emerges from this narrative has been rendered a relic of Askar's past, removed from her central position in his life, while he is out of range of any claims she might make on him. Duniya's self-narration in *Gifts* is again a transformation of a self originally shaped by others. Having thoughtlessly accepted the gift of a horse as a young girl, she later finds herself, as a consequence, remade as someone else's gift, given by her father to Zubair. The elaborate reinvention of herself that is the novel, accordingly, involves her in debates about the dynamics of gift giving and receiving, and in consequence her entire world of domestic relations is reconfigured. In *Secrets* Farah offers the most literal possible representation of a character reinventing herself, the shape-shifter Sholoongo, who not only physically transforms herself into other creatures but does so for the purpose of discovering and bringing to light the secret transformations of others: Nonno, who fled from the north and took on a new name and identity; Yaqut and Damac, who remade themselves as a family from the human ruin in which they were left by rape; and Kalaman, who affirms his own invented identity as the inheritance of these transformed selves.

The notional power of language as Farah's characters wield it, then, is not locked up in an interior play of imagination. Rather, through language the force of imagination enters the social world, projects into that world new versions of identity, and thereby affects the lives of other imagining subjects who must negotiate these versions in political relationships. By this mode of action the imagination becomes an ethical faculty because self-invention, the product of the imagination, acts outwardly as a source of pressure on other lives, pressure that is political in the sense in which we have defined it in chapter 4: a force that inevitably shifts, expands, or restricts the terms available for the negotiation of human possibilities. We have described the whole of Farah's work as an investigation of the power of language to support or to suppress intellectual debate. We can now see that the result he seeks by that investigation, most fundamentally, is a clearer view of the workings of the ethical imagination.

The search for that clarity is apparent from the beginning of *From a Crooked Rib,* but the clarity itself emerges slowly over the long progression of Farah's novels and plays. The starting point is Ebla's failure of imagination. She knows that she wants "to be free and be herself" (*FCR,* 12) but can conceive of freedom only as escape and has no idea of how to make good on it: "To escape. To be free. To be free. To be free. To escape. These were inter-related. How to escape? Where to escape to?" (*FCR,* 14). Never does the new life at the empty center of this dream of freedom as escape assume shape or substance. She opens for herself—and for readers who will follow Farah's subsequent work—the question of notional truth but does so in a way that separates mind from action: "But what is truth—that which corresponds to the notions we have in mind or that which corresponds to our doings? Why do we think differently from the way we behave?" (*FCR,* 18). Consequently Ebla puts physical distance between herself and the threatened marriage to Giumaleh, but Giumaleh's idea of her as a woman follows and controls her to the end of the novel. These ruminations on the nature of truth are an explicit attempt to justify a convenient lie and part of an effort throughout the novel to rationalize the effects of her actions on others, to escape responsibility for escape. This inability to account for herself ethically also diminishes her reinvention of self. Farah's initial insight into the ethical imagination is important, then, in establishing a link between self-invention and social responsibility. The same insight emerges from *A Naked Needle,* in which Koschin slips the hold of one commitment after another but fails to imagine himself as anything more than an absence of commitment.

One of Farah's clearest early images of the active struggle for imaginative freedom in the projection of notional truth—in anticipation of Askar's maps—is the ball on which the twins draw a map of the world in *Sweet and Sour Milk.* This image is developed throughout the novel in recurring memories that come to Loyaan of himself and Soyaan as children playing on a beach with the globe they have drawn:

> And out of the blue clearness of the waters emerges Keynaan, the tyrant: in his right hand, he grips a club at its butt-end; in his left, the rubber ball which he has torn in two, the rubber ball upon which the twins had together drawn a complete and an illustrated mini-atlas. A world with no frontiers. A world of their own fantasies. "I don't want you to believe everything these whites teach you. I want you simply to get some kind of certificate so that you can get jobs as clerks with the government. Just

that. 'The world is round. The sun is stationary.' What nonsense is that?"
(*SSM*, 131)

Here is a stark, graphic, and quite literal encounter among three different ideas of the world. From the standpoint of the reader, all are at odds
with reality. Keynaan, it is important to notice, does not object to the
round-world version simply because he knows no better. He does so
explicitly because he identifies it as an idea of the world promoted by
"whites," part of their effort to persuade his children to conduct their
lives in ways that correspond to that idea. Having different lives for
them in mind, he literally transforms their world in such a way as to
match his own narrative, in which, as we have seen, he is "the Grand
Patriarch." In reshaping it, he does not, as we might expect, flatten it,
though he carries a club that could have served that purpose. Instead he
tears it in two, asserting once again his right as patriarch to cut his own
children in two if he chooses. For the twins, this "world of their own fan-
tasies" is a world "without frontiers," one that corresponds neither to
their father's patriarchal idea of the world and his role in it nor to the
Europeans' colonial idea of the world and their own controlling presence. As an "illustrated mini-atlas," their world is varied and detailed,
not a blank emptiness, but no political borders exist to impede movement within it. In response to Keynaan's act, Soyaan swears that he will
kill his father one day. Like Keynaan, though from a very different position, he is alert to the profound ethical import of the notional truths
that engage one another at this moment, to the power each of these
incommensurate ideas of the world has to undermine the others. Soyaan's eventual participation in the group of ten, continued through Loyaan, is, at its most fundamental, an engagement in this ethical struggle
of the imagination.

Soyaan and Loyaan, then, bring to the imagined freedom sought by
Ebla and Koschin the presence of a responsible self at the center of a
world shaped by ideas. In Medina, as we have seen, the consciousness
grows of the other voices one must displace in order to assert the autonomy of that presence. Deeriye represents yet a further step toward an
understanding of the workings of the ethical imagination.

For Deeriye the advancement of insight is that, in displacing other
voices to develop his own, he cannot simply dispose of them, because
they are not all hostile voices, enemies who can be cut from the pack
and separately targeted, like Keynaan, the General, or Idil. His lifelong
self-invention, the history of world and self that he narrates, is created

out of and in continuing relation to a whole, complex society of voices and ideas. We can hear this insight in the explanation he offers Zeinab for his habit of what she calls his "imagining things": "Did I ever tell you," he asks, "why I conjure up interlocutors, why I have visions, why it is that I invent histories, why I try to create symbolic links between unrelated historical events . . . ?" (*CS,* 229). By way of answer, he reviews a lifetime of people and events, insisting that what he invented was not the fact that they existed or that they existed in relation to himself but only the meaning that their existence took on within those relationships. He takes his marriage as an example: "What did I invent? A link with my wife Nadiifa whom I loved and still love and whose feet I washed and will wash any day in heaven or earth, did I invent that? No, I did not. I made myself available to her and therefore since she loved me too *she* invented me; and I, her" (*CS,* 229, emphasis in the original). He concludes this review with one of the clearest formulations to this point in Farah's writing of the essentially social nature of self-invention:

> I could talk on and on, describing how I came by the thoughts of which I am made, for I am a collage of many notions and some of them are yours and some are Mursal's and some are Nadiifa's and some come from Natasha and some from Rooble; and so someone never goes away for ever—one can always call that part of oneself which is from the vanished person and talk to *it* or *him* or *her.* We are not only ourselves, we are *others* too, those whom we love, those who have influenced our lives, who have made us what we are. Do you understand? (*CS,* 231, emphasis in the original)

Zeinab may not in fact understand—but Askar does, and Duniya, and Kalaman, and other characters who inhabit the world of Farah's second trilogy, who understand that the most personal of self-inventions, if it is genuine, is immediately and enduringly social, and many of whom experience, as literally as Deeriye, the persistence of other lives within their own.

As we have pointed out, Deeriye is utterly unlike his author, who chooses an elderly, asthmatic, devoutly religious, politically militant clan patriarch to be the crucible of this insight. In the second trilogy, however, the same insight is developed through characters who share with their author much in the way of experience and perspective: Askar, who grows up in Kallafo in a multiethnic, multilingual community and goes to Mogadiscio as an adolescent to finish his education; Duniya, Bosaaso, and Mire, who are highly educated urban professionals; Kalaman, a cosmopolitan young man who earns his living as the very young Farah first earned his, preparing written texts for others.

In the second trilogy this developing understanding of the ethical imagination is brought down from the heights of Deeriye's august wisdom and its workings allowed to develop in a much wider (if still, in the main, socially elite) world. In *Maps* the wisdom of the aged, as we find it in the previous novel, is introduced in germinal form as the mentality of the infantile and the maternal in the characters of Askar and Misra. In one of his narrative voices Askar says of his outlook as a very young child, "To you, she was the cosmos and hers was the body of ideas upon which your growing mind nourished," a view that Misra shares: "He cannot imagine a world without my reassuring self" (*M,* 10–11). When Askar is seven years old, Misra finds him "behaving as though he were a man and she a creature of his own invention," while "she believed she was the one who made him who he was" (*M,* 107). This initial instinct of oneness between infant and mother is still far from the subtle culmination of understanding that Deeriye expresses to Zeinab, but its importance is precisely that it *is* a starting point in a process of maturing consciousness, that Farah's choice of a child, for the first time, as his protagonist allows him to investigate the development of this way of situating one's imaginings in relation to others. Askar's identification of himself with his foster-mother, Misra, is compounded by his even closer identification of self with his mother, Arla, and the intensity of these does not fade, despite his futile attempts at denial.

Maps is not, however, a story of arrested development—once again, psychological realism is not Farah's aim. Instead he traces the development of a character who, as he matures, grows more, not less, conscious of his own notional power of self-invention and of the fact that much of the substance of his inventions comes from the lives of those closest to him. Askar's predicament is that he is unable to alter that fact, unable to draw instead on the resources of his own autonomous self as he grows into an adult's knowledge of social complexity and the variety of claims on his identity. It is not a happy predicament, but the crisis of consciousness that he narrates in the novel results precisely from this intersection of personal self-invention and social responsibility. Askar's unmet challenge to narrate his life in a way that preserves his own imaginative freedom while allowing for the seemingly irreconcilable conditions of freedom of those he knows to be part of his self-invention—the Oromo woman Misra and those Somali political subjects with whom he identifies himself—is a crisis of the ethical imagination.

Having staged that crisis in such stark terms in the opening of the second trilogy, Farah goes on in *Gifts* and *Secrets* to develop characters working to resolve it. Duniya enters adult life a product of exchanges of material goods and interpersonal power. She reinvents herself as a being who exists outside such a system of exchange and expresses the notional force of this reinvention by excluding gift giving and coercion from the sphere of her family and friendships while opening her own imagination to a different kind of exchange, a sharing of dreams. Kalaman enters adult life a product of received ideas about families and lovers and what he ought to expect for himself from these. Exposed to the truth of his own origins and of the lives of his parents and grandfather, he joins willingly in a collective reinvention of this history. Nonno responds to the challenge of the ethical imagination more fully than any of Farah's characters to date, presenting a model of self-consciousness as a "collage of many notions" that surpasses even Deeriye's. A victim of his own hunger to control others as a youth, he has been forced to "overhaul his identity" (*Secrets*, 113). As a family elder he now understands and accepts, with all the "tolerance" and "magnanimity" that Talaado attributes to him, the importance of the many roles he plays in the identity constructions of those around him (*Secrets*, 297). Allowing the reconstructed versions of himself that these entail to stand, he preserves at the same time his own space of imaginative freedom, a pattern he describes in one of his conversations with himself:

> I am asking if somebody of my age nobility, my description and disposition, has an identity outside the perimeters of the one which other persons have invented, each constructed identity having a value, the mintage of a made-up currency. To Kalaman, for instance, I am a place, a vase capable of receiving the affections with which he fills it. To Yaqut, I am the threshold of an imagined hurdle of self-appraisal, an offspring's tread traversing the face of a huge mountain, a most risky undertaking, especially when there is no foothold. To Kalaman's mother, I am a serpent of the aquatic variety, dark as the mysteries it guards. . . . In short, I am many in one, and I am *other* too. (*Secrets*, 107)

At the representational level of Farah's practice as a writer, then, the second trilogy is the fruition of a long process of development. Although it was written during a period of disintegrating public order in Somalia, a disintegration that is in evidence in the background of *Secrets,* the answer it makes to its own era in Somali history is to portray the construction of a different kind of social order in the domestic sphere, one generated in the ethical imaginations of its inhabitants and established through the interplay of the notional power of language.

We next turn our attention from the representational to the artistic level of Farah's treatment of language and imagination, from the fictional characters and events he depicts to the rhetorical presence of the writer in the text. It is a strong presence, one that is established, not by means of a specific persona addressing the reader as author, but through conspicuous artistic choices about the elements arrayed in the text. Indeed, it would be surprising if Farah's novels and dramas of consciousness did not include a prominent, self-conscious role for the writer. That role is to offer in his own narrative practices a model of a world of social discourse established on the order of the ethical imagination.

Farah has said, "What I like to do, in telling a story, is . . . to allow very many different competing views to be heard, which in a sense points to the democratic drift of my writing, the drift of *tolerance*. Tolerating the views of other people and coexisting with the contradictions . . . means to me what democracy is" (Interview, 1993a, 63). In his writing the text itself represents just such a democracy, even though its subject may be one or another form of oppression and even though some of its characters may not be the least bit tolerant. What makes Farah's text a democracy is the writer's distribution of voice, his extension of the notional power of language to the characters he invents. This development of voice in his characters, as we have described it, has directly related but contrary consequences for the writer's own narrative voice: a muting of the writer's judgment to allow the debate among his characters to arise freely and be heard. Because his characters are analytically conscious of their own positions in the world and of those of others around them, and because they are capable of articulating those positions, the "business of intellectually analysing" their ideas, as Farah calls it, is work that the writer delegates to them to do in their own voices. Characters developed in such a way do not require a narrator to perform that analysis for them. With few exceptions, therefore, statements of judgment in Farah's writing—and such statements fill the pages of his novels and plays—are formulated, either directly or indirectly, from the position of one character or another, not from the independent position of the writer.

In this relationship between the voices of characters and the voice of the writer we can see an analogy that is constantly and crucially at play in Farah's work between each character's own self-invention and the writer's invention of the larger world of the text. Like Deeriye—and

like every one of us, according to Farah's understanding of human subjectivity—the writer of these texts is a "collage of many notions," of
many ideas and voices, all present and alive, contending to be heard
and to work their influence on an imaginatively evolving version of the
world in which each holds an interest. Deeriye hears and acknowledges
these other life possibilities intersecting with his own as do, in different
ways and to different degrees, Medina, Askar, Hilaal, Duniya, Nonno,
and others; and their most important use of language is to give voice to
ideas that arise from these intersecting possibilities. It is by the active
workings of this analogy—and not by his own discursive statements—
that Farah renders judgments of his characters: the "drift of tolerance"
by which the writer imagines these characters is the visible standard by
which their own imaginations are to be measured; at the same time,
the positions they take and the projects to which they commit themselves give direction, shape, and limits to that drift in the imaginative
activity of the writer. In this analogical relationship, the voices of characters and the writer's voice serve different but complementary purposes. In Farah's writing, characters have voices in order to articulate
ideas. The work of the writer's own distinctive forms of language is to
create in the text conditions in which a democracy of voices can thrive,
that is, in which different voices not only are heard but must be
attended to.

This intimate analogical relationship between the imagination of the
writer in the text and the imaginations of his characters anchors the
indeterminacy of Farah's writing and turns it from the purposes of
"postmodern experimentalism" to those of intellectual debate centered
on human freedom. Indeterminacy—the lingering presence of simulta-
neous possibilities, unresolved ambiguities, alternative "versions" of the
truth—is not an inescapable condition of writing for Farah, as it is for
the postmodernist; it is a self-conscious instrument of the ethical imagination and one of the distinctive forms of the writer's language in the
text. It does not signal epistemological failure but is a strategy for conceiving the world that holds multiple possibilities in willed suspension.
It is a strategy that recognizes that while truth is not absolute, it is also
not illusory or infinitely variable—it is notional: a negotiation between
an idea of the world suited to the expression of one's own freedom and
the ideas of those with whom one shares that world. While mysteries
abound, therefore, in the writing of Farah, while they often seem to have
more than one solution, and while readers, characters, and the writer
himself are often unable to see these solutions, we are asked in his writ-

ing to believe that the available explanations do matter and must be considered.

From *Sweet and Sour Milk* onward, indeterminacy is an increasingly common imaginative strategy in the work of Farah. Among the more startling open questions in *Maps,* to select an example, is that of Askar's menstruation. The text provides several possible accounts of this event. Although we have no way of determining which is accurate, and therefore all remain possible, we can nonetheless grasp what is at stake in that determination. If the blood on Askar's groin is a natural and ordinary effect of infection or tension, his separably male identity is preserved. If Misra smeared it on him during the night while pretending otherwise, he is justified in seeing in her, as he sometimes does, a psychic predator whose intention is to swallow his identity in hers. If it is actually his menstrual blood, his imaginative engagement in the condition of women becomes imperative, for it establishes a real and organic connection between that condition and his own. If that menstrual blood is his mother's, he is further compelled to attend to her voice as it survives inside him and to the more specific injustices of which she is the victim. Moreover, the question of Askar's menstruation is explicitly associated with another form of anomalous bleeding that he experiences, not once, but repeatedly: "I awoke and there was a taste of blood in my mouth. . . . I could not account for it. . . . And I couldn't help recalling the day I 'menstruated' " (*M,* 214). In some of these episodes he reports only the taste of blood and in others the actual presence of blood in his mouth, associating his experience of menstruation with the oft repeated and deep-seated connection in the text between blood and enmity: "In short, life *is* blood, and the shedding of one's blood for a cause and for one's country; in short, life is the drinking of enemy blood and vengeance" (*M,* 244). Identification of the "cause" and of the "enemy" is a shifting affair, however, though it is an insistent one, as the images of violence here and elsewhere suggest. Because the writer holds as indeterminate the truth of Askar's menstruation, therefore, Askar is compelled to attend to the claims of competing causes and voices in apportioning his own life energies, despite his wish to hear, in a single, clear voice, the answer to the question "Who is Askar?"

An equally puzzling and unresolved matter in *Gifts* (again, one among many) concerns the dreams that Duniya and Bosaaso appear to share. Asleep and alone in his bed, Bosaaso "diverted his mind by telling himself (and Duniya in her dream, of which he was part) the story of an only son of an only parent," that is, Bosaaso's own story (*G,* 40). As

Bosaaso wakes the next morning, the reader awakens to the possibility that Bosaaso and Duniya have shared more than a dream:

> Certain that Duniya was with him and had enjoyed hearing the story of his childhood, Bosaaso postponed the instant when he opened his eyes. Somewhere in the echoey two-storey house where he lived alone, a door opened and banged shut, a bath-tub was run and a toilet flushed. His face tightened in the sad expectation of finding her gone or that she might not hear him or answer his call. Yet with his eyes still closed, his outstretched hand informed him that in his bed there was a depression to his right, where she had slept; and his cheeks felt stroked, touched by her lips, kissed. (*G,* 44)

Duniya is not, in fact, physically there when he rises—and her decision to sleep with Bosaaso comes much later in the book—though perhaps she is present by a kind of proxy: "He gave a start when he heard a high-pitched whistle and then saw a half-collared kingfisher in the kitchen, settled in the very chair where Duniya might have been" (*G,* 44), a bird that, by its description, appears to be the same one that earlier enters Duniya's room as she is reminiscing at length about her own childhood and her first marriage (*G,* 32). At breakfast Bosaaso's memories turn to *his* former marriage, and to the death of his wife and baby. The next chapter bears a heading that begins, "Duniya wakes from a dream in which Bosaaso tells her a story" (*G,* 51). Remembering that dream, she recalls details that come not from the version of Bosaaso's dream that we have just read but from his waking reminiscence (possibly occurring at the same moment)—but these details concerning Bosaaso's wife and baby (whom Duniya knew in her capacity as nurse) are different from those passing through his own memory (*G,* 52).

Farah's intentional practice in his writing is not to "blur the line between the real and the fantastic," not to leave the reader in doubt as to whether a passage represents a dream or waking reality—"I'm tempted now and again to do it," he has said, "but I don't" (Interview, 1992, 51). Though that temptation seems especially strong in *Gifts*—in the preternatural behavior of birds and insects, for example—dreams and memories are carefully labeled as such in the text. What is indeterminate is the nature of the connection, if any, between the consciousness of Bosaaso and that of Duniya, an indeterminacy that Farah is at pains to make the reader aware of. The reason that this open question is brought so strongly to our attention is that the different possible explanations have different implications for the issues placed before the ethi-

cal imagination, issues having to do, in this novel, with the power of personal exchange. One such explanation (consistent with the numerous references to the supernatural in the text) is that some spiritual force is at work in the world of the novel, operating through the medium of their dreams and thoughts and providing a specific attachment between Duniya and Bosaaso. If so, they are not merely drawn to each other but fated for each other, and such a spiritual connection is a form of belonging that is not to be denied by Duniya's desire to control her participation in relations of exchange. Another possible explanation is that these partially overlapping dreams and memories bespeak the extraordinary mental (as distinct from spiritual) openness of Duniya and Bosaaso toward each other. If so, these dreams and memories point toward a mode of exchange quite different from that of gifts, an exchange of consciousness, a mode of exchange from which obligation may be absent but in which vulnerability to power may be a serious threat. Yet another possibility is that these dreams, daydreams, and perceptions are the quite separate products of separate consciousnesses sharing knowledge in common and driven by powerful desires in common. If so, the emphasis must be placed not on what they share but on how they differ, on the ethical responsibilities entailed in the fact that each, according to this explanation, plays a quite different role in his or her own narrative from the role invented for him or her in the narrative of the other.

Both of these examples, then, are instances of *strategic* indeterminacy. They do not arise out of the limitless, free-floating nature of truth or the inherent poverty of human resources for apprehending truth. They are instead products of the richness of human means for understanding and distinguishing the ethical consequences of the truths we might choose to invent. This same strategic indeterminacy accounts for the multiple "versions" of the reality of Soyaan's death, Medina's marital separation, Deeriye's visions, Yussuf's involvement in attacks on the government, Misra's betrayal, or the origin of Kalaman's name. In all of these instances the reader is required to pay attention in the same way to the differing consequences of these alternative versions. Strategic indeterminacy is therefore one of the ways in which Farah uses the power of language to "tolerate coexisting contradictions" and thereby to make the text a democracy of voices, one in which readers also participate through their own acts of interpretation.

Another equally distinctive form of language by which the writer's voice performs this work in the text is the extended metaphor, which

Farah began developing in his first novel. The following example comes as Ebla is trying to decide where to go when she makes her initial escape:

> Outside, the morning was lonely as if it were a widow whose second husband had just died and who intended never to re-marry but to face hardship and loneliness. The wind was sad as if it were a poor student whose ink-bottle had just broken into pieces and whose ink had coloured the ungrateful ground. The trees were standing apart as if they were afraid of each other and as if they would contaminate each other had they shaken and touched. Silence was the only refuge they all knew. That was the only language they could comprehend. The morning did not expect to be followed by another morning and another morning and another morning. The wind was glad to be sad for a change, maybe just as the student would be glad at breaking the bottle of ink to give him a legitimate excuse to stay outside the school premises. The trees were delighted to stay apart lest they should multiply and quarrel over space.
>   Ebla had reached a decision in the meantime. (*FCR*, 15)

In this very early instance we can see already the direction of Farah's development of the extended metaphor as a self-contained text within the text. In addition to its sheer length, several features of the passage are significant. Nothing in this cluster of similes, neither in the tenors nor in the vehicles, is directly involved in or related to the action of the narrative at this point. Rather the passage introduces another world, superimposed like a cinematic *mise en abime*. Nothing in the context surrounding the passage provides an "inside" by which to locate the opening reference to the morning outside, and it comprises elements of which Ebla has no knowledge: the feelings of a widow, a student's ink bottle. The action of the main narrative, in fact, appears to continue uninterrupted while a second rhetorical action, the development of the metaphor, is occurring simultaneously, a layering that we see confirmed in the concluding sentence, "Ebla had reached a decision *in the meantime*." The passage asserts the active and controlling presence of the writer not only in its disconnection from the narrative action but in the arbitrariness of the comparisons themselves—no one, reading that the sadness of the wind was like a student with a broken ink bottle, is likely to murmur "How true!" It has, nonetheless, an important contribution to make, and that is to evoke images of the conscious self taking its distance from prevailing social claims, and thereby to introduce "versions" of the debate that Ebla is engaged in with herself and with the social

voices inside her head, implicating the reader in this debate by creating
a need to close the space between metaphor and context.

The development of the extended metaphor in Farah's writing is a useful source of insight into the relationship he conceives between the power
of language and the ethical imagination. This device is especially prominent in *Sweet and Sour Milk,* where each chapter opens with *half* a simile, a
long vehicle beginning with the word *like,* whose tenor is left unstated
and, because the simile has no literal connection to the context, whose
meaning is once again dependent upon the imagination of the reader.
Chapter 1 of the novel, having to do with the disposition of Soyaan's body
after his death at the end of the Prologue, opens with the following: "Like
two tyres of a bicycle that never touch, never come together, to tell each
other of a wish to retire from serving an ungrateful master—each remains
isolated within its own limits of space, a system, a code of behaviour that
perpetuates and makes possible the serving; each is, for a purpose, locked,
tied, screwed to a bar which runs between, which makes possible the moving, gives the article an existence, offers the metallic composition a
name—and a label at that" (*SSM,* 19). One might wish to see here a comparison between the twin brothers and the two wheels of a bicycle, but a
more productive reading allows the simile to stand apart from literal connections to the text and to evoke instead a "version" of the debate in the
text concerning the roles of individual beings who find themselves elements in a larger order turned to purposes not their own.

What gives this device its significant and characteristic function in
Farah's work is not the technical form of the metaphorical comparison
but the features we have mentioned: length, self-containment, and an
evocation of debates that animate the larger text in which the metaphor
operates. Indeed, the device of the extended metaphor takes a variety of
forms in later texts, but recognizing that they *are* forms of the same
device allows us to make clearer sense of their meaning. Chapter 4 of
Sardines, for example, opens with a vignette, set off from the rest of the
chapter by ellipsis points, that operates in just this way. It differs in form
from previous examples in that it directly involves one of the characters
in the novel, but the passage, in which further metaphors are embedded,
stands apart from the context in the same way as earlier extended
metaphors and serves the same function. In this long paragraph (too
long to quote in its entirety) Samater is at his washbasin:

> His glance fell on a black ant which was caught in the overwhelming
> tide. Samater turned off the tap. In the quietness which followed, he gave

hints to the ant, hints by which it cleverly understood the subtle meaning of his moving hands. . . . Like a child's paper boat, the ant floated to
the rim of the sink. Then something quite unexpected took place, as sud-
den as an attack of hiccups: Samater thoughtlessly turned on the tap.
Not only that—his facial expression hardened, he seemed a person upon
whom a nightmare had called. . . . Then he saw what he had done and he
turned off the tap. A second later, he decided to throw the ant his hand
as a bridge. Its trembling legs climbed wristwards. . . . And the ant
started to feel freer, like a prisoner in a prison yard where the air is fresher
than that of the cell. (*Sardines*, 68)

The ant eventually falls to the floor and escapes. The incident is trivial in
the extreme and is hardly less so if one tries to read it as an insight into
Samater's character (his alternating cruelty and kindness toward an
insect). As an extended metaphor of the type we see in *Sweet and Sour
Milk,* however, the passage is immediately recognizable as an evocation
of the relationships of power and especially of the interplay of dependency and resistance that are at issue for Samater and others in *Sardines.*
What is significant about this development of the device is that it takes
a form in which not only the reader contemplates it but the character as
well.

In this convergence of reader and character in contemplation of the
metaphor, we can see—as we have seen in Farah's use of strategic indeterminacy—the notional power of language operating through the voice
of the writer. These are metaphors that reposition both reader and character to consider from different perspectives a world in which the terms
of individual autonomy are continually subject to renegotiation. The
extended metaphor, read in this way, takes a more powerful form still in
Maps in the dreams of Askar. In Chapter 4, for example, he dreams that
he changes into a very old man and then again into a young woman who
exchanges her body, piece by piece, for his in an attempt to escape being
the object of lust, leaving Askar feeling that he is in a foreign country
and that there is "something unfinished" about him (*M,* 59–63). In the
Interlude he dreams that he meets "a girl without a name, without a
country, without parents," who is wearing a "borrowed" skin and who
accuses him of being concerned only with the surface of things, not their
depth (*M,* 128–31). In Chapter 10 he dreams that he is floating with
others in a flood, that he dives repeatedly to the bottom and returns to
the surface each time feeling as if he were "an entirely different person,"
and that he is given water to drink from a skull, unable to determine
"whether it had belonged to a small person or a heavily built man or

woman" (*M*, 205 –7). In these and other dreams his state of mind is one of straining to understand what these events and images mean and how they come to be as they are—straining, in other words, to read his own dreams both as their dreamer and as their narrator to the audience of his listening selves. These dreams are clearly identified as such, having no direct consequence in Askar's waking world. Although they develop according to the transformational logic of dreams, they are not convincing or illuminating as projections of Askar's unconscious, because little of the material they transform has its source in Askar's experience. As extended metaphors, however, they function rhetorically in precisely the same manner as the earlier examples we have seen, drawing reader and character together in the contemplation of notions under debate in the larger text. In this particular novel and in each of these dream-metaphors, these debates center on the problem of absorbing other identities into one's own in the process of self-invention. Alert to the possible transmutations of the extended metaphor in Farah's writing, one can recognize it in still other forms, such as the persistent stream of birds and insects that fly in and out of Duniya's home and dreams in *Gifts,* evoking debates raised elsewhere in the novel about the openness of exchange in domestic relations.

Through strategic indeterminacy and extended metaphor, then, the writer in Farah's texts operates as a "collage of many notions" and the text itself as a carefully constituted democracy of voices, both in the service of the ethical imagination. The writer's voice becomes a "collage" in a more literal manner still—and to the same effect—by its incorporation of other texts, voices, and languages into itself, a device that further strengthens the analogy between writer and characters. It is important to notice both the variety of ways in which this happens and the sheer volume of references to and quotations from other texts in Farah's work. One such technique is the frequent incorporation of untranslated passages in other languages into Farah's English-language texts. A reader encounters Somali, Arabic, and Italian in most of the novels and plays, in addition to Russian and Latin in *A Naked Needle*. These passages vary in length from a few words embedded in a longer sentence of dialogue to the 11 lines in Somali from a poem by the Sayyid in *Close Sesame.* Another characteristic practice is the embedding of quotations in English (or English translation) from a great variety of other texts, ranging (to cite only a few instances) from Qur'anic verses in *A Naked Needle,* to a poem by John Wain in *Sweet and Sour Milk,* to a passage from Chinua Achebe's *Things Fall Apart* in *Sardines,* to a long quote from a 1956 speech by Haile Selassie in *Maps*, to excerpts from news-agency reports at the ends of half of the chapters in *Gifts*. A great many other writers and texts are invoked by name in Farah's work without being quoted. In *Sardines* alone these include the myth of Prometheus, *The Thousand and One Nights*, the Somali newspaper *Xiddigta Oktoober*, and works by Ivan Goncharov, Flann O'Brien, Anne Sexton, Bertolt Brecht, Malcolm X, Jean-Paul Sartre, György Lukács, LeRoi Jones, Eldridge Cleaver, Albert Camus, Hart Crane, Virginia Woolf, Allen Ginsberg, and Jack Kerouac.

Somali and Arabic proverbs and folktales provide still other voices to which Farah opens his writing. Proverbs, in fact, furnish the titles and epigraphs to his first two novels: "God created Woman from a crooked rib; and any one who trieth to straighten it, breaketh it" (*FCR,* 1); "The needle that stitches the clothes of people remains naked itself" (*NN,* n.p.). In one case, in fact, the same Somali proverb—"A stone thrown at a culprit hits nobody but the innocent" (*NN,* 143)—shows up with minor variations in wording in four different novels and one of the plays. Folktales and legends are more extensive examples of the same technique at work, the longest of these occurring in *Close Sesame,* in which Deeriye tells his grandson stories of the legendary sultan Wiil-Waal, and in *Gifts*, in which Mataan recounts tales of the northern African trickster figure Juxaa. All of these examples are of voices brought into the text from outside that the characters themselves hear or evoke, as they do the indeterminacies and some of the extended metaphors that we have examined.

Still another register in which such voices speak is one that only the reader hears: the epigrammatic quotes that precede sections of five of Farah's novels. These include passages of varying length and diverse sources: Samuel Beckett and Arthur Miller in *From a Crooked Rib;* Marianne Moore, Mary Webster, Wilhelm Reich, Philip O'Connor, Derek Walcott, W. B. Yeats, and James Dickey in *Sweet and Sour Milk;* Ho Chi Minh, Herman Melville, Malcolm Muggeridge, Moamed Iqbal, Bertolt Brecht, Rabindranath Tagore, William Blake, Paul Valéry, Ted Hughes, and Franz Kafka in *Sardines;* Patricia Beer, W. B. Yeats (twice), Hermann Hesse, George Lamming, Dylan Thomas, Oscar Wilde, Forrester Reid, and Czeslaw Milosz in *Close Sesame;* and Socrates, Charles Dickens, Søren Kierkegaard, Joseph Conrad, and the book of *Romans* in *Maps*.

This extensive (though far from exhaustive) catalogue of other textual voices incorporated into the writer's own voice underscores both their number and their variety. It is not surprising to learn that the writer in these texts, like every writer and every human being, is, in part, an amalgamation of many ideas and experiences that come from others. The important thing to notice about that amalgamation here, however, is that these ideas and experiences, these other voices, are not synthesized or fused. Instead they assert their separate identities and make their separate statements. They remain identifiable parts of a "collage," self-contained in the same manner, and to the same effect, as Farah's extended metaphors. In this way they make themselves available as part of the debate, the formulation of notional truths in the ethical imagination. "Proverbial" truths in Farah, for example, become notional because they are used in contexts in which they do not carry the automatic authority of folk wisdom but lend themselves instead to competing ideas in the mouths of different characters. An instance of this in Farah's first novel is the way in which Awill and Ebla struggle for control of the same proverb (the one that gives the book its title) and, in the process, use it to emphasize the differences in their positions. Awill tries to put Ebla in her place by telling her how woman was created. She responds,

> "Why should you tell me? I know it. I know where woman was created from."
> "But don't tell me. Let me tell you that they [*sic*] were created from the crooked rib of Adam." After saying this, Awill kept silent for a while. Then Ebla, who had been also talking and not listening to him, added, "And if anyone tries to straighten it, he will have to break it." (*FCR*, 179)

Awill quotes only the first half of the proverb, figuratively emphasizing Ebla's dependence on him for her existence. She calls attention to the second half and to its corollary proposition that if Awill is to enjoy her continued existence he will have to respect the separate shape it takes. A similar instance occurs in *Sweet and Sour Milk* as Loyaan and his mother argue as to whether there is any harm in accepting gifts from the government on behalf of the dead Soyaan. Once again the same proverb is bent to opposing positions in a debate on principle: "He could instantaneously think of concepts that would render meaningless and insignificant the Somali proverb which, he felt, she would quote at him. 'A dead man isn't as useful to one as his pair of shoes are' " (*SSM*, 79).

Folktales and legends contribute in especially significant ways to the "drift of tolerance," the openness of the text to debate. This element is an effect of Farah's careful selection from the rich repertoire of material available in Somali folklore. Ahmed Artan Hanghe, in his collection of Somali folktales, describes the great variety of themes and tropes within that repertoire, among them "tales with moral-teaching in which both humans and the lower animals are actors."[7] The tales from this last category in Hanghe's collection demonstrate the moral qualities that are their themes by, again, a great variety of narrative devices. One of these devices is to disclose a flaw in the conventional way of reasoning about a problem and to suggest that other ways of reasoning are possible and may be preferable. All of the folk stories that Farah incorporates into his texts are of this type. *From a Crooked Rib* furnishes an example as Ebla calls to mind a tale she has heard:

> The story goes that a certain tribe had a sackful of sugar: it was the first time they had ever got the chance to own so much of this sweet thing. . . . There was not enough and a riot began somewhere in the dwelling. . . . After a long time, an old man put forward a suggestion that the sugar should be poured into the common river, which would then become sweet. The idea was acceptable to everyone, and so they dumped the sugar into the river.
>
> Ebla heard that the townspeople thought that the countrypeople had done an unwise thing. "But," she thought to herself, "The old man only wanted to bring the squabble to an end: he was wise. But they are only townspeople and they don't understand. And even if they do they ignore it." (*FCR,* 93–94)

The predicament described in the tale and the theme of greed that it develops have nothing to do with events at this point in the novel. The tale is significant instead as an exercise for Ebla in critical consciousness, in which she thinks not only about competing solutions to a problem but about competing interpretations of the story. Another example occurs in *Close Sesame* when Deeriye tells Samawade a story—a tale completely divorced from the action of the novel—of the Somali sultan Wiil-Waal, whose wife contrives to make him question his own reasoning and to recognize thereby wisdom other than his own among his subjects (*CS,* 53–55). Still other examples are the two Juxaa stories that Mataan tells in *Gifts,* which are again not directly connected to the action of the text (*G,* 70–71, 113). While both are generally relevant to the larger theme of gift giving in the novel, their most significant contribution is to portray Juxaa in a positive light (which is not the case in many stories in this tradition) for countering one form of logic with another.

Many of Farah's epigraphs work in similar ways, calling the reader's attention not only to specific thematic issues in the texts they introduce

but also evoking larger issues of interpretation and raising questions
concerning memory, imagination, and logic: " 'Like bastard children,
hiding in their names . . . forests / Of history thickening with amne-
sia.'—Derek Walcott" (SSM, 167); " 'Memory does not return / Like
experience, more like imagination / How it would have been if, how it
must'—Patricia Beer" (CS, 1); " 'All is illusion—the words written, the
mind at which they are aimed, the truth they are intended to express,
the hands that will hold the paper, the eyes that will glance at the lines.
Every image floats vaguely in a sea of doubt—and the doubt itself is lost
in an unexplored universe of uncertitude.'—Joseph Conrad" (M, 133).

The reader's own position among these many voices—the foreign
languages, the proverbs and folktales, the epigraphs—should not escape
notice. In the matter of languages other than English, for example, it is
likely that many Somalis old enough to have been colonial subjects are
capable of following the passages in Somali, Arabic, and Italian—
though not of comprehending the other languages that Farah incorporates into his texts. Such readers, however, constitute a very minor proportion of his audience, and he has made it clear on many occasions that
his intended audience is anyone in the world who is literate in English.
The typical reader of Farah, therefore, must contend with the same situation as his characters, that is, with a textual world in which not all
utterances are comprehensible, in which other voices occupy positions
alongside of, but outside, the reader's own. To understand at a literal
level every word in the text requires translation and, therefore, collabo-
ration with other readers. The cultural specificity of the proverbs and
tales and the encyclopedic range of the other texts and writers named or
quoted in Farah's work produce the same result. This device is not an
idle show of erudition but another means—like the indeterminacies and
extended metaphors—of ensuring the reader's awareness of the multiplicity of voices, all contending for a hearing, that the writer's voice
makes heard in these texts.

We have described Farah's work as an investigation of the power of
language to support or to suppress intellectual debate and thereby to
enlarge or to restrict human freedom. That investigation, we have seen,
significantly shapes his practice as a writer, both in his representation of
fictional characters and actions and in his manipulation of the devices
available to him as a verbal artist. By virtue of that same investigation,
his work is also and inevitably a study in the artist's role within larger
social discourses of power.

As an African writer, he is already implicated in such discourses for sociological reasons, as he often acknowledges: "In Africa, the writers themselves belong to the same elite as the people about whom they are writing, the politicians. . . . In some countries . . . it's possible that the head of state has gone to school with the man who is writing the books, or the man who is the head of the secondary school. It's very incestuous" (Interview, 1987a, S7). (Farah did not attend school with Siyad Barre but did tutor Siyad Barre's son-in-law in English.) Some level of engagement in politics, in the service of one political agenda or another, is inescapable in these circumstances: "The writer in Africa and other countries in the Third World, because of his *nearness* (remember: he is a member of the privileged elite) to the central questions of decision-making and power, is engaged (unlike his counterpart in Western Europe and North America) in the unfolding of history in its rawness; engaged in the making of history" ("Fences," 179). Though he has never possessed notable wealth or occupied a position of power apart from his work as writer and teacher, Farah has always acknowledged that, relative to most of his compatriots, his life has indeed been one of material and social privilege. In writing about the "privilegencia" of Somalia, he demonstrates the logical interdependence, in their lives as in his own, of personal privilege and political engagement—not only because they see most clearly the relationship between political power and individual autonomy, as we have shown in chapter 4, but also because their privileged existence almost necessarily locates them close to the centers of power in the social structures they inhabit. In these ways Farah accepts as natural that his audience will listen to his voice with a political ear, as it would to the voice of almost any African writer.

In other significant ways, however, Farah's work keenly attunes his reader to the resonances of power in the voice of the writer; again and again, in essays and interviews—and indeed in his plays *The Offering* and *A Spread of Butter*—Farah returns to the relationship of the writer to the politician. One of his fullest treatments of the matter is the 1984 essay we have discussed in chapter 5, "The Creative Writer and the Politician." "Do the two have anything in common?" he asks. "If they do, it is that they both make use of words" ("Politician," 28). Having identified this similarity, however, he is at pains to enumerate the differences: the writer invents new idioms, while the politician falls back on old ones; the writer speaks in images, symbols, and metaphors, the politician in statistics, generally deceptive ones; the writer is content to leave judg-

ments of his or her own worth to posterity, while the politician tries to
control such judgments; the writer's allegiance is to ideals, the politician's to whatever audience applauds most loudly.

The relationship of the writer and the politician in Farah's own work,
however, is much more complex than this account suggests. To see that
complexity we need first to understand that all political power, in
Farah's representation of it and regardless of the social formation in
which it operates, ultimately rests not on physical force but on the
notional power of language to assert a narrative of political identities
and relationships. Keynaan's power to cut his children in two if he
chooses is not a matter of superior size and strength but of his ability to
assert successfully his identity as "the Grand Patriarch." The legal bind-
ing of Ebla to Awill by the sheikhs, the inclining of Samater's head to
Idil, the punishments accepted by Aw-Adan's students, the banishment
of Nonno from Berbera: all these are consequences of social narratives of
power by which roles of authority and submission are invented and
these inventions sustained. All such inventions, coercive though they
are, proceed from the ethical imagination, the same faculty by which
Loyaan, Sagal, Deeriye, Duniya, and others of Farah's characters seek to
reinvent themselves and others as more autonomous. To speak of the
"ethical" imagination in the work of Farah is not to say that all of its
products are ethically positive but only that all of its products have ethical consequences. The same notional power of language, therefore,
makes possible the very different ethical visions of Margaritta and Qumman, of Medina and Idil, of Hussen and Yussuf, of Abshir and Shiriye.

The coercive potential of language as the enabling instrument of
political power is nowhere as intensely realized in Farah's work as in the
figure of the General, who, in fact, makes language and power virtually
synonymous and identifies himself as the source of both. One of the
General's rhetorical devices for doing this is to associate himself,
through language, with the god of Islam. The expression he places in
the mouth of the dead Soyaan, "there is no General but our General,"
resonates with the profession of faith intoned every day by the practicing Muslim, "There is no god but God" (*SSM,* 97). Loyaan sees this as
part of a generalized strategy: "In one hand, the Blue Book of the General and Lenin's writings in improvised translations; in the other, the
Holy Koran. In one instant: 'We have blind faith in Allah's doctrine'; in
the same: 'We are Marxist-Leninist and Mohammedan' " (*SSM,* 133).
The association of the word of the General with the word of God runs
much deeper, however, for in the case of Somalia it was, in effect, the

dictator who created and bestowed/imposed upon his people not only his political message but the very ability to read and write that message, the language itself. Nasser makes this connection explicitly in *Sardines*: "Through the irony of history, . . . an illiterate 'prophet' changed a people from being oralists and forced them to belong to the written tradition. That was Prophet Mohammed. And through another irony of history, an illiterate general who models himself on God has tried to do the same thing" (*Sardines,* 170). This is an irony that is lost, though the force of the association is not, on Farah's most ironic character, Koschin, in his praise of the government for establishing an official Somali script: "I worship them for this, I worship them" (*NN,* 120). It is a strategy, moreover, that the General inherits from his colonial predecessors in Somalia and elsewhere, as Hilaal explains to Askar: "History has proven that whoever is supported by the written metaphysics of a tradition wins, in the long run, the fight to power" (*M,* 168). Askar uses this insight to explain to himself "the logic of why the first sentence of *Book One Oxford English* had to be 'This is a pen,' and the second sentence, 'This is a book,' " remembering "the first words the Archangel Gabriel dictated to the then illiterate Mohammed, thereafter Prophet—. . . 'Read, read in the name of Allah who created you out of clots of blood, read!' " (*M,* 168–69). Herein lies the force of Keynaan's commandment to Loyaan at the end of *Sweet and Sour Milk* to "Read!" from the Qur'an, and of Loyaan's refusal to do so (*SSM,* 241–42).

By this "deification" of himself (the professor's term in *A Spread of Butter*) as the very power and source of language, the General gains control over access to language, both oral and written, a power that he uses to divide his subjects from one another. By such control, as Loyaan explains, "people were kept in their separate compartments of ignorance about what happened to other people and what became of other things" (*SSM,* 198–99). Deeriye too comments on the divisiveness of language in the service of political power: "Information . . . is the garden the common man in Somalia or anywhere else is not allowed to enter . . . ; keep the populace underinformed so you can rule them; keep them apart by informing them separately; . . . feed them with the wrong information, give them poisonous bits of what does not count, a piece of gossip here, a rumour there, an unconfirmed report" (*CS,* 74). Such conditions strengthen the dictator's ability to refashion events and their meanings into a story that sustains the coherence and legitimacy of his authority in the imaginations of his subjects. This is the power by which the government rewrites the truth of Soyaan's death, of Amina's rape, and of the deaths of Mukhtaar and Jibriil Mohamed-Somali. This is the power by which the General collapses all stories into his story, merges all voices into his voice.

Farah shows us this power at work and he shows us the dictator's subjects struggling with the hold of this power on their own imaginations—but nowhere does he show us the dictator himself. As we have indicated in chapter 4, the General stands apart from all other human representations in Farah's writing in that he is never manifested as a character, never appears on stage. His whole existence, in the four novels in which he plays a part, is as a voice—not the voice of an individual like Keynaan's or Yussuf's but a voice directly analogous to that of the writer in the text, a voice that controls the conditions of language itself. We have seen already the important analogical relationship between the writer's voice in the text and the voices of his characters; here is another and more problematic analogy.

The problem arises in that this description of the dictator's voice reveals no inherent distinction between the language of politics and the language of art. The power of the writer's voice in Farah's texts and the power of the politician are the same. Both exist by virtue of their control of the conditions of language and both have the potential to exercise that power in the manner of a dictator. Indeed the writer controls his invented subjects, his characters, far more completely than the politician, however dictatorial, controls his; and the writer's public is potentially far wider and more numerous. The challenge to the writer's ethical imagination is the same challenge faced by the politician and by every political subject: to invent narratives that are open to many voices.

We have seen that Farah's novels and plays offer examples of characters who, despite their struggle to free those whose autonomy is denied, succumb to the temptation of tyranny and attempt to resist power by speaking in the closed and singular voice of power: Medina, for instance, who dictates strategy to the community of women to whom she is mentor, or Yussuf, who usurps the role of God in defining the nature of the nationalist's commitment, or Askar, who suppresses all voices but the nationalist's in accusing Misra of betrayal. Like these characters, the General asserts a single truth in a single voice, and it is that singleness of voice that makes him a dictator. Like these characters and like the General, the writer too is capable of synthesizing the collage of his imagination into a single voice, of usurping debate and rendering the text a dictatorship rather than a democracy. This potential collapsing of separate voices and selves into one is the very nightmare that is staged in *A*

Spread of Butter. In the epigraph to our previous chapter, Farah states that "a writer . . . is in a sense everybody; he is a woman, he is a man: . . . he is as many other selves as the ones whose tongues he employs to articulate his thoughts; he is as many other selves as there are minds and hearts he dwells in" ("Politician," 29). This is the same claim made by the nationalist ideologue Yussuf: "I am a man . . . and at the same time a woman and a child rolled into one" (*YB,* 100). It is, in turn, this same Yussuf who assures his brothers, "I am you in the same way as you are the nation"; "we're all one person" (*YB,* 52, 94), a pronouncement that differs little from the General's claim that Medina struggles to deny: "He is . . . all of us" (*Sardines,* 3). Only Farah's multivoiced use of the notional power of language separates his practice from that of the dictator. If we attend closely to Farah's treatment of the power of language and of the ethical imagination, we are forced to conclude that art is not an inherently privileged and liberatory practice, that, if it is to be democratic, it must be self-critical in its exercise of the instruments of power that it shares, and will always share, with politics.

This insight, that artistic language and political language are one and that the artist must be as mindful as the politician of the double-edged nature of its power, grows logically out of Farah's practice as a writer and, at the same time, connects him directly to the tradition of Somali oral poetry as we have described it in chapter 1. It is this connection, ultimately, that defines the work of Nuruddin Farah, if any single definition is possible. Like the Somali oral poet, he turns his art to intellectual debate in the service of political struggle; like a member of a traditional Somali political community, he plies his politics by the power of language. The connection is stronger, however, than mere likeness. By his novels and plays Farah is a direct participant in the Somali tradition of verbal art, and his art is a defense of the very principles that underlie that tradition. It is true that he is a writer, not an oralist; that he writes in English, not Somali; that he claims a vast and varied literary inheritance; that he is a feminist in a historically patriarchal society; and that in many others ways he bears little resemblance to the classic pastoralist poet. The political struggles that he writes about, however, are in large part a crisis of the Somali verbal tradition itself, an undermining of the conditions under which language operates. The viability of verbal art and of political culture alike in Somalia, as we have seen, has historically been strongest when the power of language is the property of all, is open to the light of critical scrutiny, and is deployed under conditions of strict accountability. The pressure exerted on that tradition in this century,

however, by colonialism, nationalist resistance, and eventually dictatorship has weakened the conditions necessary to safeguard the practice of
public discourse and set loose the power possessed by the *afmiishaar,* the
destructive potential of language that has always been the concomitant
of its productive power in Somali culture. Farah's work is a demonstra-
tion that the response of the verbal artist within that tradition, at the
particular historical juncture of Farah's writing and from his particular
position, must be to resist that pressure and to reconstitute language as
a social practice that nourishes individual autonomy.

It is, therefore, not only a generalized crisis of Africa and of our time
but the very particular crisis of the Somali verbal tradition that is
enacted at the center of Farah's art. This is the historical importance of
the democracy of voices that Farah constructs within each text and in his
work as a whole. Where the traditional poet speaks strongly in an individual voice and attends the responses of other voices, Farah aspires to
contain within the text the whole discursive space, the whole range of
voices, that made traditional poetic debate possible. This is where the
traditional and the contemporary meet and merge in the art of Nuruddin Farah.

Notes and References

Preface

1. A striking example of the extent to which interpreting a single work by Farah in isolation from the whole can affect reading may be found in two essays that appear back to back in a collection of commentary on approaches to Islam in African literature. Maggi Phillips characterizes *Close Sesame* as "a thoroughly Islamic novel, a metaphorical mosque of words in which the puzzles of creation and sanctity are contemplated and praised anew." A few pages later, in a reading of Farah's next novel, *Maps*, Alamin Mazrui comments that "Farah seems to be informed by a brand of Eurocentric ideology that has considered Islam as retrograde in its cultural dispensation, and as socially and historically decadent in its doctrines." (Maggi Phillips, "The View from a Mosque of Words: Nuruddin Farah's *Close Sesame* and the Holy Qur'an," and Alamin Mazrui, "Mapping Islam in Farah's *Maps*," in *The Marabout and the Muse*, ed. Kenneth W. Harrow [Portsmouth, N.H.: Heinemann; London: James Currey, 1996], 192, 205.)

Chapter One

1. Nuruddin Farah, *Maps* (London: Pan Books, 1986), 166; hereafter cited in text as *M*.

2. Lee V. Cassanelli, *The Shaping of Somali Society* (Philadelphia: University of Pennsylvania Press, 1982), 25; hereafter cited in text.

3. B. W. Andrzejewski and I. M. Lewis, *Somali Poetry: An Introduction* (Oxford: Clarendon Press, 1964), 28.

4. Lidwien Kapteijns, "Women and the Crisis of Communal Identity: The Cultural Construction of Gender in Somali History," in *The Somali Challenge: From Catastrophe to Renewal?*, ed. Ahmed I. Samatar (Boulder, Colo.: Lynne Reinner, 1994), 211–32.

5. Lidwien Kapteijns, *Women and the Somali Pastoral Tradition: Corporate Kinship and Capitalist Transformation in Northern Somalia* (Boston: Boston University African Studies Center, 1991), 7.

6. Pia Grassivaro Gallo, "Female Circumcision in Somalia (Overall Review)," in *Proceedings of the Third International Congress of Somali Studies,* ed. Annarita Puglielli (Rome: Il Pensiero Scientifico Editore, 1988), 438–43.

7. Leonard J. Kouba and Judith Muasher, "Female Circumcision in Africa: An Overview," *African Studies Review* 28 (1985): 95–110.

8. Quoted in John Markakis, *National and Class Conflict in the Horn of Africa* (Cambridge: Cambridge University Press, 1987), 17; hereafter cited in text. Cassanelli and other historians note an exception to this pattern, a pastoralist dynasty within the Ajuraan clan in southern Somalia during the sixteenth century (Cassanelli, 84–118).

9. John Markakis, "Ethnic Conflict and the State in the Horn of Africa," in *Ethnicity and Conflict in the Horn of Africa,* ed. Katsuyoshi Fukui and John Markakis (London: James Currey; Athens: Ohio University Press, 1994), 220.

10. Said S. Samatar, *Oral Poetry and Somali Nationalism* (Cambridge: Cambridge University Press, 1982), 56; hereafter cited in text.

11. Amina H. Adan, "Women and Words," *Ufahamu* 10, no. 3 (1981): 140.

12. Bronislaw [*sic,* Bogumil W.] Andrzejewski, "Alliteration and Scansion in Somali Oral Poetry and Their Cultural Coordinates," *Journal of the Anthropological Society of Oxford* 13 (1982): 76.

13. Said S. Samatar, "Oral Poetry and Political Dissent in Somali Society: The Hurgamo Series," *Ufahamu* 17, no. 2 (1989): 49.

14. Nuruddin Farah, interview by Feroza Jussawalla and Reed Way Dasenbrock, in *Interviews with Writers of the Post-Colonial World* (Jackson: University Press of Mississippi, 1992), 50; hereafter cited in text.

15. I. M. Lewis, *A Modern History of Somalia,* rev. ed. (Boulder, Colo: Westview Press, 1988), 46–47.

16. Hussein M. Adam, "Language, National Consciousness and Identity—The Somali Experience," in *Nationalism and Self Determination in the Horn of Africa,* ed. I. M. Lewis (London: Ithaca Press, 1983), 38.

17. Said S. Samatar, "Historical Setting," in *Somalia: A Country Study,* ed. Helen Chapin Metz (Washington, D.C.: Library of Congress, 1993), 44.

18. B. W. Andrzejewski, "Language Reform in Somalia and the Modernization of the Somali Vocabulary," in *Language Reform: History and Future,* vol. 1, ed. Istvan Fodor and Claude Hagege (Hamburg: Buske Verlag, 1983), 75–76.

Chapter Two

1. Nuruddin Farah, "Childhood of My Schizophrenia," *Times Literary Supplement,* 23–29 November 1990, 1264.

2. Nuruddin Farah, interview by Funso Aiyejina and Bob Fox, in *Ife Studies in African Literature and the Arts* 2 (1984): 26; hereafter cited in text.

3. Nuruddin Farah, interview by authors, tape recording, Oxford, England, 17–18 May 1996; hereafter cited in text.

4. Nuruddin Farah, "Coming Out of the Oral Tradition to Write about Dictatorship," interview by Mary Langille, *The Varsity* (University of Toronto), 26 November 1987, S7; hereafter cited in text as Interview, 1987a.

5. Nuruddin Farah, "False Accounting," *Granta* 49 (Fall 1994): 173.

6. Nurrudin Farah, letter to James Currey, 22 October 1973, Heinemann African Writers Series archives, Overstone Library, University of Reading.

7. Nuruddin Farah, "A Combining of Gifts: An Interview," by Maya Jaggi, *Third World Quarterly* 11 (1989): 182–83; hereafter cited in text as Interview, 1989.

8. Nuruddin Farah, "Why I Write," *Third World Quarterly* 10 (1988): 1595; hereafter cited in text.

9. Memorandum signed "Elizabeth," 20 August [1975], Heinemann African Writers Series archives, Overstone Library, University of Reading.

10. Nuruddin Farah, "Homing In on the Pigeon," *Index on Censorship* 5 and 6 (1993): 17.

11. A contemporary of Farah's who was an active member of the dissident movement in Italy at the time has spoken, in conversation with the authors, of recognizing actual figures in the movement among the minor characters in *Sardines*.

12. Nuruddin Farah, "Farah—Living in a Country of the Mind," interview by Maggie Jonas, *New African,* December 1987, 61; hereafter cited in text as Interview, 1987b.

13. Nuruddin Farah, interview by Robert Elliot Fox, *Daily Times* (Lagos, Nigeria), 9 September 1989, 11.

14. Nuruddin Farah, "Wretched Life," interview by Patricia Morris, *Africa Events,* September 1986, 54; hereafter cited in text.

15. Nuruddin Farah, "Savaging the Soul of a Nation," *In These Times,* 28 December 1992, 14; hereafter cited in text as "Savaging."

16. Nuruddin Farah, "Author in Search of an Identity," interview by Julie Kitchener, *New African,* December 1981, 61; hereafter cited in text as Interview, 1981a.

17. Nuruddin Farah, "In Praise of Exile," *Third World Affairs* (1988): 182; hereafter cited in text as "Exile."

18. Nuruddin Farah, "Do Fences Have Sides?," in *The Commonwealth in Canada: Proceedings of the Second Triennial Conference of CACLALS,* pt. 2, ed. Uma Paramenswaran (Calcutta: Writers' Workshop, 1983), 182 (emphasis added); hereafter cited in text as "Fences."

19. Nuruddin Farah, "Somali Paradox," interview by Anya Schiffrin, *City Limits,* 22–29 January 1987, n.p.

20. Nuriddin [sic] Farah, "The Creative Writer and the Politician," *The Classic* 3 (1984): 27; hereafter cited in text as "Politician."

21. Nuruddin Farah, "Fear Is a Goat," *The Guardian* (Lagos), 1 June 1990, 9.

22. Nuruddin Farah, "A Country in Exile," *Transition* 57 (1992): 4 (emphasis in the original).

Chapter Three

1. Nuruddin Farah, personal communication, 15 March 1998.

2. The only exception is *The Offering,* which is set in a jail cell in Ethiopia. Farah relocates that cell to Somalia, however, in reworking the play as *A Spread of Butter.*

3. Nuruddin Farah, *From a Crooked Rib* (London: Heinemann, 1970), 8; hereafter cited in text as *FCR.*

4. Nuruddin Farah, *A Naked Needle* (London: Heinemann, 1976), 106; hereafter cited in text as *NN.*

5. Siyad's name occurs in several passages in *Secrets.* All, however, come in revisions to the original manuscript, written after Siyad's death in 1995.

6. Nuruddin Farah, letter to James Currey, 16 June 1972, Heinemann African Writers Series archives, Overstone Library, University of Reading.

7. Nuruddin Farah, *Sweet and Sour Milk* (St. Paul, Minn.: Graywolf Press, 1992), 97; hereafter cited in text as *SSM.*

8. Nuruddin Farah, *Sardines* (St. Paul, Minn.: Graywolf Press, 1992), 3; hereafter cited in text.

9. Nuruddin Farah, *Close Sesame* (St. Paul, Minn.: Graywolf Press, 1992), 103; hereafter cited in text as *CS.*

10. Nuruddin Farah, *The Offering, Lotus (Afro-Asian Writings)* 30, no. 4 (1976): 80; hereafter cited in text as *O.*

11. Nuruddin Farah, *A Spread of Butter* (1978, TS), 2; hereafter cited in text as *SB.*

12. Nuruddin Farah, *Yussuf and His Brothers* (1982, TS), 93–94; hereafter cited in text as *YB.*

13. Though *Maps* is partially set in Farah's childhood home and its protagonist, like Farah, flees from the war there to Mogadiscio, he has stated that "the book is not autobiographical; there is nothing that I can think of, or that I know about my own life, that is in any way similar to Askar's, or any other character's in the novel" (Interview, 1989, 185).

14. Nuruddin Farah, *Gifts* (London: Serif; Harare, Zimbabwe: Baobab Books, 1992), 114, 128; hereafter cited in text as *G.*

15. Nuruddin Farah, *Secrets* (New York: Arcade, 1998) 164; hereafter cited in text.

Chapter Four

1. Hilarie Kelly, "A Somali Tragedy of Political and Sexual Confusion: A Critical Analysis of Nuruddin Farah's *Maps," Ufahamu* 16, no. 2 (1988): 25, 27–28; hereafter cited in text.

2. Derek Wright, "Somali Powerscapes: Mapping Farah's Fiction," *Research in African Literatures* 21, no. 2 (1990): 33.

3. Scott L. Malcomson, "Family Plot," *The New Yorker,* 15 June 1998: 79.

4. Nuruddin Farah, interview by Theo Vincent, in *Seventeen Black African Writers on Literature and Life* (Lagos, Nigeria: Centre for Black and African Arts and Civilization, 1981), 47; hereafter cited in text as Interview, 1981b.

5. Barbara Turfan, "Opposing Dictatorship: A Comment on Nuruddin Farah's *Variations on the Theme of an African Dictatorship*," *Journal of Commonwealth Literature* 24 (1989): 183.

6. In our interview of Farah he cites the argument of Benedict Anderson that nations, historically, are very recent and by no means necessary inventions and that their status as inevitable and primordial entities exists only in the imaginations of their citizens. "Substitute clan for nation" in this formula, Farah says (Interview, 1996). See Benedict Anderson, *Imagined Communities* (London: Verso, 1983). Also directly relevant to this analysis is Eric Hobsbawm and Terence Ranger, eds., *The Invention of Tradition* (Cambridge: Cambridge University Press, 1983).

7. In the only previously published study of this play, Jacqueline Bardolph reaches the conclusion that "since men are hopelessly divided both within themselves and from one another, action can only be meaningful if it restores collective unity and a sense of belonging, hence the fight for national freedom. Thus, on a political level, the message can only concern collective will and identity. . . . The only meaning to life is the willingness to die for a cause." Jacqueline Bardolph, "*Yussuf and His Brothers* by Nuruddin Farah," *Commonwealth Essays and Studies* 7, no. 1 (1984): 68–69. In our view Bardolph has correctly interpreted Yussuf's own position, but it is a position that the text as a whole subjects to intense critical scrutiny. None of Farah's protagonists speaks for his or her author, Yussuf perhaps least of all.

8. Rhonda Cobham, "Misgendering the Nation: African Nationalist Fictions and Nuruddin Farah's *Maps*," in *Nationalisms and Sexualities*, ed. Andrew Parker (New York: Routledge, 1992), 49–50.

9. Sallie Ann Hirsch, "Voice, Consciousness, and Patriarchal Politics: The Development of Female Characters in Nuruddin Farah's *From a Crooked Rib, Sardines,* and *Gifts*" (honors thesis, University of Richmond, 1997), 38–39.

Chapter Five

1. Juliet Okonkwo, "Nuruddin Farah and the Changing Roles of Women," *World Literature Today* 58 (1984): 217.

2. Nuruddin Farah, "A View of Home from the Outside," interview by James Lampley, *Africa,* no. 124 (December, 1981): 81.

3. Islam has been assimilated into various societies across the Middle East, Arabia, and Africa, and in the process its interpretation and practice have been affected by other traditions and discourses present in these regions. According to Leila Ahmed, "in its account of the creation of humankind the Qur'an gives no indication of the order in which the first couple was created,

nor does it say that Eve was created from Adam's rib. In Islamic traditionist literature, however, which was inscribed in the period following the Muslim conquests, Eve, sure enough, is referred to as created from a rib." Farah's work registers some of the ways in which Somalis have understood Islamic doctrine; often he indicates that the local understanding is at variance with the Qur'an. Leila Ahmed, *Women and Gender in Islam* (New Haven: Yale University Press, 1992), 4–5.

4. Jacqueline Bardolph, "Women and Metaphors in Nuruddin Farah's *Sweet and Sour Milk* and *Sardines,*" in *Proceedings of the Second International Conference of Somali Studies, 1–6 August 1983,* vol. 1, ed. Thomas Labahn (Hamburg: Buske Verlag, 1984), 441; hereafter cited in text.

5. Jacqueline Bardolph, "Nuruddin Farah: L'écriture du nomade," *Politique Africaine* 35 (1989): 125. Derek Wright, *The Novels of Nuruddin Farah* (Bayreuth: Eckhard Breitinger, Bayreuth University, 1994), 107; hereafter cited in text.

Chapter Six

1. Juliet Okonkwo, "Farah and the Individual's Quest for Self-Fulfilment," *Okike* 29 (1989): 67.

2. For a fuller discussion of Farah's "post-modernist tendencies" see also Wright's "Zero Zones: Nuruddin Farah's Fiction," *Ariel* 21, no. 2 (1990): 21–42.

3. Nuruddin Farah, interview by Armando Pajalich, *Kunapipi* 15 (1993): 64–65; hereafter cited in text.

4. Nuruddin Farah, radio interview by Rebekah Presson, *New Letters on the Air* (Kansas City: University of Missouri, 1993), audiocassette

5. Jim Crace, "Drowning in Style," review of *Close Sesame, South,* April 1984, 50.

6. Maggi Phillips also emphasizes the importance of this passage, calling Deeriye's insight at this moment a " 'turn-about' revelation." For Phillips, however, the revelation bears on Deeriye's spiritual faith, rather than on his understanding of how he constructs his own identity (Phillips, 201).

7. Ahmed Artan Hanghe, *Folktales from Somalia* (Uppsala, Sweden: Ahmed Artan Hanghe and Nordiska afrikainstitutet, 1988), 106.

Selected Bibliography

PRIMARY SOURCES

Published Works

NOVELS

From A Crooked Rib. London: Heinemann, 1970.

A Naked Needle. London: Heinemann, 1976.

Sweet and Sour Milk. London: Allison & Busby, 1979; London: Heinemann, 1980; Saint Paul, Minn.: Graywolf Press, 1992.

Sardines. London: Allison & Busby, 1981; London: Heinemann, 1982; Saint Paul, Minn.: Graywolf Press, 1992.

Close Sesame. London: Allison & Busby, 1983; Saint Paul, Minn.: Graywolf Press, 1992.

Maps. London: Pan Books; New York: Pantheon, 1986.

Gifts. London: Serif Publishers; Harare, Zimbabwe: Baobab Books, 1992.

Secrets. New York: Arcade, 1998.

PLAY

The Offering. Lotus (Afro-Asian Writings) 30, no. 4 (1976): 77–93.

ESSAYS

"Do Fences Have Sides?" In *The Commonwealth in Canada: Proceedings of the Second Triennial Conference of CACLALS*. Pt. 2, ed. Uma Parameswaran, 174–82. Calcutta: Writers' Workshop, 1983. The predicament and responsibility of the African writer as a member of the privileged elite.

"The Creative Writer and the Politician." *Classic* 3 (1984): 27–30. Defends his decision to be in exile and contrasts the activity of the writer with that of the politician.

"In Praise of Exile." *Third World Affairs* (1988): 181–82. Reprinted in *Literature in Exile,* ed. John Glad, 64-67. Durham, N.C.: Duke University Press, 1990. Comments on the censorship of his work, the nature of his exile, and the relationship between the oral and the written.

"Why I Write." *Third World Quarterly* 10 (1988): 1591–99. Important discussion of his development as a political writer.

"Fear Is a Goat." *The Guardian* (Lagos), 1 June 1990, 9. The fearful uncertainty as to whether one is a target of the state.

"Childhood of My Schizophrenia." *Times Literary Supplement,* 23–29 November
    1990, 1264. The experience of living in the occupied Ogaden as a
    "divided" child in an age of colonial contradiction.
"A Country in Exile." *Transition,* no. 57 (1992): 4–8. Questions his earlier
    claims that he was not in exile and that distance is good for a writer. Con-
    siders his own role as a Somali male in sexual oppression.
"Savaging the Soul of a Nation." *In These Times,* 28 December 1992, 14–17.
    Account of his clash with Museveni of Uganda over the solution to the
    Somali crisis. Senses failure recently in ability to raise an instinct of
    humanity in the Mogadiscio residents he writes about.
"Homing In on the Pigeon." *Index on Censorship* 22, nos. 5–6 (1993): 16–20.
    Revised and reprinted as "Bastards of Empire: Writing and the Politics of
    Exile." *Transition,* no. 65 (1995): 26–35. Excerpt from *Awake, When
    Asleep,* his nonfiction study of refugees currently in preparation. A coun-
    try is a working hypothesis; when it ceases to work, one must invent a
    country of the imagination. Those who cannot do that must flee across
    borders to recover the fullness of their natures.
"False Accounting." *Granta,* no. 49 (1994): 171–81. Money as economic impe-
    rialism. The suspicions he faces as a foreigner and "rich" man among his
    neighbors in Nigeria.
"People of a Half-Way House." *London Review of Books,* 21 March 1996, 19–20.
    Personal identity and the status of a refugee. Account of his first meeting
    with his father after 17 years.
"The Women of Kismayo." *Times Literary Supplement,* 15 November 1996, 18. A
    political demonstration by women in Kismayo challenged the clan-based
    character of men's political action and revealed the extent to which men
    think of women as secret enemies.
"My Father, the Englishman, and I." *Under African Skies: Modern African Stories,*
    ed. Charles Larson, 290-92. New York: Farrar, Straus & Giroux, 1997.
    Account of meeting the British Administrator of the Ogaden while a
    child. Memories of his father's complicity in securing acceptance of a
    treaty ceding the Ogaden to Ethiopia.

Unpublished Works

Plays
A Spread of Butter, broadcast by BBC African Service, 1978. Typescript.
Yussuf and His Brothers, produced at University of Jos, 1982. Typescript.

SECONDARY SOURCES

Interviews

Aiyejina, Funso, and Bob Fox. "Nuruddin Farah in Conversation with Funso
    Aiyejina and Bob Fox." *Ife Studies in African Literature and the Arts* 2

(1984): 24–37. Account of his own language experience. Important statements on the power of the word as used by the writer and the politician and on the relation of the oral to the written.

Fox, Robert Elliot. "Art Personality: Nuruddin Farah." *Daily Times* (Lagos, Nigeria), 19 August 1989, 12; 2 September 1989, 10; 9 September 1989, 10–11; 16 September 1989, 15. Reprinted in *Masters of the Drum: Black Lit/oratures across the Curriculum*, by Robert Elliot Fox, 157-70. Westport, CT: Greenwood Press, 1995. Assessment of his own position among African writers, especially in relation to Ngugi. The spirit of Somaliness in his work and the relevance of his writing to the larger concerns of Africa.

Jaggi, Maya. "A Combining of Gifts: An Interview." *Third World Quarterly* 11, no. 3 (1989): 171–87. Very important interview. Comments on language choice, audience, Somali nationalism and pan-Africanism, and the role of the writer in changing the consciousnesses that are responsible for political problems.

Jonas, Maggie. "Living in a Country of the Mind." *New African,* December 1987, 60–61. Account of his choices in regard to exile.

Jussawalla, Feroza, and Reed Way Dasenbrock. *Interviews with Writers of the Post-Colonial World,* 42–62. Jackson: University Press of Mississippi, 1992. Comments on the question of language choice, the oral tradition, his readership, and the relation of the first trilogy to the second.

Langille, Mary. "Coming Out of Oral Tradition to Write about Dictatorship." *The Varsity* (University of Toronto), 26 November 1987, S7. Description of watching his mother compose oral poems. His privileged position as a male writer.

Moss, Robert. "Mapping the Psyche." *West Africa,* 1 September 1986, 1827–28. His purposes in developing women characters.

Pajalich, Armando. "Nuruddin Farah Interviewed by Armando Pajalich." *Kunapipi* 15 (1993): 61–71. Important comments on his creation of character and voice and his imagining of the conditions for democracy.

Presson, Rebekah. "Nuruddin Farah." *New Letters on the Air.* Kansas City: University of Missouri, 1993. Audiocassette. His identification with all of his characters, even the "bad" ones, holding their different world views in tension. Reads aloud from several of his novels.

Vincent, Theo. "Nuruddin Farah, Somalia." *Seventeen Black and African Writers on Literature and Life,* 46–53. Lagos, Nigeria: Centre for Black and African Arts and Civilization, 1981. The supposed communal nature of Africans and his practice of isolating them to study them as characters. Every human act is a political act.

Special Issues of Journals.

Journal of Commonwealth Literature 24, no. 1 (1989). Though Somalia is not a member of the British Commonwealth, the journal published a collection of four essays on Farah in recognition of his impact on Commonwealth

literature. The essays, all included in this bibliography, are by Jacqueline
Bardolph, Fiona Sparrow, Barbara Turfan, and Derek Wright.

World Literature Today 72, 4 (1998). This issue is devoted to Farah as winner of
the 1998 Neustadt International Prize for Literature. The final composition of the issue is still in progress as this book goes to press. It is
expected to include a lecture by Farah and articles by Jacqueline Bardolph, Michael Eldridge, Simon Gikandi, Claudio Gorlier, Charles Sugnet, Itala Vivan, Abdourahman Waberi, Derek Wright, and ourselves, as
well as other material related to Farah.

Books and Articles

Adam, Ian. "Nuruddin Farah and James Joyce: Some Issues of Intertextuality."
World Literature Written in English 24 (1984): 34–43. Influences and
echoes of Joyce in *A Naked Needle, Sweet and Sour Milk,* and *Sardines.*

———. "The Murder of Soyaan Keynaan." *World Literature Written in English*
26 (1986): 203–11. *Sweet and Sour Milk* resembles the detective novel
structurally but departs from its usual pattern of closure.

Ahmed, Ali Jimale. "Farah and the (Re)Writing of Somali Historiography: Nar-
rative as a Politically Symbolic Act." In *Daybreak Is Near: Literature,
Clans, and the Nation-State in Somalia,* 75–99. Lawrenceville, N.J.: Red
Sea Press, 1996. Discussion of ways in which *From a Crooked Rib* and *A
Naked Needle* reveal contradictions in Somali society, relating various ref-
erences in the novels to Somali culture and history.

Alden, Patricia. "Mapping the Personal and the Political: The Child-Geographer
in Nuruddin Farah's *Maps.*" In *African Literature—1988: New Masks,*
ed. Hal Wylie, Dennis Brutus, and Juris Silenieks, 119–24. Washington,
D.C.: Three Continents Press, 1990. *Maps* merges the generic potentials
of the political bildungsroman, the ironized epic, and the psychoanalytic
family romance.

———. "New Women and Old Myths: Chinua Achebe's *Anthills of the Savannah* and Nuruddin Farah's *Sardines.*" *Matatu* 8 (1991): 67–80. A comparison of Farah's development of female characters in *Sardines* to
Achebe's in *Anthills of the Savannah;* it is Farah who draws women as gen-
uinely world-historical characters and captures the diversity of women's
experiences.

Alden, Patricia and Louis Tremaine. "Reinventing Family in the Second Trilogy
of Nuruddin Farah." *World Literature Today* 72, no. 4 (1998). An extension of our argument in this book concerning the conceptual unity, political bearing, and narrative complexities of Farah's second trilogy.

Bardolph, Jacqueline. "Women and Metaphors in Nuruddin Farah's *Sweet and
Sour Milk* and *Sardines.*" In *Proceedings of the Second International Conference
of Somali Studies, 1–6 August 1983.* Vol. 1, ed. Thomas Labahn, 429–45.
Hamburg: Buske Verlag, 1984. The images and metaphors connected
with women show that these novels are more complex than a single ide-

ology and that no one character speaks for the author. An African vision of tension between freedom and identity.

————. "*Yussuf and His Brothers* by Nuruddin Farah." *Commonwealth: Essays and Studies* 7 (1984): 57–70. The only critical essay on this play in print, apart from the present study. Based on an unpublished script of the play as performed at the University of Jos in 1982. (Our own treatment of the play is based on a more recent revision of the script.) The mode of composition of the play is aimed at an African public. The message of the play concerns collective will: the only meaning to life is the willingness to die for a cause.

————. "L'évolution de l'écriture dans la trilogie de Nuruddin Farah: Variations sur le thème d'une dictature africaine." *Nouvelles du Sud* 6–7 (1986–1987): 79–91. The three novels of the first trilogy show a range of technical and aesthetic innovations in support of a complex political analysis.

————. "*Maps* de Nurrudin [*sic*] Farah et l'identité somalie." *Bulletin des Etudes Africaines de l'INALCO* 7 (1987): 249–66. Farah's poetic exploration of the themes of blood, language, and maps as signs of belonging in *Maps*.

————. "Time and History in Nuruddin Farah's *Close Sesame*." *Journal of Commonwealth Literature* 24 (1989): 193–206. This novel is organized around two interconnected temporal orders: Deeriye's life and the history of Somalia. The Sayyid's "Death of Corfield" is the fundamental intertext for the novel.

Cobham, Rhonda. "Misgendering the Nation: African Nationalist Fictions and Nuruddin Farah's *Maps*." In *Nationalisms and Sexualities*, ed. Andrew Parker, 42–59. New York: Routledge, 1992. "This essay argues that the transformation of the anti-imperialist struggle in Africa into a nationalist movement exacerbated a crisis of individual and collective identity that is staged in the African novel." Sensitive analysis of the relationship between the unstable categories of gender and nationality in *Maps* as the basis for an important critique of common critical readings of other African novels.

Ewen, D. R. "Nuruddin Farah." In *The Writing of East and Central Africa*, ed. G. D. Killam, 192–210. Exeter, N.H.: Heinemann, 1984. Discussion of the first four novels, emphasizing, by comparison to British novelists, Farah's control of language.

Hawley, John C. "Nuruddin Farah—Tribalism, Orality, and Postcolonial Ultimate Reality and Meaning in Contemporary Somalia." *Ultimate Reality and Meaning* 19 (1996): 189-20. A philosophical treatment of the Dictatorship Trilogy (factually inaccurate at several points) that argues that most of Farah's characters in those novels "have become politicized at the expense of their moral grounding" and lack a "clear sense of ultimate reality and meaning."

Kazan, Francesca. "Recalling the Other Third World: Nuruddin Farah's *Maps*." *Novel* 26 (1993): 253–67. A complex reading of the pronoun shifts and merging of bodies in *Maps* to produce a conception of identity in which self and other are complementary, rather than oppositional.

Kelly, Hilarie. "A Somali Tragedy of Political and Sexual Confusion: A Critical Analysis of Nuruddin Farah's *Maps*." *Ufahamu* 16, no. 2 (1988): 21–37. Critical of Farah for his "stylistic peccadilloes," his "neurotic" characters, and the way he "fetishizes women."

Kidawi, Shuaib Ahmed. "The Two Novels of Nuruddin Farah." In *Somalia and the World: Proceedings of the International Symposium Held in Mogadishu, October 15–21, 1979.* Vol. 2, ed. Hussein M. Adam, 191–201. Mogadishu: HALGAN, 1980. Of historical interest as a reading of Farah's first two novels presented in the context of a Somali-government sponsored conference. Depicts Farah as "blatantly hostile to women" in *From a Crooked Rib.*

Mazrui, Alamin. "Mapping Islam in Farah's *Maps*." In *The Marabout and the Muse*, ed. Kenneth W. Harrow, 205-17. Portsmouth, N.H.: Heinemann; London: James Currey, 1996. In *Maps* Farah, like Salman Rushdie, considers Islam to be morally bankrupt and culturally retrograde. His views of the Qur'an "border on sacrilege."

Okonkwo, Juliet. "Nuruddin Farah and the Changing Roles of Women." *World Literature Today* 58 (1984): 215–21. "Farah seems virtually alone among African writers in depicting the progress which women have made within the constricting African social landscape."

———. "Farah and the Individual's Quest for Self-Fulfilment." *Okike* 29 (1989): 66–74. The individual's quest for self-fulfillment, for the good life, is the common theme that binds the first four novels together into a single entity.

Petersen, Kirsten Holst. "The Personal and the Political: The Case of Nuruddin Farah." *Ariel* 12, no. 3 (1981): 93–101. Farah battles for individual freedom and differs from other African writers in criticizing both traditional and modern society.

Phillips, Maggi. "The View from a Mosque of Words: Nuruddin Farah's *Close Sesame* and the Holy Qur'an." In *The Marabout and the Muse*, ed. Kenneth W. Harrow, 191-204. Portsmouth, N.H.: Heinemann; London: James Currey, 1996. *Close Sesame* is a "deeply theological novel" that is primarily concerned not with political justice but with Deeriye's ailing faith and the imperfection of human knowledge.

Smith, Angela. "The Novel in East Africa." In *East African Writing in English,* 12–42. London: Macmillan, 1989. Half of the essay is devoted to Farah, emphasizing the parallels between family and national conflict as themes in the novels.

Sparrow, Fiona. "Telling the Story Yet Again: Oral Traditions in Nuruddin Farah's Fiction." *Journal of Commonwealth Literature* 24 (1989): 164–72. Concerned primarily with the representation and incorporation of oral materials in *Close Sesame.*

Stratton, Florence. "The Novels of Nuruddin Farah." *World Literature Written in English* 25 (1985): 16–30. Compares structures of oppression at the levels of sexual relations, family, and government in Farah's novels.

Turfan, Barbara. "Opposing Dictatorship: A Comment on Nuruddin Farah's *Variations on the Theme of an African Dictatorship*." *Journal of Commonwealth Literature* 24 (1989): 173–84. Sharply critical of the first trilogy because it deals with members of a privileged elite who are out of touch with the masses.

Wright, Derek. "Unwritable Realities: The Orality of Power in Nuruddin Farah's *Sweet and Sour Milk*." *Journal of Commonwealth Literature* 24 (1989): 185–92. Ontological and epistemological uncertainties in the oral code are repeated in the written language of Farah's text.

———. "Zero Zones: Nuruddin Farah's Fiction." *Ariel* 21, no. 2 (1990): 21–42. Reviews "post-modernist tendencies" in Farah's fiction.

———. "Oligarchy and Orature in the Novels of Nuruddin Farah." *Studies in Twentieth Century Literature* 15 (1991): 87–99. There is an interpenetration of the oral and written modes in Farah's fiction; both are "off-centered" in a postmodernist way.

———. "Fabling the Feminine in Nuruddin Farah's Novels." In *Essays on African Writing: A Re-Evaluation,* ed. Abdulrazak Gurnah, 70–87. Portsmouth, N.H.: Heinemann, 1993. Mainly concerned with *Maps*. The inadequacy of allegorical schemes in interpreting Farah's writing, especially with regard to gender.

———. *The Novels of Nuruddin Farah.* Bayreuth: Eckhard Breitinger, Bayreuth University, 1994. A lively and useful critical introduction to Farah's published novels and the only book-length study of Farah prior to the present volume. A brief introduction to Farah and Somalia is followed by separate chapters on each novel. Wright is by far the most prolific scholar of Farah's work; from among his articles on the subject we have selected, for this bibliography, only those that explore significantly different topics from those discussed in his book.

Index

The Authors

Patricia Alden is professor of English at St. Lawrence University, where she is also on the faculty of the African Studies Program. She is the author of *Social Mobility and the English Bildungsroman* and coeditor of *African Studies and the Undergraduate Curriculum*. She has conducted research as a Fulbright scholar in Zimbabwe and published essays on British and Zimbabwean novelists as well as on Nuruddin Farah.

Louis Tremaine is associate professor of English and international studies at the University of Richmond, where he coordinates the concentration in African studies. He is the author of articles and papers on a number of African and African-American novelists, including Nuruddin Farah, and is a translator of the work of the Algerian novelist Mohammed Dib.

The Editor

Bernth Lindfors is a professor of English and African literatures at the University of Texas at Austin. He has written and edited more than 30 books, including *Black African Literature in English* (1979, 1986, 1989, 1995), *Popular Literatures in Africa* (1991), *Comparative Approaches to African Literatures* (1994), *Long Drums and Canons: Teaching and Researching African Literatures* (1995), *Loaded Vehicles: Studies in African Literary Media* (1996), and (with Reinhard Sander) *Twentieth-Century Caribbean and Black African Writers* (1992, 1993, 1996). From 1970 to 1989 he was editor of *Research in African Literatures*.